LEVEL 8

motivation
MATH

TEKS–Based Alignment to STAAR®

student edition

Critical Thinking for Life!
Mentoring Minds

Publisher
Michael L. Lujan, M.Ed.

Editorial Director
Teresa Sherman, B.S.E.

Production Coordinator
Kim Barnes, B.B.A.

Digital Production Artist
Ashley Francis, B.A.A.S.

Illustrators
Judy Bankhead, M.F.A.
Ashley Francis, B.A.A.S.

Content Development Team
Marian Rainwater, M.Ed.
Amanda Byers, B.S.
Paula Jones, M.S.
Angela Ruark, M.A.
Ladona Cook, M.Ed.
Karen Lane, M.Ed.
Cara Smith, M.S.
Laura Duncan, B.A.
Monica Ventress, B.B.A.
Stephanie Rieper, B.S.I.S.
Jennifer Hart, M.Ed.

Content Editorial Team
Marian Rainwater, M.Ed.
Amanda Byers, B.S.
Paula Jones, M.S.
Angela Ruark, M.A.
Allison Wiley, B.S.E.
Cathy Cutler, B.S.E.
Anne Altamirano, M.A.T.
Ladona Cook, M.Ed.
Laura Duncan, B.A.
Diane Sorrels, B.A.
Sheila Thurmond, M.Ed.

Critical Thinking for Life!™
Mentoring Minds

[p] 800.585.5258 · [f] 800.838.8186

For other great products from Mentoring Minds,
please visit our website at:

mentoring**minds**.com

ISBN: 978-1-938935-69-5

motivationmath™
Table of Contents

Unit 1 – Describe relationships between sets of real numbers 8.2(A)–S 7

Unit 2 – Approximate the value of an irrational number and
locate the value on a number line 8.2(B)–S 15

Unit 3 – Convert between standard decimal and scientific notations 8.2(C)–S 23

Unit 4 – Order sets of real numbers 8.2(D)–R 31

Unit 5 – Generalize that ratios of corresponding sides of similar shapes
are proportional 8.3(A)–S 39

Unit 6 – Compare and contrast attributes of a shape and its dilation 8.3(B)–S 47

Unit 7 – Use an algebraic representation to explain the effect of a scale factor
applied to two-dimensional figures 8.3(C)–R 55

Unit 8 – Use similar right triangles to develop an understanding of slope 8.4(A)–S ... 63

Unit 9 – Graph proportional relationships 8.4(B)–R 71

Unit 10 – Use data from a table or graph to determine the rate of change
or slope and y-intercept 8.4(C)–R 79

Unit 11 – Represent linear proportional and non-proportional situations with tables,
graphs, and equations 8.5(A)–S, 8.5(B)–S 87

Unit 12 – Contrast bivariate sets of data that suggest a linear relationship
with sets that do not 8.5(C)–S 95

Unit 13 – Use a trend line to make predictions 8.5(D)–R 103

Unit 14 – Solve problems involving direct variation 8.5(E)–S 111

Unit 15 – Distinguish between and identify examples of proportional and
non-proportional situations 8.5(F)–S, 8.5(H)–S 119

Unit 16 – Identify functions 8.5(G)–R 127

Unit 17 – Write an equation in the form $y = mx + b$ to model a linear relationship
between two quantities 8.5(I)–R 135

Unit 18 – Describe the volume formula of a cylinder in terms of
its base area and height 8.6(A)–S 143

Unit 19 – Model the relationship between the volume of a cylinder and a cone 8.6(B) . . 151

Unit 20 – Use models and diagrams to explain the Pythagorean Theorem 8.6(C)–S . . . 159

Unit 21 – Solve problems involving the volume of cylinders, cones, and
spheres 8.7(A)–R 167

Unit 22 – Determine solutions for lateral and total surface area problems involving
rectangular prisms, triangular prisms, and cylinders 8.7(B)–R 175

Unit 23 – Use the Pythagorean Theorem and its converse to solve problems 8.7(C)–R . . 183

Unit 24 – Determine the distance between two points on a coordinate plane using the
Pythagorean Theorem 8.7(D)–S 191

Unit 25 – Write one-variable equations or inequalities that represent problems and
write real-world problems given one-variable equations or
inequalities 8.8(A)–S, 8.8(B)–S 199

Unit 26 – Model and solve one-variable equations with variables on both sides
of the equal sign 8.8(C)–R 207

Unit 27 – Use informal arguments to establish facts about angle relationships
8.8(D)–S 215

Unit 28 – Identify and verify values of x and y that simultaneously satisfy two linear
equations 8.9(A)–S 223

Unit 29 – Generalize properties of orientation and congruence of transformations and
differentiate between transformations that preserve congruence and those
that do not 8.10(A)–S, 8.10(B)–S 231

Unit 30 – Explain the effect of transformations on a coordinate plane using an algebraic
representation 8.10(C)–R 239

Unit 31 – Model the effect of dilations on linear and area measurements 8.10(D)–S . . 247

Unit 32 – Construct a scatterplot and describe the association between
bivariate data 8.11(A)–S 255

Unit 33 – Determine the mean absolute deviation using a data set of
no more than 10 data points 8.11(B)–S 263

Unit 34 – Simulate generating random samples to develop the notion of a random sample
being representative of the population 8.11(C) 271

Unit 35 – Solve problems comparing how interest rate and loan length affect cost of credit; calculate total cost of repaying a loan using online calculators; identify and explain advantages and disadvantages of different payment methods 8.12(A)–S, 8.12(B), 8.12(E)..281

Unit 36 – Explain how regular investments grow over time; calculate and compare simple and compound interest 8.12(C)–S, 8.12(D)–R.........................287

Unit 37 – Analyze and determine if a situation is financially responsible and identify the benefits of financial responsibility and the costs of financial irresponsibility 8.12(F)..293

Unit 38 – Estimate the cost of college education and devise a periodic savings plan 8.12(G)–S 299

Performance Assessments 305

Chart Your Success 325

Math Glossary...329

Grade 8 Mathematics Reference Materials 351

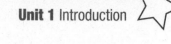

1 Complete the diagram to show the relationship between the following sets of numbers.

Rational Numbers, Counting Numbers, Irrational Numbers, Whole Numbers, Integers

The Real Number System

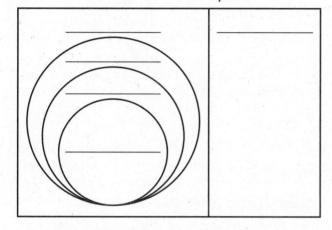

2 Record the following numbers in the correct section of the diagram in problem 1.

$$-100, -8.4, 0, 0.003, \frac{4}{9}, 1, \sqrt{2},$$

$$1.5, \sqrt{4}, \pi, 3.\overline{3}, \frac{7}{2}, -\sqrt{13}, 7.92, 17$$

3 Use the completed diagram in problem 1 to determine all sets to which each number belongs.

-2 _____

$\frac{3}{4}$ _____

$\frac{\sqrt{2}}{2}$ _____

292 _____

$-\frac{19}{3}$ _____

6.969669666... _____

4 List 3 numbers that belong to each of the following number sets.

Counting Numbers _____

Integers _____

Irrational Numbers _____

5 Label each statement *true* or *false*. Rewrite each false statement so that it is true.

All real numbers are classified as either rational or irrational.

_____

_____

If a number is an element of the set of integers, it is also an element of the set of whole numbers.

_____

_____

The set of irrational numbers is a subset of the set of rational numbers.

_____

_____

Not every counting number is an integer.

_____

_____

Every element of the set of whole numbers is a rational number.

_____

_____

1 Which diagram correctly displays the relationship between sets of numbers?

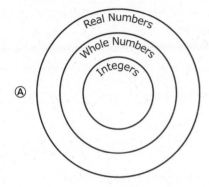

Ⓐ

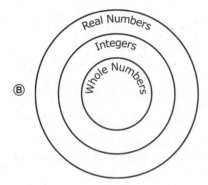

Ⓑ

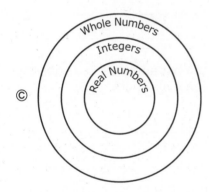

Ⓒ

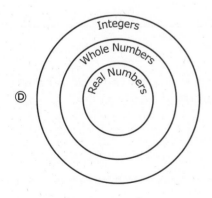

Ⓓ

2 Which statement is NOT true about elements of the set of rational numbers?

Ⓕ All integers are elements of the set.

Ⓖ Elements of the set include repeating and terminating decimals.

Ⓗ All elements of the set can be written as a ratio $\frac{a}{b}$, where $b \neq 0$.

Ⓙ The numbers π and $\sqrt{3}$ are elements of the set.

3 If a number is an element of the set of real numbers, which of the following statements must also be true?

Ⓐ The number is an element of either the set of rational numbers or the set of irrational numbers.

Ⓑ The number is an element of both the set of rational numbers and the set of irrational numbers.

Ⓒ The number is an element of the set of rational numbers but not the set of irrational numbers.

Ⓓ The number is an element of the set of irrational numbers but not the set of rational numbers.

4 To which of the following sets of numbers does $\sqrt{196}$ belong?

I. Counting numbers

II. Integers

III. Rational numbers

IV. Irrational numbers

Ⓕ I only   Ⓗ I, II, and III only

Ⓖ III only   Ⓙ IV only

1 A set of numbers is shown.

$$S = \left\{ -\frac{3}{4}, \sqrt{144}, 17.85, \frac{18}{3} \right\}$$

Which of the following best fits in the set?

Ⓐ $\sqrt{136}$

Ⓑ $\frac{27}{7}$

Ⓒ π

Ⓓ 0.12122122212222…

2 In which section of the diagram does the number $-\frac{2}{9}$ belong?

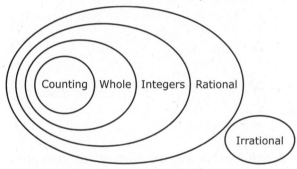

The Real Number System

Ⓕ Counting

Ⓖ Integers

Ⓗ Rational

Ⓙ Irrational

3 Set A = $\left\{ \sqrt{36}, \frac{\sqrt{100}}{2}, \sqrt{225} \right\}$. Set A is NOT a subset of which set of numbers?

Ⓐ Irrational numbers

Ⓑ Rational numbers

Ⓒ Integers

Ⓓ Whole numbers

4 Which lists the correct labels for the diagram shown?

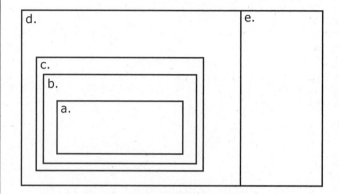

Ⓕ a. Whole Numbers
  b. Counting Numbers
  c. Integers
  d. Rational Numbers
  e. Irrational Numbers
  f. Real Numbers

Ⓖ a. Counting Numbers
  b. Whole Numbers
  c. Integers
  d. Irrational Numbers
  e. Rational Numbers
  f. Real Numbers

Ⓗ a. Counting Numbers
  b. Whole Numbers
  c. Integers
  d. Rational Numbers
  e. Irrational Numbers
  f. Real Numbers

Ⓙ a. Counting Numbers
  b. Whole Numbers
  c. Integers
  d. Rational Numbers
  e. Real Numbers
  f. Irrational Numbers

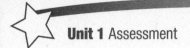

Unit 1 Assessment

1 The Venn diagram represents the relationship between rational numbers and whole numbers.

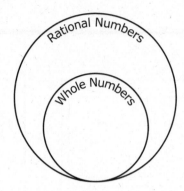

Which number is an element of the set of Rational Numbers but is not an element of the set of Whole Numbers?

Ⓐ $\frac{\sqrt{49}}{7}$

Ⓑ $\sqrt{78}$

Ⓒ $\frac{1}{3}$

Ⓓ $\frac{0}{29}$

2 Given the following set of numbers, $\left\{-\frac{13}{2}, \sqrt{37}, \frac{35}{5}, \frac{\sqrt{18}}{2}, -9.45\right\}$, which elements belong to the set of irrational numbers?

Ⓕ $-\frac{13}{2}$ and -9.45 only

Ⓖ $\sqrt{37}$ and $\frac{\sqrt{18}}{2}$ only

Ⓗ $-\frac{13}{2}, \frac{35}{5}$, and $\frac{\sqrt{18}}{2}$ only

Ⓙ $\sqrt{37}$ and -9.45 only

3 The set of irrational numbers includes all of the following except—

Ⓐ π

Ⓑ 0.454554555...

Ⓒ $\sqrt{169}$

Ⓓ $\sqrt{124}$

4 According to the diagram, which statement is NOT true?

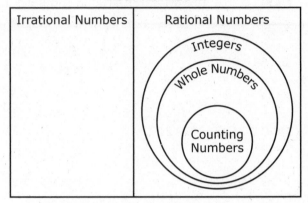

Ⓕ All counting numbers are also rational numbers.

Ⓖ All rational numbers are real numbers.

Ⓗ All whole numbers are integers.

Ⓙ All rational numbers are integers.

5 Which best describes all possible classifications for this set of numbers?

$$\left\{-\frac{28}{7}, 18, \sqrt{64}, -95\right\}$$

   I. Whole numbers

   II. Integers

   III. Rational numbers

   IV. Real numbers

Ⓐ I and II only

Ⓑ II and III only

Ⓒ II, III, and IV only

Ⓓ III and IV only

1 Create a set of numbers, Set X, using the guidelines shown.
- Must contain a minimum of 10 elements
- Exactly 1 element must be a whole number
- At most 1 element may be a counting number
- Exactly 3 elements must be integers
- At least 2 elements must be rational numbers only
- No more than 2 elements may be irrational numbers

Set X = _____

Justify that Set X is correct using a visual representation.

2 For each statement, circle the correct response that makes the statement true.

a. (All/Some/No) rational numbers are also integers.

b. An irrational number is (always/sometimes/never) an element of the set of rational numbers.

c. The set of whole numbers (is/is not) a subset of the set of integers.

d. An element of the set of rational numbers is (always/sometimes/never) an element of the set of real numbers.

e. (All/Some/No) counting numbers are also integers.

f. The set of rational numbers (is/is not) a subset of the set of whole numbers.

g. (All/Some/No) irrational numbers can be expressed as the ratio of two integers.

h. The square root of a number is (always/sometimes/never) an irrational number.

Journal

Ariceli and Maya disagree over the classification of $\frac{22}{7}$. Ariceli says $\frac{22}{7}$ is a rational number, while Maya says it is irrational because it is equal to pi. Which student is correct? Explain your answer.

_____

_____

_____

_____

Vocabulary Activity

Study the list of numbers. Complete the steps below. Numbers may be used more than once, but every number must be used at least once.

$$0 \qquad \sqrt{75} \qquad -0.\overline{3} \qquad 95 \qquad \sqrt{205} \qquad -\frac{76}{4} \qquad \sqrt{121} \qquad -\frac{2}{9}$$

a. Circle a number that may be written in the form $\frac{a}{b}$, where a and b are both integers, and b is not 0.

b. Draw a triangle around two numbers that are *elements* of the set of *counting numbers*.

c. Place a star below a number that is classified as a *rational number*, an *integer*, and a *whole number*, but not a *counting number*.

d. Draw a pentagon around two numbers that are *elements* of the set of *irrational numbers*.

e. Underline a number that is classified as both a *rational number* and an *integer*, but not a *whole number*.

f. Place a hashtag (#) above two numbers that may be written as *repeating decimal numbers*.

g. Draw a heart around a number that is an *element* of the set of *rational numbers* but not a member of the set of *integers*.

Color the Number Set

For each section in the picture, a number is shown. Color the section according to the rules given.

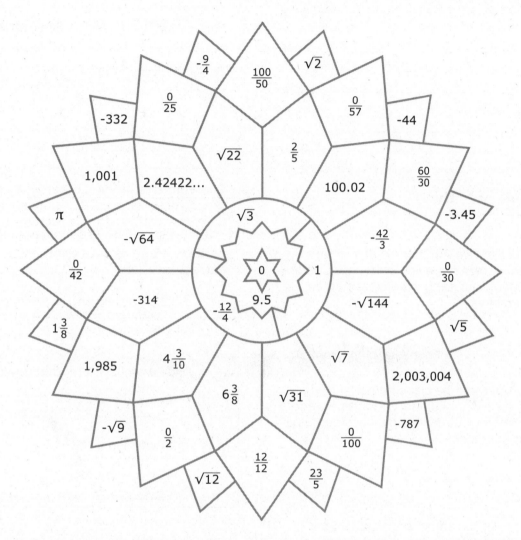

If the number can be classified as a counting number, a whole number, an integer, and a rational number, color the section purple.

If the number is not a counting number and can be classified as a whole number, an integer, and a rational number, color the section black.

If the number is not a whole number and can be classified as an integer and a rational number, color the section green.

If the number is not an integer and can be classified as a rational number, color the section red.

If the number can be classified as an irrational number, color the section blue.

1 List all the sets in which the numbers shown can be classified.

a. 0 _____

b. $-\frac{12}{4}$ _____

c. π _____

d. -3.9 _____

e. 57 _____

f. $\sqrt{16}$ _____

2 Write a set of five numbers that can be classified as real numbers, rational numbers, and integers, but cannot be classified as whole numbers.

3 What number can be classified as a real number, a rational number, an integer, and a whole number, but cannot be classified as a counting number?

4 Write a set of four numbers that can be classified as real numbers and irrational numbers only.

5 Place an X on one number from each set so that the set meets the given classification.

a. $\left\{0, -\frac{1}{2}, 2, 3, -\frac{4}{2}\right\}$; integers

b. {-1, 0, 1}; whole numbers

c. $\{\sqrt{16}, \sqrt{20}, \sqrt{64}, \sqrt{81}\}$; rational numbers

d. $\left\{\frac{15}{3}, \frac{24}{3}, \frac{45}{3}, \frac{56}{3}\right\}$; counting numbers

6 The numbers in the diagram may or may not be correctly located. If a number is in the correct location, draw a rectangle around it. If a number is in an incorrect location, draw an X on it and rewrite the number in the correct location.

The Real Number System

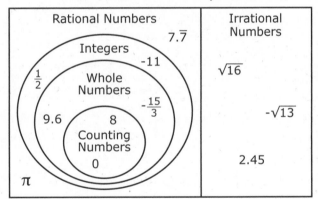

Connections

1. Use the Internet to research the origin of the real number system. Write a one-page report on the origin of the number system, including the order in which the different classifications were named.

2. Make a game of finding items around your house that display a counting number, a whole number, an integer, a rational number, or an irrational number. Try to find at least one example of each number.

1 The areas of different squares are shown. For each square, write an expression using a square root that can be used to estimate the length of one side.

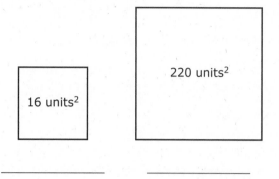

_____   _____

_____   _____

2 In each blank, record the appropriate letter from the number line that shows the approximate location of the irrational number.

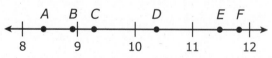

_____ $\sqrt{71}$ _____ $\sqrt{140}$

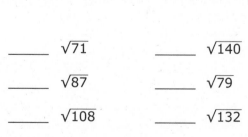

_____ $\sqrt{87}$ _____ $\sqrt{79}$

_____ $\sqrt{108}$ _____ $\sqrt{132}$

3 Locate and label the points on the number line by estimating the value of the irrational number.

A $\sqrt{53}$ B $\sqrt{88}$ C $\sqrt{110}$

4 For each number shown, list the perfect square values between which the number lies on the number line. Place a star above the perfect square that is closest to the number.

a. 115: between _____ and _____

b. 73: between _____ and _____

c. 200: between _____ and _____

d. 38: between _____ and _____

5 For each irrational number shown, list the whole number values between which the number lies on the number line. Place a star above the whole number value that is closest to the number on a number line.

a. $\sqrt{115}$: between _____ and _____

b. $\sqrt{73}$: between _____ and _____

c. $\sqrt{200}$: between _____ and _____

d. $\sqrt{38}$: between _____ and _____

Use the number line as needed to answer the following questions.

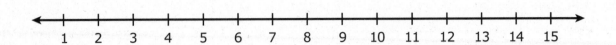

1 Between which two whole numbers on a number line is $\sqrt{108}$ located?

Ⓐ 11 and 12

Ⓑ 10 and 11

Ⓒ 9 and 10

Ⓓ 8 and 9

2 The area of a square is 32 square inches. Which equation best represents the length of one side of the square?

Ⓕ $\sqrt{32} \approx 16$ in.

Ⓖ $32^2 = 1,024$ in.

Ⓗ $\sqrt{32} \approx 5.7$ in.

Ⓙ $\frac{32}{4} = 8$ in.

3 Which point on the number line best represents $\sqrt{8}$?

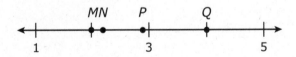

Ⓐ Point *M*

Ⓑ Point *N*

Ⓒ Point *P*

Ⓓ Point *Q*

4 Which of the following irrational numbers lies between 5 and 6 on the number line?

Ⓕ $\sqrt{23}$

Ⓖ π

Ⓗ $\sqrt{37}$

Ⓙ $\sqrt{29}$

5 Which value best represents point *Z* shown on the number line?

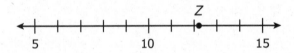

Ⓐ $\sqrt{146}$

Ⓑ $\sqrt{12}$

Ⓒ $\sqrt{165}$

Ⓓ $\sqrt{13}$

6 Which whole number is closest to the value of $\sqrt{54}$?

Ⓕ 6

Ⓖ 7

Ⓗ 8

Ⓙ 9

1 For which number line is the value of B approximately $\sqrt{37}$?

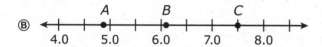

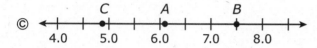

Ⓓ Not here

2 Which of the following irrational numbers has a value closest to 11?

Ⓕ $\sqrt{12}$

Ⓖ $\sqrt{22}$

Ⓗ $\sqrt{88}$

Ⓙ $\sqrt{120}$

3 A square tile has a diagonal line drawn on it as shown.

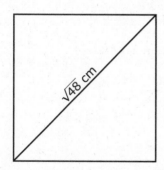

What is the approximate length of the square's diagonal?

Ⓐ 7 cm

Ⓑ 8 cm

Ⓒ 12 cm

Ⓓ 24 cm

4 Line segment PR is shown on the coordinate plane.

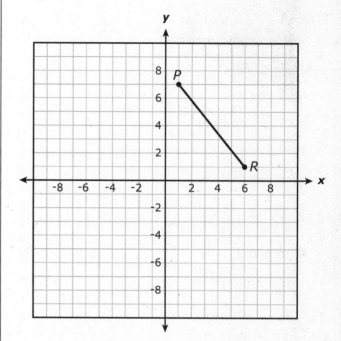

If $PR = \sqrt{61}$, between which two integers does the length lie on a number line?

Ⓕ 30 and 33

Ⓖ 60 and 62

Ⓗ 7 and 8

Ⓙ 6 and 7

5 The longest side of a right triangle measures $\sqrt{17}$ inches. Which point on the number line most closely represents the value of $\sqrt{17}$?

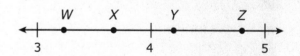

Ⓐ Point W

Ⓑ Point X

Ⓒ Point Y

Ⓓ Point Z

6 Which of the following has a value that is closest to 3?

Ⓕ $\sqrt{3}$

Ⓖ π

Ⓗ $\sqrt{12}$

Ⓙ $\sqrt{7}$

1 Which best shows the values of the labeled points on the number line?

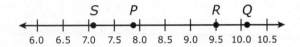

6.0 6.5 7.0 7.5 8.0 8.5 9.0 9.5 10.0 10.5

Ⓐ $P = \sqrt{64}$ $R = \sqrt{86}$
     $Q = \sqrt{102}$ $S = \sqrt{50}$

Ⓑ $P = \sqrt{62}$ $R = \sqrt{91}$
     $Q = \sqrt{101}$ $S = \sqrt{50}$

Ⓒ $P = \sqrt{62}$ $R = \sqrt{86}$
     $Q = \sqrt{102}$ $S = \sqrt{48}$

Ⓓ $P = \sqrt{64}$ $R = \sqrt{91}$
     $Q = \sqrt{101}$ $S = \sqrt{48}$

2 Lane paints a square-shaped section of a fence with an area of 75 square feet. What is the approximate height of the section Lane paints?

Ⓕ 8.1 ft

Ⓖ 8.3 ft

Ⓗ 8.6 ft

Ⓙ 8.9 ft

3 The square root of 88 is found between which two numbers on a number line?

Ⓐ 7 and 8

Ⓑ 8 and 9

Ⓒ 9 and 10

Ⓓ 10 and 11

4 Which point on the number line best represents $\sqrt{57}$?

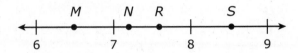

6   7   8   9

Ⓕ Point M

Ⓖ Point N

Ⓗ Point R

Ⓙ Point S

5 Mr. Watson built a ramp so that his dachshund, Fritz, could climb onto the sofa.

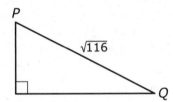

Between which two whole numbers does the length of $\overline{PQ}$ lie on a number line?

Ⓐ Between 4 and 5

Ⓑ Between 10 and 11

Ⓒ Between 12 and 13

Ⓓ Between 115 and 117

motivation**math**™LEVEL 8
mentoring**minds**.com

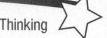

1   Place a point on each number line to represent the approximation of $\sqrt{12}$. Explain your reasoning for each placement.

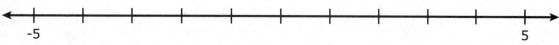

-5   5

Explanation: _____

_____

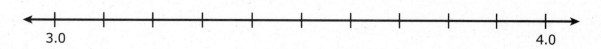

3.0   4.0

Explanation: _____

_____

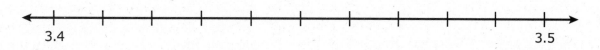

3.4   3.5

Explanation: _____

_____

2   Between which two whole numbers does the value of $\sqrt{5}$ lie? _____

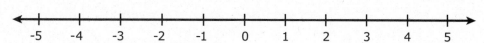

-5   -4   -3   -2   -1   0   1   2   3   4   5

Consider -$\sqrt{5}$. How does the location change on a number line? Are there any similarities to the placement of $\sqrt{5}$? Explain your answer.

Unit 2 Journal/Vocabulary Activity

Journal

Explain how to approximate the value of the square root of a rational number, such as $\sqrt{5.6}$.

_____

_____

_____

Vocabulary Activity

Marcus has been studying his vocabulary terms for math. He has cards with terms printed on them and matching cards with examples or definitions of each term. Marcus dropped his cards, and they are no longer paired. Help Marcus match each vocabulary term with the correct example by drawing a line between each matching pair of cards.

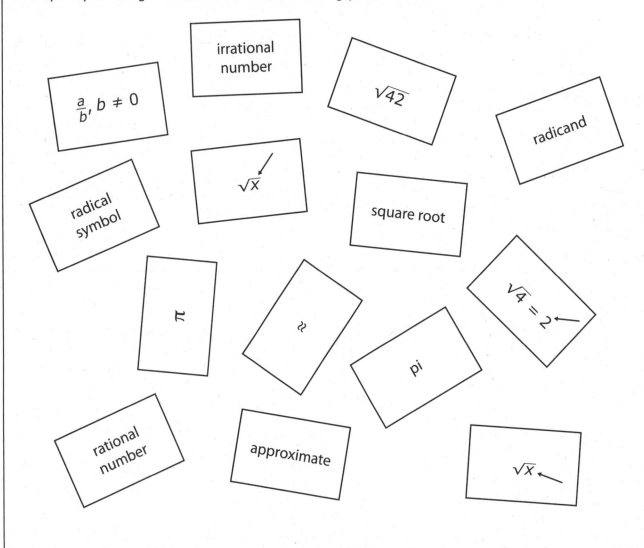

Claim and Color

Play *Claim and Color* with a partner. Each pair of players needs a game board, a pencil, and a paper clip to use with the spinner. Each player needs a different color marker or colored pencil to shade squares on the game board. Player 1 spins the spinner and selects a square so that the value of the irrational number falls between the two numbers on the spinner space. If the square is selected correctly, player 1 colors the square to claim it. If incorrect, player 1 does not color the square. Play then passes to player 2. If there are no more squares containing a value that falls between the numbers spun, the player loses a turn. Play continues until the teacher calls time. The player with more colored squares is the winner.

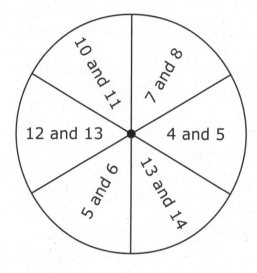

$\sqrt{52}$	$\sqrt{180}$	$\sqrt{118}$	$\sqrt{60}$	$\sqrt{35}$
$\sqrt{152}$	$\sqrt{22}$	$\sqrt{63}$	$\sqrt{195}$	$\sqrt{150}$
$\sqrt{20}$	$\sqrt{32}$	$\sqrt{172}$	$\sqrt{102}$	$\sqrt{19}$
$\sqrt{31}$	$\sqrt{190}$	$\sqrt{58}$	$\sqrt{120}$	$\sqrt{145}$
$\sqrt{62}$	$\sqrt{28}$	$\sqrt{17}$	$\sqrt{50}$	$\sqrt{165}$

Unit 2 Homework

1 Write equations to show all the perfect squares from 1 to 225. The first two have been done for you.

$1^2 = 1$ _____ _____

$2^2 = 4$ _____ _____

_____ _____

_____ _____

_____ _____

_____ _____

_____ _____

_____

2 Use the number line to approximate, to the nearest tenth, the value of the irrational numbers shown.

a. $\sqrt{11} \approx$ _____

b. $\sqrt{14} \approx$ _____

c. $\sqrt{18} \approx$ _____

d. $\sqrt{24} \approx$ _____

3 A number line is shown.

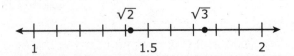

Write one statement describing a similarity for $\sqrt{2}$ and $\sqrt{3}$ and one statement describing a difference between $\sqrt{2}$ and $\sqrt{3}$.

_____

_____

_____

_____

4 For each irrational number shown, write the whole number it lies closest to on a number line.

a. $\sqrt{222}$ _____

b. $\sqrt{104}$ _____

c. $\sqrt{85}$ _____

d. $\sqrt{17}$ _____

e. $\sqrt{157}$ _____

f. $\sqrt{26}$ _____

Connections

1. Find five examples of irrational numbers in newspapers or magazines. Cut out and tape the numbers to a sheet of paper. Record the whole number values that the irrational numbers lie between on a number line.

2. Research Euler's number, *e*. Find out about the origin of the irrational number and its use in mathematics. Write a one-page paper and share with the class.

1 Using a calculator, write each power as an integer or a rational number.

10^2 _____

10^3 _____

10^4 _____

10^{-1} _____

10^{-2} _____

10^{-3} _____

2 Rewrite each number using scientific notation.

300 _____

106,000 _____

0.0000397 _____

4,356,000 _____

0.0157 _____

3 Rewrite each number using standard notation.

4.8×10^4 _____

5.72×10^9 _____

3.72×10^1 _____

1.9284×10^{-2} _____

3×10^{-13} _____

4 Is 5.067×10^{-7} a positive or negative number? Explain your answer.

_____

_____

_____

5 A number greater than 1 requires the decimal point to be moved seven times in order to write the number using scientific notation. What power of 10 is used to write the number? Explain your answer.

_____

_____

_____

6 If the number shown is written correctly using scientific notation, write *correct*. If the number is written incorrectly using scientific notation, explain why it is incorrect. Then rewrite the number correctly.

a. 0.5045×10^{-6} _____

_____

b. 2.804×10^9 _____

_____

c. 12.04×10^3 _____

_____

d. 0.39×10^{12} _____

_____

e. 1.004×10^{-8} _____

_____

1 The human eye blinks an average of 4.2×10^6 times per year. Which of the following is equivalent to 4.2×10^6?

Ⓐ 4,200,000

Ⓑ 42,000,000

Ⓒ 420,000

Ⓓ 420,000,000

2 The distance light travels in one light year is 9,500,000,000,000 miles. Which of the following shows this distance using scientific notation?

Ⓕ 9.5×10^{10} miles

Ⓖ 9.5×10^{11} miles

Ⓗ 9.5×10^{12} miles

Ⓙ 9.5×10^{13} miles

3 The diameter of a xylem cell in a redwood tree is 3.0×10^{-5} meters. What is the diameter of the cell written using standard notation?

Ⓐ 0.000003 meter

Ⓑ 0.00030 meter

Ⓒ 0.00003 meter

Ⓓ 0.00300 meter

4 June completes a science homework sheet in which one of the values she records is 0.0000000000052. Since her math class has been working on writing numbers using scientific notation, June decides to record the very small number using what she has learned.

$$5.2 \times 10^{\square}$$

What value should June record in the box?

Record your answer and fill in the bubbles on the grid below. Be sure to use the correct place value.

5 The distance, in meters, to reach the star Vega from Earth is 239,000,000,000,000,000. What is this distance using scientific notation?

Ⓐ 239×10^{15} m

Ⓑ 2.39×10^{17} m

Ⓒ 239×10^{17} m

Ⓓ 2.39×10^{15} m

1 A grain of sand with a diameter of 0.06 millimeter has a mass of approximately 3.0×10^{-13} gram. How is the mass of a grain of sand expressed using standard notation?

Ⓐ 0.00000000000003 g

Ⓑ 0.0000000000003 g

Ⓒ 0.000000000000003 g

Ⓓ 0.000000000003 g

2 The human retina contains cells called rods and cones that absorb light and change it to electric signals sent to the brain. There are approximately 120,000,000 rods and 6,000,000 cones in a retina. How is the number of rods in a human retina written using scientific notation?

Ⓕ 12.0×10^{9}

Ⓖ 1.2×10^{7}

Ⓗ 1.2×10^{8}

Ⓙ 12.0×10^{7}

3 Americans eat an average of 100 acres of pizza per year. That is equivalent to 4,356,000 square feet of pizza per year. How is the area expressed using scientific notation?

Ⓐ 4356×10^{3} ft^2

Ⓑ 435.6×10^{4} ft^2

Ⓒ 43.56×10^{5} ft^2

Ⓓ 4.356×10^{6} ft^2

4 Which of the following uses scientific notation incorrectly?

Ⓕ 9.1×10^{4}

Ⓖ 75.3×10^{2}

Ⓗ 8×10^{-6}

Ⓙ 4.23×10^{-2}

5 William Shakespeare died on his birthday at age 52. Approximately how many seconds did Shakespeare live? (Hint: There are 31,536,000 seconds in one year.)

Ⓐ 16.4×10^{10} seconds

Ⓑ 16.4×10^{9} seconds

Ⓒ 1.64×10^{9} seconds

Ⓓ 1.64×10^{10} seconds

6 The surface area of Earth is 5.101×10^{8} square kilometers. Which of the following is equivalent to this measure?

Ⓕ 5,101,000,000 km^2

Ⓖ 510,100,000,000 km^2

Ⓗ 51,010,000 km^2

Ⓙ 510,100,000 km^2

1 A national charitable foundation collected an estimated 38.2 million dollars last year. How is this amount written using scientific notation?

Ⓐ 38.2×10^7

Ⓑ 38.2×10^5

Ⓒ 3.82×10^6

Ⓓ 3.82×10^7

2 Donna writes the following number using scientific notation.

$$96,080,000,000$$

What number does Donna use as the power of ten?

Record your answer and fill in the bubbles on the grid below. Be sure to use the correct place value.

3 Ryan records four numbers from his science homework using scientific notation.

$$35 \times 10^5, \; 2.6 \times 10^3, \; 1.6 \times 10^{-6}, \; 7.9 \times 10^2$$

Which number did Ryan record incorrectly?

Ⓐ 35×10^5

Ⓑ 2.6×10^3

Ⓒ 1.6×10^{-6}

Ⓓ 7.9×10^2

4 The wavelength of an x-ray measures 1.0×10^{-11} meter. How is this number written using standard notation?

Ⓕ 0.000000001 meter

Ⓖ 0.0000000001 meter

Ⓗ 0.00000000001 meter

Ⓙ 0.000000000001 meter

5 There are 1,000 milligrams in 1 gram and 1,000 grams in 1 kilogram. Expressed as a number in scientific notation, how many milligrams are in 1 kilogram?

Ⓐ 1.0×10^3 mg

Ⓑ 1.0×10^4 mg

Ⓒ 1.0×10^5 mg

Ⓓ 1.0×10^6 mg

motivation**math**™LEVEL 8

mentoring**minds**.com

1 The estimated diameter of the observable universe is 9.3×10^{26} meters. Neutrinos are subatomic particles measuring 1.0×10^{-24} meter in diameter. If the measure of one neutrino is subtracted from the measure of the observable universe, what conclusion may be drawn about the difference? Explain your answer.

2 The table shows the approximate populations for several countries in 2010.

Populations

Country	Population
China	1.337×10^9
Russian Federation	142,000,000
Finland	5.36×10^6
USA	309,000,000

During a class discussion, Whalen states that the United States has the largest population at 3.09×10^9 people. Is Whalen's statement correct? Explain your answer.

_____

_____

_____

Journal

When might recording numbers using scientific notation be preferred over using standard notation? Explain your answer.

_____

_____

_____

Vocabulary Activity

Compare and contrast *standard notation* and *scientific notation*. Include at least two examples of each.

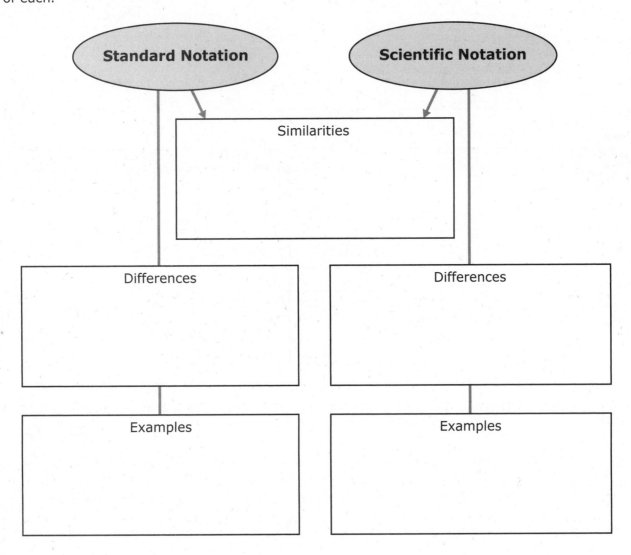

Scientifically Standard

Play *Scientifically Standard* with a partner. Each pair of players needs a spinner and a paper clip to use with the spinner. Each player needs a pencil. Player 1 spins the spinner. If the number in the space is written in scientific notation, player 1 records the number using standard notation. If the number is written using standard notation, player 1 records the number using scientific notation. If the number is written correctly, player 1 initials the space along the outside edge. If incorrect, player 1 loses a turn, and player 2 spins the spinner to repeat the process. If the spinner lands on a space that is already initialed, the player moves clockwise to the next open space. The game ends when all spaces have initials. The player with more spaces initialed is the winner.

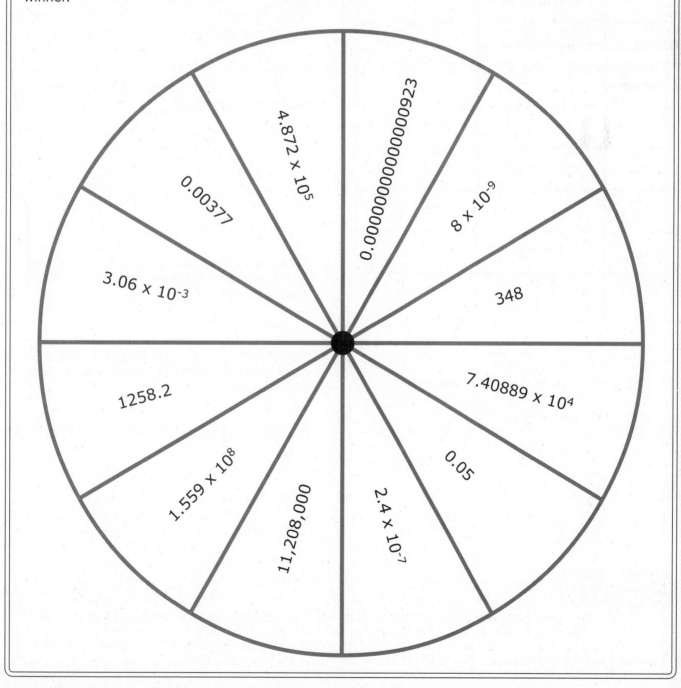

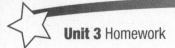
1 The table shows the distance, in miles, of each planet from the sun. Complete the table.

Distance from the Sun

Planet	Approximate Distance from the Sun	Scientific Notation Form
Earth		9.3×10^7
Jupiter	484,000,000	
Mars	142,000,000	
Mercury		3.63×10^7
Neptune		2.8×10^9
Saturn	888,000,000	
Uranus		1.78×10^9
Venus	67,200,000	

2 The width of a plant cell is approximately 0.00001276 meter. Use scientific notation to write the width of the plant cell.

3 The land area of Russia is about 6.6×10^6 square miles. Use standard notation to write the approximate area of Russia.

4 The number of seconds in one week is 604,800. If this number is written using scientific notation, what is the numeric value of the exponent?

Use scientific notation to write the number of seconds in one week.

5 When a number between 0 and 1 is written using scientific notation, what is true about the exponent?

When a number greater than 1 is written using scientific notation, what is true about the exponent?

Connections

Create a set of flash cards to practice converting numbers from standard notation to scientific notation and vice versa. Record a number in standard notation on one side of an index card. On the reverse side of the card, record the same number written using scientific notation. Use the cards to quiz your friends, or ask a family member to quiz you.

1 Mark and label the following numbers on the number line.

$$\sqrt{3}, \ 1.85, \ \frac{16}{10}, \ 1\frac{3}{4}$$

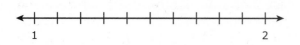

2 Termiyah is asked to order the following set of numbers from least to greatest.

$$-1.4, \ 0.75, \ -2\frac{1}{3}, \ 21\%, \ \frac{4}{5}$$

Termiyah's response is as follows.

$$-1.4, \ -2\frac{1}{3}, \ 21\%, \ \frac{4}{5}, \ 0.75$$

Did Termiyah correctly order the numbers? Explain your answer.

_____

_____

_____

3 Order the following set of numbers in ascending order.

$$\left\{-\sqrt{72}, \ 18, \ \sqrt{100}, \ -\frac{70}{9}, \ 8.25\right\}$$

4 Penny makes a Sunshine Cake for her friend's birthday. The table shows some of the ingredients she uses.

Sunshine Cake Ingredients

Ingredient	Amount
Shortening	$\frac{2}{3}$ c
Sugar	$1\frac{1}{2}$ c
Cake flour	$2\frac{1}{2}$ c
Milk	$\frac{3}{4}$ c

List the cake ingredients in descending order.

5 Place the following numbers in order from least to greatest.

$$-4.5, \ 3\frac{5}{6}, \ -\sqrt{16}, \ \frac{8}{3}, \ 2\pi$$

6 The following set of numbers is ordered from greatest to least.

$$1\frac{1}{3}, \ \frac{2}{7}, \ 0.035, \ {}^-\sqrt{2}$$

Place the following numbers in the list. Explain your reasoning for each placement.

$$\sqrt{2}, \ \frac{1}{12}, \ -\frac{3}{2}$$

_____

_____

_____

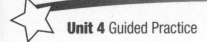
1 Which list shows the rational numbers in descending order?

Ⓐ $-2\frac{1}{3}$, -1.4, 0.75, 21%, $\frac{4}{5}$

Ⓑ $\frac{4}{5}$, -1.4, $-2\frac{1}{3}$, 21%, 0.75

Ⓒ 0.75, $\frac{4}{5}$, 21%, -1.4, $-2\frac{1}{3}$

Ⓓ $\frac{4}{5}$, 0.75, 21%, -1.4, $-2\frac{1}{3}$

2 Chauncey needs to order the following list of numbers from least to greatest.

$$\frac{1}{2}, \frac{5}{2}, -\frac{3}{4}, \sqrt{4}, \sqrt{5}, -\frac{1}{2}$$

Which list shows the correct order?

Ⓕ $-\frac{1}{2}$, $-\frac{3}{4}$, $\frac{1}{2}$, $\sqrt{4}$, $\sqrt{5}$, $\frac{5}{2}$

Ⓖ $-\frac{3}{4}$, $-\frac{1}{2}$, $\frac{1}{2}$, $\sqrt{4}$, $\sqrt{5}$, $\frac{5}{2}$

Ⓗ $-\frac{1}{2}$, $-\frac{3}{4}$, $\sqrt{4}$, $\sqrt{5}$, $\frac{1}{2}$, $\frac{5}{2}$

Ⓙ $-\frac{3}{4}$, $-\frac{1}{2}$, $\frac{1}{2}$, $\sqrt{4}$, $\frac{5}{2}$, $\sqrt{5}$

3 Roland records the deposit and withdrawal transactions in his bank account.

$15.20, -$23.44, -$3.75, $9.01, -$1.68

Which list shows these transactions in increasing order?

Ⓐ -$1.68, -$3.75, -$23.44, $9.01, $15.20

Ⓑ $15.20, $9.01, -$1.68, -$3.75, -$23.44

Ⓒ -$23.44, $15.20, $9.01, -$3.75, -$1.68

Ⓓ -$23.44, -$3.75, -$1.68, $9.01, $15.20

4 The captain of a submarine orders the crew to dive to a depth of 380 feet below sea level, then rise to a depth of 200 feet below sea level. Next, the crew is ordered to dive again to 922 feet below sea level, rise to 600 feet below sea level, and then surface. Which list shows the depths of the submarine in declining order?

Ⓕ -922 ft, -600 ft, -380 ft, -200 ft, 0 ft

Ⓖ 0 ft, -922 ft, -600 ft, -380 ft, -200 ft

Ⓗ 0 ft, -200 ft, -380 ft, -600 ft, -922 ft

Ⓙ 0 ft, -600 ft, -922 ft, -380 ft, -200 ft

5 Which list of real numbers is NOT ordered correctly?

Ⓐ -3.50, -2.75, -2.25, -1.05, 0.05

Ⓑ $-\frac{1}{5}$, $-\frac{1}{7}$, $\frac{1}{7}$, $\frac{1}{5}$, 40%

Ⓒ $-\sqrt{11}$, $-\sqrt{9}$, $\sqrt{5}$, 3, $\sqrt{10}$

Ⓓ $-\frac{4}{3}$, $-\sqrt{4}$, $-\sqrt{1}$, -0.08, -0.07

6 A weather balloon took temperature readings at various heights in the lower atmosphere. Balloons at lower altitudes had higher temperature readings. Which list shows balloons in order of increasing altitude?

Ⓕ 10.8°, 30.1°, 55.4°, 68.9°, 71.2°

Ⓖ 42.1°, 40.5°, 39.7°, 34.4°, 30.0°

Ⓗ 30.0°, 50.0°, 40.0°, 60.0°, 20.0°

Ⓙ 75.2°, 63.3°, 51.8°, 59.3°, 47.7°

1 Which list shows numbers ordered from smallest to largest?

Ⓐ -3.28, -3.47, 8.25, 14.38

Ⓑ -4.82, $\frac{1}{2}$, $\sqrt{21}$, 18

Ⓒ $\sqrt{9}$, $\frac{17}{2}$, $7\frac{3}{8}$, 21%

Ⓓ $8\frac{3}{4}$, $\sqrt{50}$, $33\frac{1}{3}$%, 40.5

2 The students in Mr. Woods' shop class measure several boards and record the lengths in a table as shown.

Board Lengths

Board Number	Length (inches)
1	$13\frac{3}{4}$
2	14
3	$13\frac{3}{8}$
4	$13\frac{1}{4}$
5	$13\frac{2}{3}$

Which list shows the lengths of the boards in order from greatest to least?

Ⓕ 14, $13\frac{3}{8}$, $13\frac{3}{4}$, $13\frac{2}{3}$, $13\frac{1}{4}$

Ⓖ 14, $13\frac{3}{4}$, $13\frac{2}{3}$, $13\frac{1}{4}$, $13\frac{3}{8}$

Ⓗ 14, $13\frac{3}{8}$, $13\frac{2}{3}$, $13\frac{1}{4}$, $13\frac{3}{4}$

Ⓙ 14, $13\frac{3}{4}$, $13\frac{2}{3}$, $13\frac{3}{8}$, $13\frac{1}{4}$

3 Demichael orders a set of numbers on his homework. In descending order, the first number is $5\frac{1}{2}$ and the last number is $5\frac{1}{3}$. Which of the following numbers is NOT in Demichael's list?

Ⓐ $\sqrt{25}$

Ⓑ 5.45

Ⓒ $5\frac{5}{12}$

Ⓓ 5.34

4 Mr. Duncan creates a pop quiz for his students. On the quiz, students must order the following numbers from least to greatest.

$$\left\{\frac{5}{12}, -1.15, \sqrt{14}, \frac{9}{2}, -\sqrt{8}\right\}$$

Which list shows the correct response to the question on Mr. Duncan's quiz?

Ⓕ -1.15, $-\sqrt{8}$, $\frac{5}{12}$, $\frac{9}{2}$, $\sqrt{14}$

Ⓖ -1.15, $-\sqrt{8}$, $\sqrt{14}$, $\frac{5}{12}$, $\frac{9}{2}$

Ⓗ $-\sqrt{8}$, -1.15, $\frac{5}{12}$, $\sqrt{14}$, $\frac{9}{2}$

Ⓙ $-\sqrt{8}$, -1.15, $\frac{5}{12}$, $\frac{9}{2}$, $\sqrt{14}$

5 The circumferences of several circles are shown.

$\frac{160}{7}$ 7π 20.2 $\frac{67}{3}$

Which shows the circumferences ordered from longest to shortest?

Ⓐ $\frac{160}{7}$, $\frac{67}{3}$, 20.2, 7π

Ⓑ $\frac{67}{3}$, $\frac{160}{7}$, 7π, 20.2

Ⓒ 20.2, 7π, $\frac{160}{7}$, $\frac{67}{3}$

Ⓓ $\frac{160}{7}$, $\frac{67}{3}$, 7π, 20.2

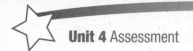
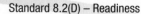
1 Savon has the following set of numbers to order on his math homework.

$$\left\{\pi, -3.14, -3\tfrac{1}{4}, 9, \tfrac{23}{7}\right\}$$

Which list correctly orders the numbers in increasing order?

Ⓐ π, $\tfrac{23}{7}$, -3.14, -3$\tfrac{1}{4}$, 9

Ⓑ -3.14, π, $\tfrac{23}{7}$, -3$\tfrac{1}{4}$, 9

Ⓒ π, -3.14, -3$\tfrac{1}{4}$, $\tfrac{23}{7}$, 9

Ⓓ -3$\tfrac{1}{4}$, -3.14, π, $\tfrac{23}{7}$, 9

2 Rosa orders blinds for all the windows in her new house. Before ordering, she measures the widths of the windows.

Window Measures

Room	Window Width (feet)
Living room	6.5
Kitchen	4.25
Master bedroom	6$\tfrac{1}{4}$
Guest bedroom	6
Study	7

Which list shows the rooms, arranged by the widths of the windows, in descending order?

Ⓕ Master bedroom, Kitchen, Living room, Study, Guest bedroom

Ⓖ Study, Living room, Master bedroom, Guest bedroom, Kitchen

Ⓗ Kitchen, Guest bedroom, Master bedroom, Living room, Study

Ⓙ Study, Master bedroom, Living room, Guest bedroom, Kitchen

3 Nadine finds the median of the following set of numbers: 5.79, 5$\tfrac{3}{4}$, 5$\tfrac{7}{8}$, 5.9, 5$\tfrac{4}{5}$. Which shows Nadine's work to find the median?

Ⓐ 5$\tfrac{3}{4}$, 5$\tfrac{4}{5}$, ⎛5$\tfrac{7}{8}$⎞ 5.79, 5.9

Ⓑ 5.9, 5.79, ⎛5$\tfrac{3}{4}$⎞ 5$\tfrac{4}{5}$, 5$\tfrac{7}{8}$

Ⓒ 5.79, 5$\tfrac{3}{4}$, ⎛5$\tfrac{7}{8}$⎞ 5$\tfrac{4}{5}$, 5.9

Ⓓ 5.9, 5$\tfrac{7}{8}$, ⎛5$\tfrac{4}{5}$⎞ 5.79, 5$\tfrac{3}{4}$

4 Which list shows the numbers in increasing order?

Ⓕ -0.5, 1.5, -2, -0.75, $\sqrt{7}$

Ⓖ -0.5, -2, -0.75, 1.5, $\sqrt{7}$

Ⓗ -2, -0.75, -0.5, 1.5, $\sqrt{7}$

Ⓙ $\sqrt{7}$, 1.5, -0.5, -0.75, -2

5 Karla orders a set of four numbers from least to greatest. The smallest number she orders is $\sqrt{17}$, and the largest is 4$\tfrac{3}{4}$. Which shows two possible numbers that could be in Karla's set?

Ⓐ 4.7 and $\sqrt{24}$

Ⓑ 4$\tfrac{2}{3}$ and 4.7

Ⓒ 4.05 and 4$\tfrac{2}{3}$

Ⓓ 4.1 and 4.5

1   Graph the following numbers on the number line.

$$-\sqrt{5}, \frac{\pi}{2}, \frac{\pi}{3}, 4\frac{5}{8}, \sqrt{18}$$

Explain the process you used to complete your number line.

_____

_____

_____

_____

2   Think about any two rational numbers. Will there always be an irrational number between two rational numbers? Explain your answer.

_____

_____

_____

Will there always be an irrational number between two other irrational numbers?
Explain your answer.

_____

_____

_____

Unit 4 Journal/Vocabulary Activity

Journal

Explain how to order a set of numbers containing one irrational number, one negative rational number, one positive decimal number, and one whole number.

_____

_____

_____

_____

Vocabulary Activity

For each vocabulary term, provide a synonym, an antonym, and a symbolic or pictorial representation.

Order

Synonym
Antonym
Representation

Decreasing

Synonym
Antonym
Representation

Descending

Synonym
Antonym
Representation

Ascending

Synonym
Antonym
Representation

Real Numbers

Synonym
Antonym
Representation

Increasing

Synonym
Antonym
Representation

mentoring**minds**.com

What's the Real Order?

Play *What's the Real Order?* with a partner. Each pair of players needs a game board, a number cube, and a two-color counter. Each player needs a pencil and a sheet of paper. Player 1 rolls the number cube and tosses the counter. Player 1 advances a number of spaces equal to the number rolled. He/She then orders the numbers in the space according to the side of the counter facing up: descending if red, and ascending if not red. If the numbers are ordered correctly, play passes to player 2. If the numbers are ordered incorrectly, player 1 moves back to the space where he/she began the turn, and play passes to player 2. The first player to reach *End* is the winner.

END

			-0.5, 1.5, -2, -0.75, $\sqrt{7}$
Move back 2 spaces.	$\sqrt{3}$, 1.85, $\frac{26}{10}$, $1\frac{3}{4}$	43.22, 43, 43.022	3, $\sqrt{10}$, $\frac{3}{4}$, -1.5
$-\frac{3}{4}$, 5, $\frac{9}{2}$, -2, -1			
0.2, $\frac{4}{15}$, 0.21, $\frac{1}{4}$	-1.2, -1.15, -1.1, -1.25, -1.17		
	Move ahead 1 space.		
	$5\frac{3}{4}$, $5\frac{2}{3}$, $5\frac{5}{8}$	4.12, $\sqrt{16}$, -4, $\frac{9}{2}$	
		Lose a turn.	
$\sqrt{5}$, -2.1, 0.5, $\frac{5}{100}$	$-\frac{3}{4}$, 0, -3, 0.75	-5, 2, -5.5, 3	

START

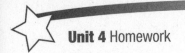
1 Record the following set of numbers in descending order.

$$-\sqrt{7}, \ 3, \ \sqrt{11}, \ \frac{3}{4}, \ -1.5, \ \pi$$

2 There are five advertisements from different car dealerships in the morning newspaper. Each dealership offers a different interest rate on car loans.

2%, 1.3%, 0.3%, 0.55%, 1.2%

Order the interest rates from least to greatest.

3 Locate and label the given numbers on the number line.

$$\frac{13}{7}, \ 2.5, \ \sqrt{9}, \ 3.5, \ -2.2, \ -4\frac{5}{9}, \ -\frac{30}{6}$$

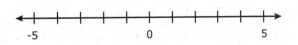

4 The table shows the lowest elevations for six different continents.

Continent Elevations

Continent	Elevation (below sea level)
Africa	156 m
Asia	417.5 m
Australia	12 m
Europe	28 m
North America	86 m
South America	105 m

Order the continents, based on their elevations, from greatest depth to least depth.

5 Steven, Linda, and Elliott check their lunch accounts in the cafeteria. Steven owes $12 on his account. Linda has $7, and Elliott has $3 remaining in his account. Order the students from least to greatest based on the amounts in their lunch accounts.

Connections

1. Locate five real numbers in a newspaper or magazine. At least one number should be irrational. Cut out the numbers and arrange them in ascending or descending order.

2. Use a measuring tape to measure the width of all the doors in your house. Make a table that includes the location of each door and its width. Order the door widths from least to greatest or greatest to least.

1 For each set of similar figures shown, record the scale factor used to dilate figure *A* as a ratio of corresponding sides.

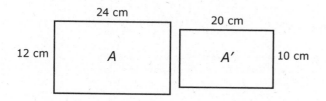

24 cm

20 cm

12 cm   *A*   *A'*   10 cm

Scale factor: _____

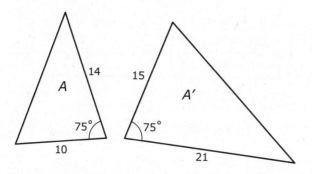

14   15

A   *A'*

75°   75°

10   21

Scale factor: _____

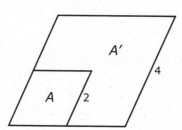

A'

4

A   2

Scale factor: _____

2 Triangle *PQR* is similar to triangle *P'QR'*.

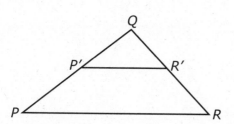

Q

P'   R'

P   R

Complete the proportion to justify that the triangles are similar.

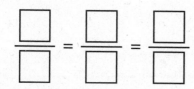

$$\frac{\square}{\square} = \frac{\square}{\square} = \frac{\square}{\square}$$

3 Parallelogram *DEFG* is dilated using a scale factor of 0.6 to form parallelogram *D'E'F'G'*. If the dimensions of parallelogram *DEFG* are 4 inches by 10 inches, write expressions to determine the dimensions of parallelogram *D'E'F'G'*.

What are the dimensions of parallelogram *D'E'F'G'*?

4 Triangle *ABC* has a perimeter of 30 meters. Triangle *DEF* has dimensions of 20 meters, 25 meters, and 15 meters. Are the two triangles similar? Explain why or why not.

_____

_____

_____

_____

5 Rectangles *ABCD* and *EFGH* are shown.

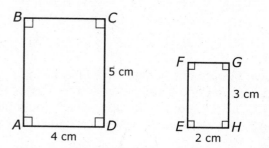

B   C

5 cm

A   D
4 cm

F   G
3 cm
E   H
2 cm

Are the rectangles similar? Use ratios to justify your answer.

Unit 5 Guided Practice

1 Triangle *EFG* is dilated to form triangle *HJK*.

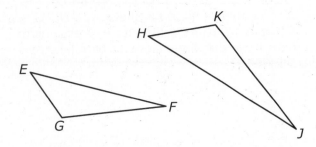

Which of the following is true about the triangles?

I. The ratio of $\overline{EG}$ to $\overline{HK}$ is equal to the ratio of $\overline{EF}$ to $\overline{HJ}$.

II. $\frac{GF}{KJ} = \frac{GE}{KH}$

III. $\frac{GF}{FE} = \frac{JH}{KJ}$

IV. The dimensions of triangle *EFG* are equivalent to the dimensions of triangle *HJK*.

Ⓐ I and II only

Ⓑ I, II, and IV only

Ⓒ III and IV only

Ⓓ I, II, III, and IV

2 Two figures are similar. The ratio of the corresponding sides between the figures is 9 to 12. Based on the ratio, which could be the scale factor used to dilate one figure to create the other?

Ⓕ 0.3

Ⓖ 3.4

Ⓗ 3

Ⓙ 0.75

3 Triangle *XYZ* is shown.

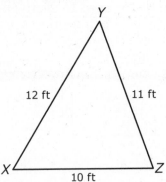

Which does NOT show a correct dilation of triangle *XYZ*?

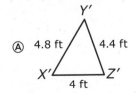

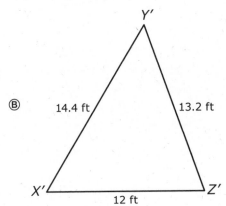

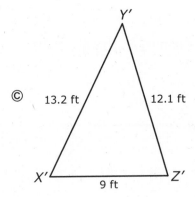

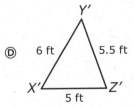

motivation**math**™LEVEL 8

mentoring**minds**.com

1 Which of the following statements is true about similar figures?

   I. The ratios of corresponding sides in similar figures are proportional.

   II. The scale factor is multiplied by the dimensions of each side of one figure to find the dimensions of each side of the dilated figure.

   III. The scale factor is multiplied by each angle measure of one figure to find each angle measure of the dilated figure.

Ⓐ I and II only

Ⓑ II and III only

Ⓒ I, II, and III

Ⓓ III only

2 Triangles *PQR* and *STR* are shown.

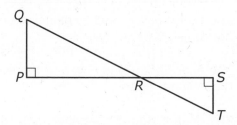

Which of the following does NOT justify △*PQR* ~ △*STR*?

Ⓕ $\dfrac{PQ}{PR} = \dfrac{ST}{SR}$

Ⓖ $\dfrac{QR}{TR} = \dfrac{QP}{TS}$

Ⓗ $\dfrac{RQ}{RT} = \dfrac{PQ}{ST}$

Ⓙ $\dfrac{PR}{SR} = \dfrac{TR}{QR}$

3 Parallelogram *MNPQ* is shown.

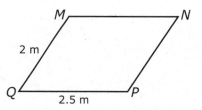

Which of the following figures is similar to parallelogram *MNPQ*?

Ⓐ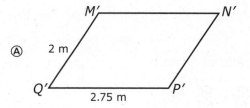

Ⓑ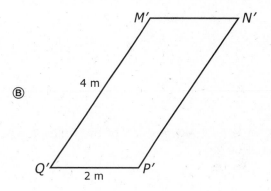

Ⓒ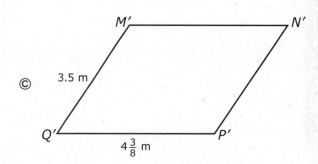

Ⓓ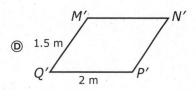

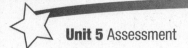

Unit 5 Assessment

1 Quadrilateral *ABCD* is dilated to form quadrilateral *A'B'C'D'*.

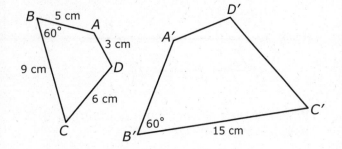

What scale factor was used to perform the dilation?

Ⓐ $\frac{3}{2}$

Ⓑ $\frac{5}{3}$

Ⓒ $\frac{3}{5}$

Ⓓ $\frac{1}{2}$

2 If $\triangle ABC \sim \triangle MNP$, which of the following is also true?

I. $\frac{AC}{BC} = \frac{MP}{NP}$

II. $\frac{BC}{NP} = \frac{AB}{MP}$

III. $\frac{AB}{BC} = \frac{MN}{NP}$

Ⓕ I only

Ⓖ II only

Ⓗ I and II only

Ⓙ I and III only

3 Which of the following is NOT true about a shape and its dilation?

Ⓐ The dimensions of a dilation are proportional to the corresponding dimensions of the original shape.

Ⓑ The ratio of the side lengths in the original shape is equal to the ratio of the corresponding side lengths in the dilation.

Ⓒ The dilation of a shape always results in a figure that is larger than the original.

Ⓓ A shape and its dilation have congruent corresponding angle measures.

4 The ratio of the corresponding side lengths of a figure and its dilation is 2 : 3. Which of the following is true?

Ⓕ The ratio of the corresponding angles of the figures is 2 : 3.

Ⓖ The scale factor used to dilate the original figure is 150%.

Ⓗ The dilated figure is one-half the size of the original figure.

Ⓙ The dilated figure is smaller than the original figure.

 motivation**math**™LEVEL 8 mentoring**minds**.com

1 Triangle *ABC* has the dimensions shown, forming a 3 : 4 : 5 ratio for the side lengths.

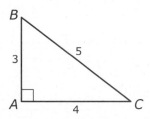

Complete the table for triangles similar to △*ABC* using the scale factor provided.

Scale Factor	Side *AB* (units)	Side *AC* (units)	Side *BC* (units)
0.5			
2			
3.25			
6			
n			

Explain how to use ratios to justify that the triangles in the table are similar to triangle *ABC*.

2 Delia makes the following generalization about three figures.

If figure A is similar to figure B, and figure A is similar to figure C, then figure B must be similar to figure C.

Is Delia correct? Justify your response and provide examples.

Journal

Explain how a scale factor is used to dilate a shape and create a similar figure.

_____

_____

_____

Vocabulary Activity

Use the clues to identify vocabulary terms studied in this unit. Record each term in the blank provided, and locate the terms in the puzzle.

a. _____
   a pair of angles located in the same
   position in two different similar shapes

b. _____
   a pair of sides located in the same
   position in two different similar shapes

c. _____
   a transformation which produces a
   figure similar to the original by
   proportionately reducing or enlarging
   the figure.

d. _____
   having a constant ratio

e. _____
   a comparison of two quantities

f. _____
   the common ratio for pairs of
   corresponding sides of similar figures

g. _____
   figures that are exactly the same shape
   with congruent corresponding angles
   and proportional corresponding sides

```
G S X K F X L M I R S Y P Z T Z D S S
O V I W B T B S Z C S L C M M N Y E D
V F D M E B H W A N S F I N W P L D H
K U Q J I D U L Y S O N G S B G Y O D
Y L E U N L E V W Q Q B W U N W I M Y
D Z W A G F A Z D L P L R A M T J U O
K H M N A B C R Z S S S G Q H L K D L
H K G C J S N P F H F N M R P E I J P
F N T H J N Q R Y I I T I V X S H S R
U O T R V G C N O D G U C U A U W M O
R G X J T U W Y N I B U C I S Q W T P
C B U V C L P O K L T L R S E L A S O
K X V W O J P Z C B R A U E N J J K R
T G S L G S G S T O V L R J S P H R T
W U I U E K C U K V F Q O Q K Q F V I
Y I S R F M J A L S E D Q Q F W K X O
Y C R F E N H F P D B I G M D X I F N
U O P Y V Y K T C N U M I W Y V H D A
C O R R E S P O N D I N G S I D E S L
Y L M I J M W W Z E N O I T A L I D J
```

Matchmaker

Play *Matchmaker* with a partner. Each pair of players needs 16 Color Tiles®, 8 each of two colors, and a game board. Place tiles on the game board squares, one color covering the scale factors and the second color covering the dilated figures. Player 1 removes two tiles, one of each color. If the scale factor revealed and the dilated figures revealed are a match, the player keeps the two tiles, and play passes to player 2. If the scale factor and figures are not a match, the tiles are replaced, and play passes to player 2. The game ends when all the tiles have been removed from the board. The player with more tiles wins.

	A	B	C	D
4	Scale Factor 2	Triangle A: 9, 15; Triangle A': 12, 20	Triangle A: 8, 10, 6; Triangle A': 12, 15, 9	Scale Factor $\dfrac{1}{3}$
3	Scale Factor 1.25	Triangle A: 6.4, 12; Triangle A': 15	Scale Factor 0.75	Rectangle A: 10, 15; Rectangle A': 20, 30
2	Triangle A: 12, 13; Triangle A': 2.5, 6	Scale Factor $\dfrac{4}{3}$	Triangle A: 12, 8, 18; Triangle A': 13.5	Scale Factor 0.5
1	Figure A / A': 2, 6	Scale Factor 3	Scale Factor $\dfrac{3}{2}$	Rectangle A: 3, 5; Rectangle A': 9, 15

Name _____

1 Quadrilateral *PQRS* is shown.

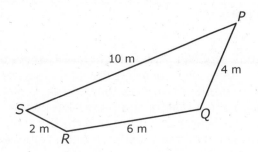

If a scale factor of $\frac{5}{4}$ is used to dilate quadrilateral *PQRS* to form quadrilateral *P'Q'R'S'*, what are the dimensions of the new figure?

P'Q' = _____   *Q'R'* = _____

R'S' = _____   *S'P'* = _____

2 Triangles *EFG* and *HJL* are shown.

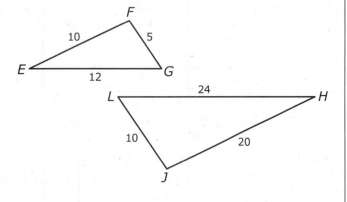

Write three ratios to prove that △*EFG* ~ △*HJL*.

3 Look at the figures shown.

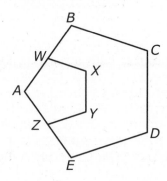

If pentagon *ABCDE* is similar to pentagon *AWXYZ*, write one statement that must be true about the figures.

_____

_____

_____

_____

4 If rectangle *FGHJ* was dilated to form rectangle *F'G'H'J'*, what scale factor was used for the dilation? Explain your answer.

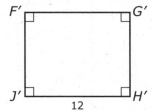

Connections

1. Find two objects in your house that you think are similar. Measure the dimensions of each, and use proportions to determine whether the objects are indeed similar.

2. Using your computer, create a figure or picture. Copy and paste the figure or picture, and use the tools to dilate it and create a similar figure. Record the scale factor you used in the dilation, and share the picture with the class.

         motivation**math**™LEVEL 8   mentoring**minds**.com

Use the graph to answer questions 1–5.

Triangle *JKL* is dilated by a scale factor of $\frac{1}{2}$ to form triangle *J'K'L'*.

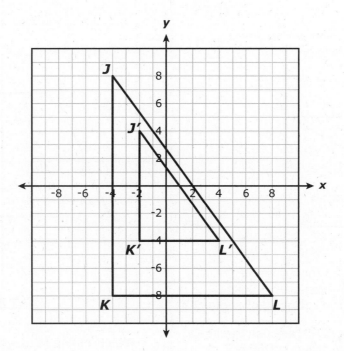

1 In triangle *JKL*, *JL* = 20 units. Use the coordinate plane to determine the lengths of the remaining sides of triangle *JKL*. Determine the lengths of the sides of triangle *J'K'L'*. Label the lengths on the graphic.

2 Write a ratio for the lengths of each pair of corresponding sides $\left(\frac{new}{original}\right)$.

3 Using a protractor, measure each angle of the triangles to the nearest degree. Label each angle with the measure.

4 Are the figures similar? Justify your answer using your responses from problems 1–3.

_____

_____

_____

_____

_____

5 Use your results from problems 1–4 to write one sentence that generalizes the relationship between any shape and its dilation.

_____

_____

Use the graph to answer questions 1 and 2.

Look at the triangle.

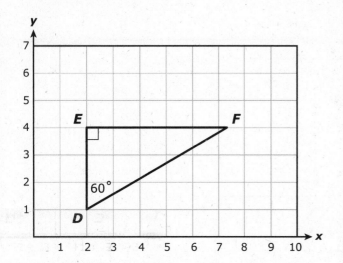

1   Triangle *DEF* is dilated to form triangle *D'E'F'*. The length of side *D'E'* measures 6 units. Which best describes the measure of angle *D'*?

Ⓐ   Angle *D'* measures 120° because the scale factor used to dilate triangle *DEF* is 2.

Ⓑ   Angle *D'* measures 60° because the corresponding angles of triangles *DEF* and *D'E'F'* are congruent.

Ⓒ   Angle *D'* measures 70° because triangle *DEF* is enlarged by a scale factor of 10% to form triangle *D'E'F'*.

Ⓓ   Angle *D'* measures 30° because the dilation is reduced by a scale factor of 50%.

2   Which statement is true about triangle *DEF* and triangle *D'E'F'*?

Ⓕ   The figures are similar and congruent.

Ⓖ   The figures are neither similar nor congruent.

Ⓗ   The figures are similar but not congruent.

Ⓙ   The figures are congruent but not similar.

3   Trapezoid *ABCD* is dilated to form trapezoid *A'B'C'D'*.

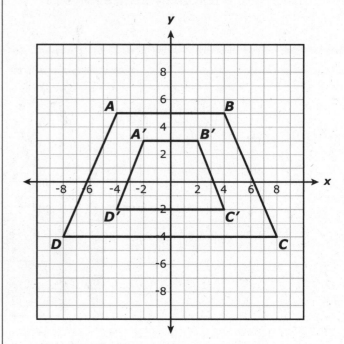

Which of the following statements are true?

I.   The ratio of *BC* to *B'C'* is equivalent to the ratio of *BA* to *B'A'*.

II.   Angle *D* is congruent to angle *D'*.

III.   Side *DC* is congruent to side *D'C'*.

IV.   Trapezoid *ABCD* is similar to trapezoid *A'B'C'D'*.

Ⓐ   I and II only

Ⓑ   I, II, and III only

Ⓒ   I, II, and IV only

Ⓓ   I, II, III, and IV

Use the graph to answer questions 1 and 2.

Triangle *XYZ* is dilated by a scale factor of 3 to form triangle *TUV*.

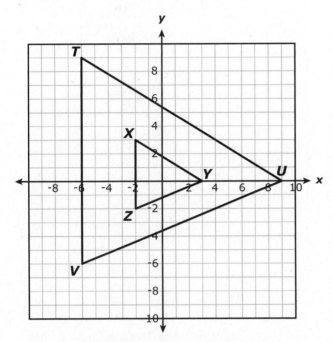

1 Which statement is NOT true?

Ⓐ The length of $\overline{TU}$ is three times the length of $\overline{XY}$.

Ⓑ Angle *V* and angle *Y* are congruent.

Ⓒ Triangle *XYZ* is similar to triangle *TUV*.

Ⓓ The measure of $\overline{YZ}$ is $\frac{1}{3}$ the measure of $\overline{UV}$.

2 If the length of $\overline{VU}$ is 16 units, which best describes the length of $\overline{ZY}$?

Ⓕ 16 units, because the figures are congruent

Ⓖ 48 units, because triangle *XYZ* is three times as large as triangle *TUV*

Ⓗ $5\frac{1}{3}$ units, because the dimensions of triangle *XYZ* are $\frac{1}{3}$ the dimensions of triangle *TUV*

Ⓙ 13 units, because the dimensions of triangle *XYZ* are decreased by 3 due to the scale factor

3 Parallelogram *Q′R′S′T′* is a dilation of parallelogram *QRST* using a scale factor of $\frac{2}{3}$.

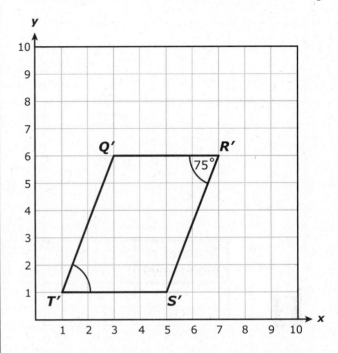

Which of the following statements are true about the figure and its dilation?

I. The ratio of $\frac{QR}{Q'R'}$ is $\frac{2}{3}$.

II. Angles *R*, *T*, *R′*, and *T′* each measure 75°.

III. The ratio of the measure of angle *Q* to the measure of angle *Q′* is $\frac{1}{1}$.

IV. The length of $\overline{TS}$ can be determined by multiplying the length of $\overline{T'S'}$ by $\frac{3}{2}$.

Ⓐ I and IV only

Ⓑ I and II only

Ⓒ II, III, and IV only

Ⓓ I, II, III, and IV

1 Triangle *ZYX* is dilated by a scale factor of $\frac{1}{4}$ to form triangle *Z'Y'X'*.

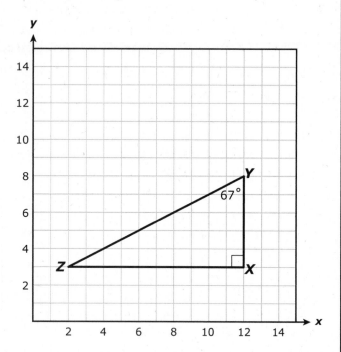

Which statement best compares the attributes of triangle *ZYX* to triangle *Z'Y'X'*?

Ⓐ The measure of angle *X'* is 22.5°, the measure of angle *Y'* is 16.75°, and the measure of angle *Z'* is 5.75°.

Ⓑ The side lengths of triangle *ZYX* are 4 times the measures of the corresponding side lengths of triangle *Z'Y'X'*.

Ⓒ The measures of the angles of triangle *Z'Y'X'* are 4 times the measures of the corresponding angles of triangle *ZYX*.

Ⓓ The side lengths of triangle *Z'Y'X'* are congruent to the corresponding side lengths of triangle *ZYX*.

2 Pentagon *ABCDE* is dilated to form pentagon *A'B'C'D'E'* as shown.

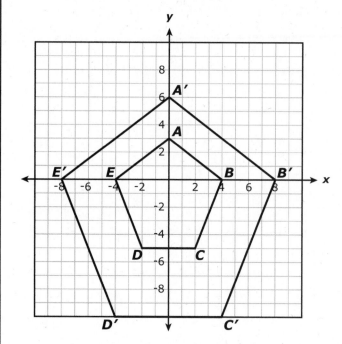

Which statement is NOT true about pentagon *ABCDE* and pentagon *A'B'C'D'E'*?

Ⓕ If the measure of angle *E* is 105°, the measure of angle *E'* is 105°.

Ⓖ The measure of angle *C'* is congruent to the measure of angle *C*.

Ⓗ $\frac{ED}{BC} = \frac{B'C'}{E'D'}$

Ⓙ $\frac{A'B'}{C'D'} = \frac{AB}{CD}$

3 Which statement is true about a shape and its dilation?

Ⓐ The corresponding angles of a shape and its dilation are not proportional.

Ⓑ The corresponding side lengths of a shape and its dilation are congruent.

Ⓒ The side lengths of a dilation are always smaller than the corresponding side lengths of the original shape.

Ⓓ The corresponding angles of a shape and its dilation are congruent.

Triangle *P'Q'R'* is a dilation of triangle *PQR*.

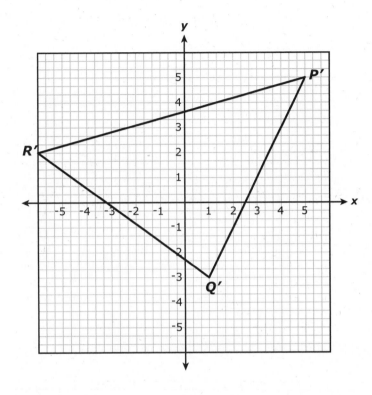

The coordinates of triangle *PQR* are $P\left(3\frac{1}{3}, 3\frac{1}{3}\right)$, $Q\left(\frac{2}{3}, -2\right)$, and $R\left(-4, 1\frac{1}{3}\right)$. Graph the triangle on the coordinate plane.

Write the following ratios of *x*-coordinates for the triangles.

$\dfrac{P'}{P}$ _____ $\dfrac{Q'}{Q}$ _____ $\dfrac{R'}{R}$ _____

Write the following ratios of *y*-coordinates for the triangles.

$\dfrac{P'}{P}$ _____ $\dfrac{Q'}{Q}$ _____ $\dfrac{R'}{R}$ _____

How do the ratios of the coordinates compare to the ratios of the corresponding sides between the two triangles?

_____

What conclusions can be made about triangle *PQR* and triangle *P'Q'R'*?

_____

_____

Journal

Explain how a scale factor is applied to the coordinates of a figure to determine the coordinates for a dilation of the figure.

_____

_____

Vocabulary Activity

A shape and its dilation are shown on the coordinate plane.

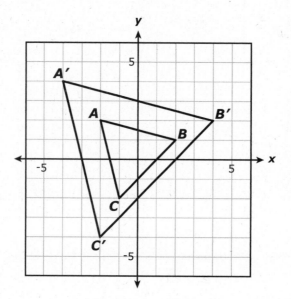

Complete the steps.

1. Draw a circle around a pair of *corresponding sides*. Express the circled sides as a ratio.

2. Draw a box around a pair of *corresponding angles*. Identify the boxed angles using a congruency statement.

3. Is the *scale factor* used to *dilate* triangle *ABC* between 0 and 1 or greater than 1? Explain your answer.

_____

_____

Justify It

Complete *Justify It* individually. For each representation shown, determine if the figures are similar. If the figures are similar, determine the scale factor. Record the information below the representation. If the figures are not similar, explain why below the representation.

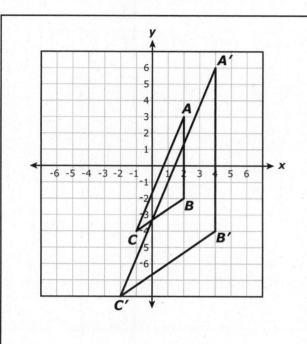

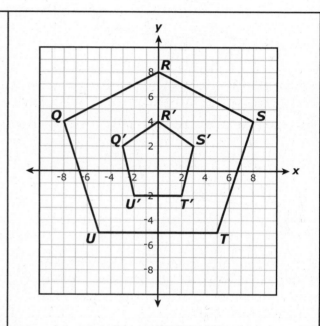

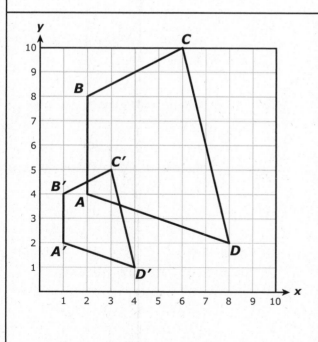

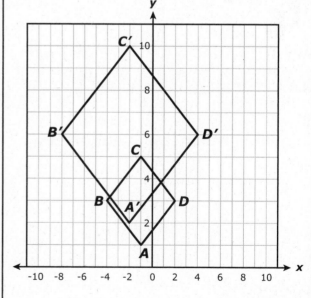

1 The dilation of parallelogram *PQRS* by a scale factor of 3 is shown.

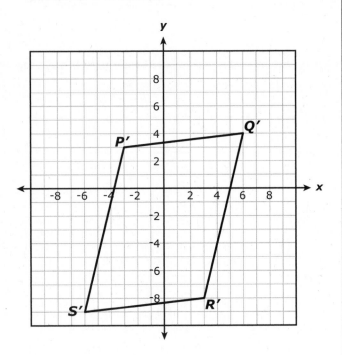

Write a statement comparing the measures of the angles of parallelogram *PQRS* to the measures of the corresponding angles of parallelogram *P′Q′R′S′*.

Write a statement comparing the side lengths of parallelogram *P′Q′R′S′* to the corresponding side lengths of parallelogram *PQRS*.

2 Trapezoid *MIND* is dilated to form trapezoid *M′I′N′D′* as shown.

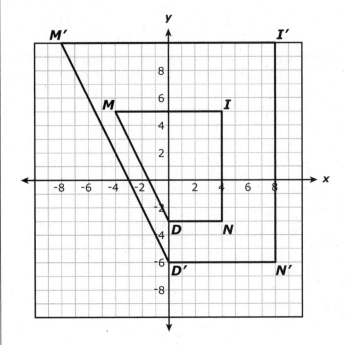

For each of the following, write *T* if the statement is true and *F* if the statement is false.

a. _____ The measure of angle *I′* is 90°; therefore, the measure of angle *I* is 90°.

b. _____ The ratio of *MD* to *M′D′* is $\frac{1}{2}$ times the ratio of *IN* to *I′N′*.

c. _____ The length of $\overline{D′N′}$ is $\frac{1}{2}$ times the length of $\overline{DN}$.

d. _____ The ratio of *IM* to *I′M′* is equal to the ratio of *ND* to *N′D′*.

e. _____ The sum of the angle measures of trapezoid *MIND* is $\frac{1}{2}$ the sum of the angle measures of trapezoid *M′I′N′D′*.

Connections

Draw a large polygon on a sheet of paper. Determine the side lengths and angle measures. Take a picture of your polygon. Measure the side lengths and angle measures of your polygon picture. Write comparisons of the angle measures, and write proportions using the side lengths. Determine the scale factor. Try this activity again using a family photo or other picture. Does your camera always use the same scale factor?

1 Triangle *DEF* is dilated by a scale factor of $\frac{1}{3}$ to form triangle *RST*.

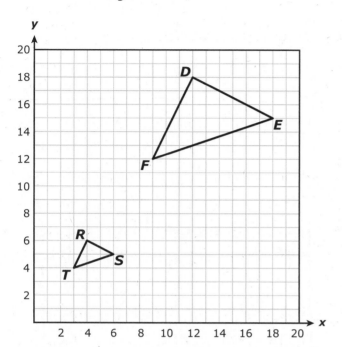

Complete the table to show the relationship between the coordinates of the original figure and the coordinates of the dilated figure.

Vertices of Triangle *DEF*	Relationship	Corresponding Vertices of Triangle *RST*

Write a general algebraic representation to describe the dilation of each *x*- and *y*-value of the vertices of triangle *DEF* to form triangle *RST*.

2 A construction company builds a rectangular parking lot.

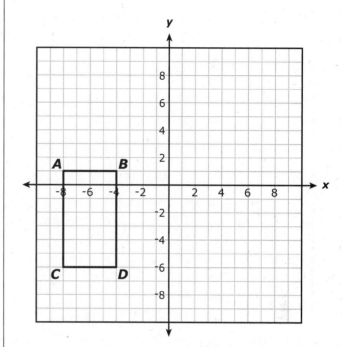

The company decides to enlarge the lot. If the new vertices can be represented by the algebraic representation (2.5*x*, 2.5*y*), what are the coordinates of point *B'*?

3 A dilation of a triangle can be represented by the coordinates (6*x*, 6*y*). How will this change the dimensions of the triangle?

What scale factor is used to dilate the triangle?

4 A rectangle is dilated by a scale factor of $\frac{2}{5}$. Use an algebraic representation to describe the effect of the scale factor on the coordinates of the original rectangle.

1 Look at the dilation shown.

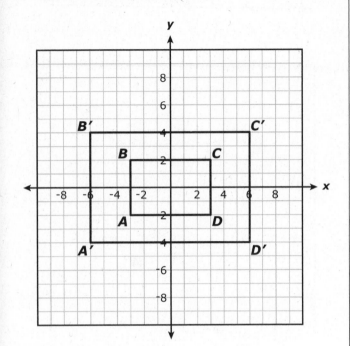

Which best represents the change in the vertices of rectangle *ABCD* to form rectangle *A'B'C'D'*?

Ⓐ $(x, y) \rightarrow \left(\frac{1}{2}x, \frac{1}{2}y\right)$

Ⓑ $(x, y) \rightarrow (2x, 2y)$

Ⓒ $(x, y) \rightarrow (4x, 4y)$

Ⓓ $(x, y) \rightarrow (3x, 2y)$

2 A triangle with a vertex at point *Y*(-3, 7) is dilated by a scale factor represented by the coordinate pair $\left(\frac{2}{3}x, \frac{2}{3}y\right)$. What is the location of *Y'*?

Ⓕ $Y'\left(-2, 4\frac{2}{3}\right)$

Ⓖ $Y'(-6, 14)$

Ⓗ $Y'\left(-3\frac{2}{3}, 7\frac{2}{3}\right)$

Ⓙ $Y'(-2, 4)$

3 Rectangle *FGHJ* has coordinates *F*(-8, 6), *G*(8, 6), *H*(8, -6), and *J*(-8, -6). The rectangle is dilated by a scale factor of 3. Which shows the effect of the scale factor on rectangle *FGHJ* to form rectangle *F'G'H'J'*?

Ⓐ $(x + 3, y + 3)$

Ⓑ $\left(\frac{1}{3}x, \frac{1}{3}y\right)$

Ⓒ $(x - 3, y - 3)$

Ⓓ $(3x, 3y)$

4 Pentagon *QRSTU* is dilated to form pentagon *Q'R'S'T'U'*.

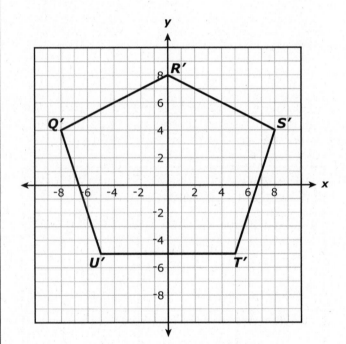

If *Q* is located at (-2, 1), which of the following can be used to determine the location of *R*?

Ⓕ $(0 \cdot 4, 8 \cdot 4)$

Ⓖ $\left(0 \cdot \frac{1}{2}, 8 \cdot \frac{1}{2}\right)$

Ⓗ $\left(0 \cdot \frac{1}{4}, 8 \cdot \frac{1}{4}\right)$

Ⓙ $(0 \cdot -2, 8 \cdot -2)$

1 A triangle with vertices $T(0, 0)$, $U(0, 3)$, and $V(4, 0)$ is dilated, and the vertices of the new triangle are $T'(0, 0)$, $U'(0, 1.5)$, and $V'(2, 0)$. Which best represents the scale factor applied to the original triangle?

Ⓐ $(1x, 1y)$

Ⓑ $(0x, 0y)$

Ⓒ $(0x, -0.5y)$

Ⓓ $(0.5x, 0.5y)$

2 The city planning committee votes to change one of the baseball fields to be used as a softball field. The softball field is shown on the grid.

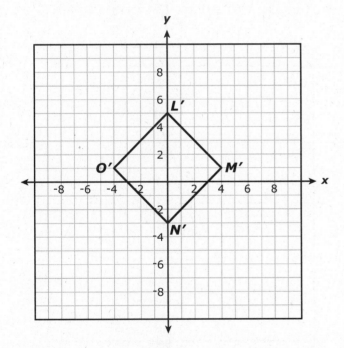

The algebraic expressions $\left(\frac{2}{3}x, \frac{2}{3}y\right)$ are used to describe the dilation of the baseball field. Which point does NOT correctly reflect the dilation?

Ⓕ $L(0, 7.5)$

Ⓖ $M(6, 1.5)$

Ⓗ $N(0, -3.5)$

Ⓙ $O(-6, 1.5)$

3 Parallelogram $UVWX$ is dilated to form parallelogram $U'V'W'X'$.

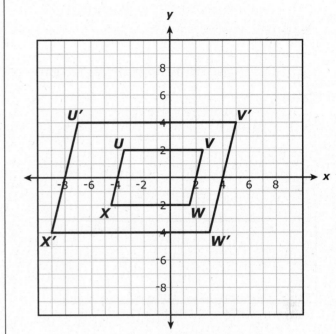

Which best represents the dilation of parallelogram $UVWX$ to parallelogram $U'V'W'X'$?

Ⓐ $\left(\frac{1}{2}x, \frac{1}{2}y\right)$

Ⓑ $(2x, 2y)$

Ⓒ $\left(\frac{2}{3}x, \frac{2}{3}y\right)$

Ⓓ $(3x, 3y)$

4 A triangle with vertices $E(-9, 6)$, $F(-6, -5)$, and $G(4, 0)$ is dilated to form a triangle with vertices $E'(-3, 2)$, $F'\left(-2, -1\frac{2}{3}\right)$, and $G'\left(1\frac{1}{3}, 0\right)$. Which best explains the effect of the scale factor applied to triangle EFG to form triangle $E'F'G'$?

Ⓕ $(x, y) \rightarrow (-3x, -3y)$

Ⓖ $(x, y) \rightarrow \left(\frac{2}{3}x, \frac{2}{3}y\right)$

Ⓗ $(x, y) \rightarrow (3x, 3y)$

Ⓙ $(x, y) \rightarrow \left(\frac{1}{3}x, \frac{1}{3}y\right)$

1 Mr. Ramirez receives blueprints for his new house. The scale used to draw the blueprints is $\frac{1}{4}$ inch equals 1 foot. The blueprint is drawn on a coordinate plane. Which algebraic representation explains the dilation used to create the blueprint of Mr. Ramirez's new house?

Ⓐ $(4x, 4y)$

Ⓑ $(12x, 12y)$

Ⓒ $\left(\frac{1}{4}x, \frac{1}{4}y\right)$

Ⓓ $\left(\frac{1}{12}x, \frac{1}{12}y\right)$

2 The figure shown is dilated using a scale factor of $(0.75x, 0.75y)$.

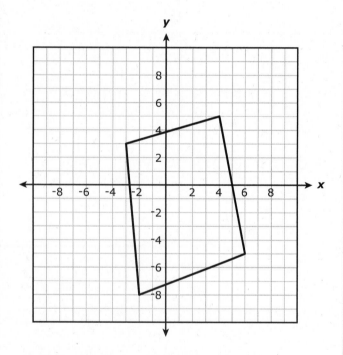

Which ordered pair will NOT be one of the new vertices?

Ⓕ $(-2.25, 2.25)$

Ⓖ $(-1.5, -6)$

Ⓗ $(3, 3.75)$

Ⓙ $(4, -2.5)$

3 A parallelogram with vertices $H(-2, 2)$, $J(5, 2)$, $K(-3, 3)$, and $L(-4, -3)$ is dilated to form a parallelogram with vertices $H'(-5, 5)$, $J'(12.5, 5)$, $K'(-7.5, 7.5)$, and $L'(-10, -7.5)$. Which representation best explains the effect of this dilation?

Ⓐ $(x, y) \rightarrow (3x, 3y)$

Ⓑ $(x, y) \rightarrow (2.5x, 2.5y)$

Ⓒ $(x, y) \rightarrow (2x, 2y)$

Ⓓ $(x, y) \rightarrow (1.5x, 1.5y)$

4 Triangle XYZ is dilated to form triangle $X'Y'Z'$.

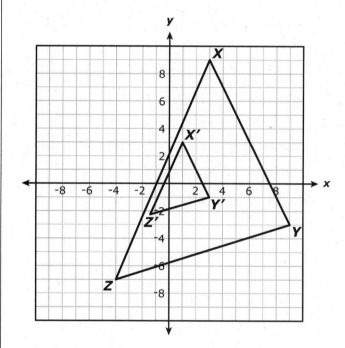

Which shows the scale factor used to dilate triangle XYZ to form triangle $X'Y'Z'$?

Ⓕ $(3x, 3y)$

Ⓖ $\left(\frac{1}{2}x, \frac{1}{2}y\right)$

Ⓗ $(2x, 2y)$

Ⓙ $\left(\frac{1}{3}x, \frac{1}{3}y\right)$

motivation**math**™LEVEL 8

Triangle *PQR* is graphed on the coordinate plane as shown.

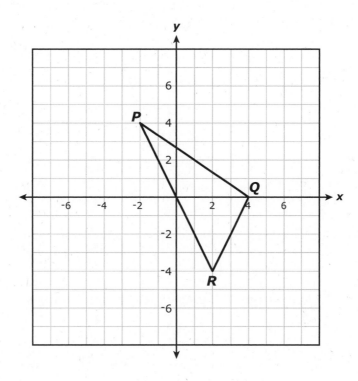

1 Dilate △*PQR* using $\left(\frac{1}{4}x, \frac{1}{4}y\right)$. Sketch and label triangle *P'Q'R'* on the coordinate plane and list the new vertices.

P' _____   Q' _____   R' _____

2 Dilate △*P'Q'R'* using (2*x*, 2*y*). Sketch and label triangle *P"Q"R"* on the coordinate plane and list the new vertices.

P" _____   Q" _____   R" _____

3 Determine a single scale factor that can be used to dilate △*PQR* to create △*P"Q"R"*. _____

Record the algebraic representation that explains the effect of the dilation on △*PQR*.

_____

4 Is it possible to still get △*P"Q"R"* if the order of the dilations is reversed, i.e. perform the dilation (2*x*, 2*y*) on △*PQR* first, followed by $\left(\frac{1}{4}x, \frac{1}{4}y\right)$? Explain your answer.

_____

_____

Journal

Anissa dilates a triangle drawn on a coordinate plane using the following: $(3x, 5y)$. Are the triangles Anissa creates similar? Explain your answer.

_____

_____

_____

Vocabulary Activity

Complete the activity with a partner. Player 1 rolls a die and uses the three terms in the row or column associated with the number rolled to create a true statement, make connections, or discuss similarities or differences between the terms. Player 1 records his/her information, briefly, in the table. The process is repeated by player 2. If a number is rolled a second time, the information given must be different than what has already been written. Players continue taking turns until time is called.

	4	5	6	Information
1	two-dimensional figure	dilation	coordinate plane	
2	coordinates	origin	scale factor	
3	axis/axes	algebraic representation (transformation)	ordered pair	
Information				

What Number Did You Dilate?

Play *What Number Did You Dilate?* with a partner. Each pair of players needs a game board and a paper clip to use with the spinner. Each player needs a pencil. Player 1 begins by spinning the spinner and using the number spun as a scale factor, using an algebraic representation to explain the effect of the scale factor on the triangle shown. Then player 1 determines the coordinate points of the dilated figure. If the points are correct, player 1 graphs the figure on the coordinate plane and initials the section of the spinner used. If the points are incorrect, play passes to player 2. If a player spins a scale factor that has already been initialed, he/she loses a turn. The game ends when all sections of the spinner have been initialed. The player with more initials on the spinner wins.

Player 1

Algebraic Representation	Coordinates
	(_____ , _____) (_____ , _____) (_____ , _____)
	(_____ , _____) (_____ , _____) (_____ , _____)
	(_____ , _____) (_____ , _____) (_____ , _____)

Player 2

Algebraic Representation	Coordinates
	(_____ , _____) (_____ , _____) (_____ , _____)
	(_____ , _____) (_____ , _____) (_____ , _____)
	(_____ , _____) (_____ , _____) (_____ , _____)

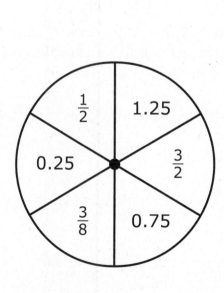

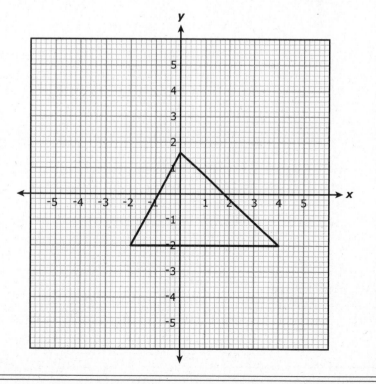

1 The neighborhood park planning committee has decided to enlarge the rose garden by a scale factor of 2.25. The original garden is shown on the graph.

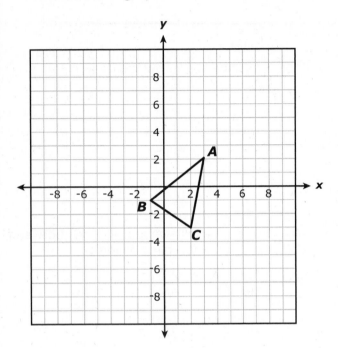

Write an algebraic representation to describe the effect of the scale factor on the original garden.

What are the coordinates of the enlarged garden?

Sketch the enlarged garden on the coordinate plane.

2 Rectangle *EFGH* with vertices *E*(-3, 5), *F*(6, 5), *G*(6, -4), and *H*(-3, -4) is dilated by a scale factor of 1.75. Use an algebraic representation to explain how the scale factor is used to find the coordinates for *F'*.

3 A dilation of quadrilateral *QRST* is shown.

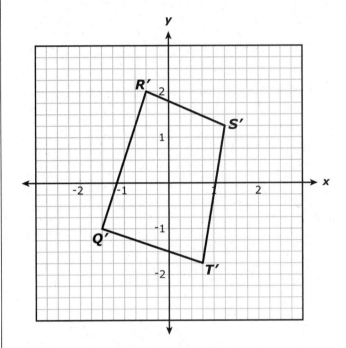

If the dilation can be represented by the ordered pair $\left(\frac{1}{4}x, \frac{1}{4}y\right)$, what are the coordinates for the vertices of *QRST*?

Connections

Measure the dimensions of a room in your house. On a sheet of graph paper, use one unit to equal one foot, and sketch the room. Dilate the room using a scale factor of $\left(\frac{1}{2}x, \frac{1}{2}y\right)$. What are the coordinates of the dilated room? Dilate the room by a scale factor of $(3x, 3y)$. What are the coordinates of the dilated room?

Use the graph to answer questions 1–4.

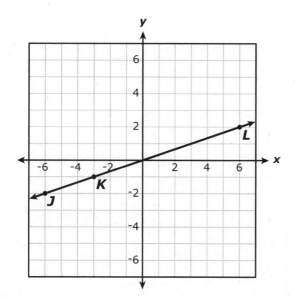

Use the graph to answer questions 5–8.

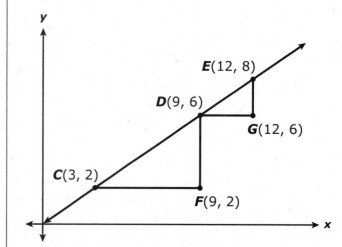

1 Beginning at point *J*, trace the vertical and horizontal distances needed to travel to point *K*. Label the vertical height and horizontal length of the triangle created.

2 Beginning at point *K*, trace the vertical and horizontal distances needed to travel to point *L*. Label the vertical height and horizontal length of the triangle created.

3 What is the ratio of the vertical height to the horizontal length for the smaller triangle?

What is the ratio of the vertical height to the horizontal length for the larger triangle?

What conclusion can be made about the two triangles?

4 Based on your responses on problem 3, what is the ratio of the side lengths *JK* to *KL*?

What information does this provide about the slope of line *JL*?

5 Find the change in *y*-values ($y_2 - y_1$) between points *D* and *F* and points *E* and *G*.

vertical change of $\overline{DF}$ _____

vertical change of $\overline{EG}$ _____

6 Find the change in *x*-values ($x_2 - x_1$) between points *F* and *C* and points *G* and *D*.

horizontal change of $\overline{FC}$ _____

horizontal change of $\overline{GD}$ _____

7 Write a ratio for each triangle $\left(\frac{y_2 - y_1}{x_2 - x_1}\right)$.

$\frac{DF}{CF} =$ _____ $\frac{EG}{DG} =$ _____

How do the two ratios compare?

8 Based on your response to problem 7, what do you know about the slope of line *CE*?

Unit 8 Guided Practice

1 Look at the graph.

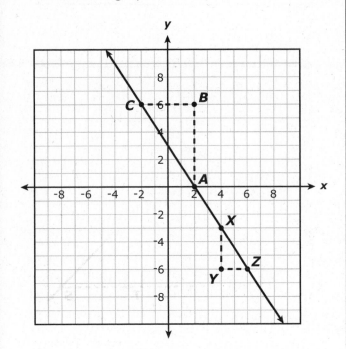

The slope of $\overline{CA}$ is $-\frac{3}{2}$. Which of the following is true about the slope of $\overline{XZ}$?

Ⓐ The slope of $\overline{XZ}$ is the negative reciprocal of the slope of $\overline{CA}$, because the triangles are flipped.

Ⓑ The slope of $\overline{XZ}$ is one-half the slope of $\overline{CA}$, because the ratio of corresponding sides between the triangles is $\frac{1}{2}$.

Ⓒ The slope of $\overline{XZ}$ is the same as the slope of $\overline{CA}$, because the ratios of the corresponding sides of the triangles are equivalent.

Ⓓ There is no relationship between the slope of $\overline{XZ}$ and the slope of $\overline{CA}$.

2 Look at the triangles.

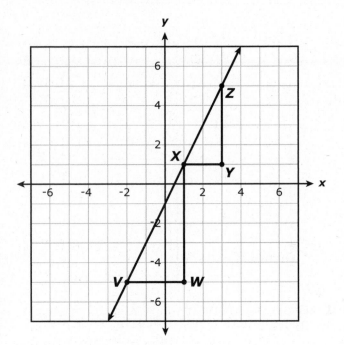

Which of the following can be used to determine the slope of line VZ?

I. $\frac{1-5}{1-3}$

II. The ratio of the vertical height to the horizontal length in triangle XYZ

III. $\frac{-5-1}{-2-1}$

IV. The ratio of the horizontal length to the vertical height in triangle VWX

Ⓕ II only

Ⓖ I and III only

Ⓗ II and IV only

Ⓙ I, II, and III only

     motivation**math**™LEVEL 8   mentoring**minds**.com

Use the graph to answer questions 1 and 2.

Look at the graph.

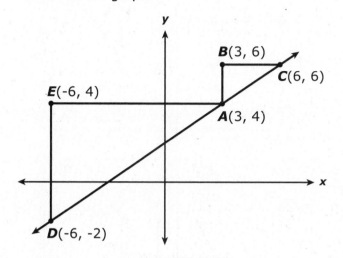

1   Given the information in the graph, how can the slope of $\overline{DC}$ be determined?

Ⓐ Find the difference between the ratios of the vertical heights to the horizontal lengths for both triangles.

Ⓑ Find the ratio of the horizontal length to the vertical height for one of the triangles.

Ⓒ Find the difference between the ratios of the horizontal lengths to the vertical heights for both triangles.

Ⓓ Find the ratio of the vertical height to the horizontal length for one of the triangles.

2   Which of the following is NOT true?

Ⓕ $\frac{-2 - 4}{-6 - 3} = \frac{6 - 4}{6 - 3}$

Ⓖ The slope of line DC is $\frac{2}{3}$, the ratio of the vertical height to the horizontal length for triangle ABC.

Ⓗ The slope of line DC is $\frac{3}{2}$, the ratio of the horizontal length to the vertical height for triangle DEA.

Ⓙ The slope of $\overline{DA}$ is equivalent to the slope of $\overline{AC}$.

3   Triangles QUS and RTS are graphed as shown.

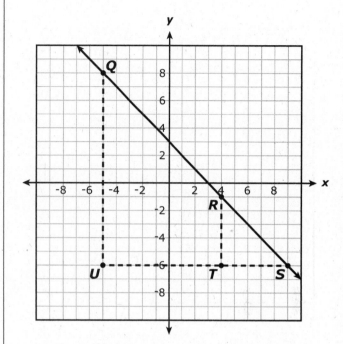

Which of the following best describes the slope of $\overline{QS}$?

Ⓐ The slope is 14, because the ratio of the vertical height to the horizontal length for triangle QUS is $\frac{14}{14}$.

Ⓑ The slope is -1, because the ratio of the vertical height to the horizontal length simplifies to -1 for both triangle QUS and triangle RTS.

Ⓒ The slope is 1, because the ratio of the horizontal length to the vertical height simplifies to 1 for both triangle QUS and triangle RTS.

Ⓓ The slope is -5, because the ratio of the horizontal length to the vertical height for triangle RTS is $-\frac{5}{5}$.

1 The graphs of triangles *LMN* and *NOP* are shown.

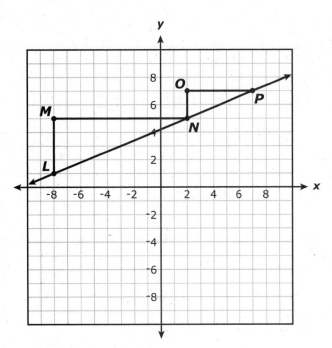

Which of the following best describes the slope of line *LP?*

Ⓐ $\frac{5}{2}$, because the ratio of the vertical side length to horizontal side length for both triangles simplifies to $\frac{5}{2}$

Ⓑ 2, because the ratio of the vertical side length of triangle *LMN* to the vertical side length of triangle *NOP* is 2

Ⓒ $\frac{2}{5}$, because the ratio of the vertical side length to the horizontal side length for both triangles simplifies to $\frac{2}{5}$

Ⓓ $\frac{1}{2}$, because the ratio of the vertical side length of triangle *NOP* to the vertical side length of triangle *LMN* is $\frac{1}{2}$

Use the graph to answer questions 2 and 3.

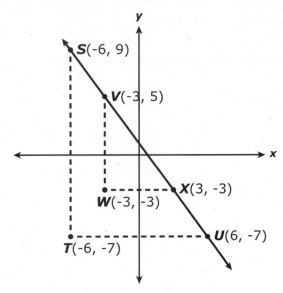

2 Given the information in the graph, how can the slope of $\overline{SU}$ be determined?

Ⓕ Find the ratio of the horizontal length to the vertical height for one of the triangles.

Ⓖ Find the ratio of the vertical height of the larger triangle to the vertical height of the smaller triangle.

Ⓗ Find the ratio of the horizontal length of the larger triangle to the horizontal length of the smaller triangle.

Ⓙ Find the ratio of the vertical height to the horizontal length for one of the triangles.

3 Which of the following is true?

Ⓐ The slope of line *SU* is $\frac{4}{3}$, the ratio of the vertical height to the horizontal length for triangle *STU*.

Ⓑ The slope of line *VX* is $-\frac{4}{3}$, the ratio of the vertical height to the horizontal length for triangle *VWX*.

Ⓒ The slope of line *SU* is $-\frac{3}{4}$, the ratio of the horizontal length to the vertical height for triangle *STU*.

Ⓓ The slope of line *VX* is $\frac{3}{4}$, the ratio of the horizontal length to the vertical height for triangle *VWX*.

motivation**math** ™LEVEL 8

mentoring**minds**.com

1 Graph a right triangle with a vertical height to horizontal length ratio of $\frac{1}{2}$. Then, extend the line opposite the right angle in both directions. Justify that the slope of the line drawn is $\frac{1}{2}$ using a second right triangle that is similar to the first. Explain the process used in your justification.

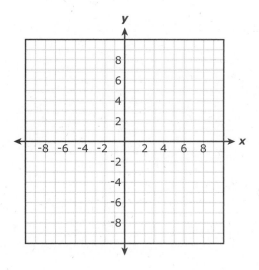

2 The graph of line l is shown.

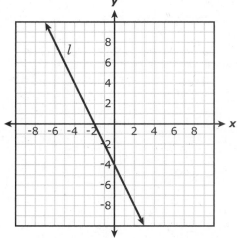

Ben and Maddie both use triangles to determine the slope of the line. Ben determines the slope of line l to be -2. Maddie says the slope of the line is $\frac{1}{2}$. Who is correct? Use similar right triangles to justify your response.

_____

_____

_____

Journal

Consider the graph shown. Explain the relationship between the points on the line, (x_1, y_1) and (x_2, y_2), and the base and height of the triangle.

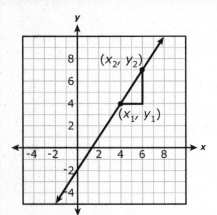

_____

_____

_____

_____

Vocabulary Activity

Each student needs a purple, a brown, a green, and a red colored pencil. The graph shows a line graphed on the coordinate plane.

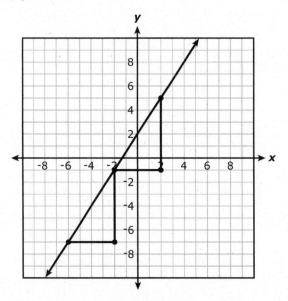

1. Use a purple pencil to shade a *vertical* height on one triangle.

2. Use a brown pencil to shade the *horizontal* length of the same triangle used in problem 1.

3. Use a green pencil to circle a representation for the *change in* y (Δy) on a different triangle than used in problem 1.

4. Use a red pencil to circle a representation for the *change in* x (Δx) on the same triangle used in problem 3.

5. Beside each of the three points on the line, write the *coordinates* for the points.

motivation**math**™LEVEL 8   mentoring**minds**.com

Tri(this)Angle

Complete *Tri(this)Angle* with a partner. Each pair of players needs a game board and a paper clip to use with the spinner. Each player needs a pencil. Player 1 spins the spinner. Using the number spun, player 1 identifies two points on the line labeled with the same number, recording the two points as (x_1, y_1) and (x_2, y_2) in the table column *Coordinates for First Triangle*. Player 1 draws a right triangle on the line between the two points. Finally, player 1 records in the table the ratio of the vertical height to the horizontal length of the triangle drawn. Player 2 then identifies two different points on the same line and repeats the process. If the ratios for both players are equal, each player initials the table next to his/her work. If the ratios are not equal, the players review the work to determine the mistake. The player with the correct ratio then initials his/her work, and the process is repeated with player 2 spinning the spinner. If a line that is already completed is spun, the player loses a turn. Players continue until the table is complete. The winner is the player with more initials on the table.

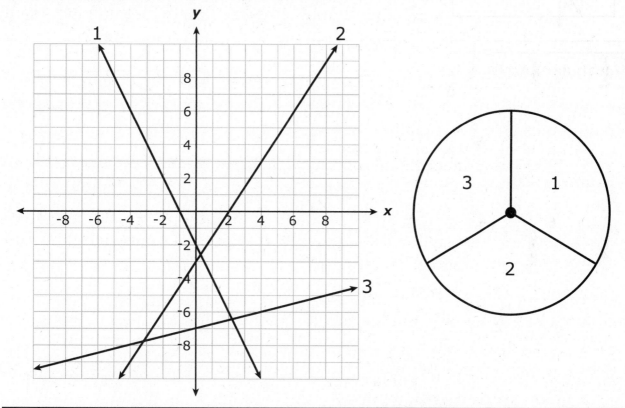

Line	Coordinates for First Triangle	$\frac{(y_2 - y_1)}{(x_2 - x_1)}$	Coordinates for Second Triangle	$\frac{(y_2 - y_1)}{(x_2 - x_1)}$
1	(___, ___) & (___, ___) x_1 y_1 x_2 y_2		(___, ___) & (___, ___) x_1 y_1 x_2 y_2	
2	(___, ___) & (___, ___) x_1 y_1 x_2 y_2		(___, ___) & (___, ___) x_1 y_1 x_2 y_2	
3	(___, ___) & (___, ___) x_1 y_1 x_2 y_2		(___, ___) & (___, ___) x_1 y_1 x_2 y_2	

1 Use the graph to answer the following questions.

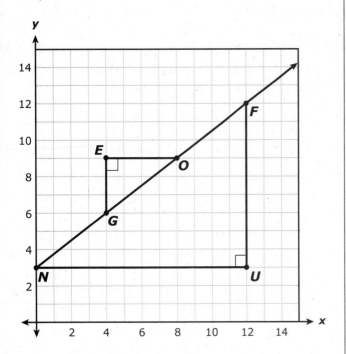

(a) What is the ratio of the change in y-values (vertical height) to the change in x-values (horizontal length) for triangle *GEO*?

(b) What is the ratio of the change in y-values (vertical height) to the change in x-values (horizontal length) for triangle *FUN*?

(c) What conclusion can be made about triangles *GEO* and *FUN*?

(d) Based on your response to part (c), what do you know about the slope of line *FN*?

2 Explain how to determine the vertical height, or change in y-values, between two points on a coordinate plane.

_____

_____

Explain how to determine the horizontal length, or change in x-values, between two points on a coordinate plane.

_____

_____

Explain how to use the vertical height and horizontal length to determine the slope of a line.

_____

_____

3 The slope of a line is 3.

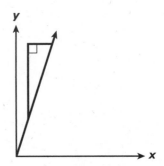

What is a possible vertical height of the right triangle?

Based on the vertical height, what is a possible horizontal length of the right triangle?

Connections

Measure the heights and widths of several steps of a staircase at home or elsewhere. Write the ratios of the vertical heights to the horizontal lengths for each step you measured. Were they all the same? Use your ratios to describe the slope of the staircase. Explain how the ratios helped you describe the slope of the staircase.

1 Myra walks at a constant rate of 8 miles every 2 hours. Graph a line to show the relationship between the time in hours, *t*, and distance in miles, *d*, that Myra walks.

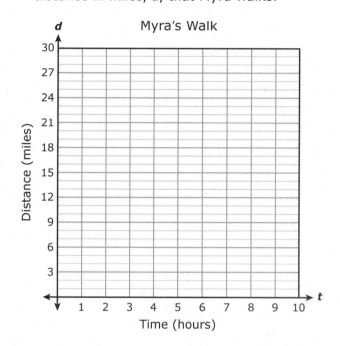

What is the unit rate in miles per hour?

What is the slope of the line graphed?

How does the slope of the line compare to the unit rate?

2 Mr. Nguyen buys rope by the foot from the hardware store. The graph shows the relationship between the rope length and cost.

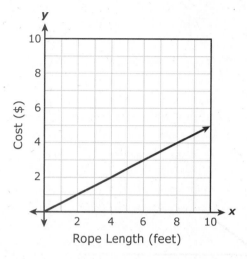

Write a statement that describes the unit rate for the rope Mr. Nguyen purchases.

3 The graph shows the relationship between the number of cups of peanut butter and the number of cups of sugar in Mrs. Myers' peanut butter cookie recipe.

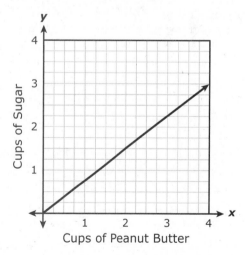

Based on the information in the graph, what is the unit rate for cups of sugar per cup of peanut butter?

1 The graph shows the relationship between the time and distance a cyclist travels.

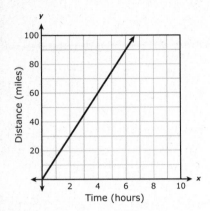

Which of the following best describes the slope of the line?

Ⓐ The cyclist travels at a speed of $1\frac{1}{2}$ miles per hour.

Ⓑ The cyclist travels at a speed of 15 miles per hour.

Ⓒ The cyclist travels at a speed of 8 miles per hour.

Ⓓ The cyclist travels at a speed of 20 miles per hour.

2 Students organized a walkathon as a fundraiser. The graph shows the amount of money earned during the fundraiser.

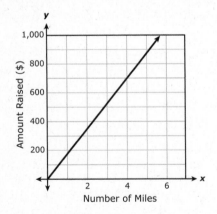

Which best describes the amount of money raised per mile?

Ⓕ The students raised $900 per mile.

Ⓖ The students raised $700 per mile.

Ⓗ The students raised $175 per mile.

Ⓙ The students raised $200 per mile.

3 A parking lot owner charges $9 per car for parking. Which line can be used to model the relationship between c, the number of cars in the lot, and d, the amount of money collected?

Ⓐ

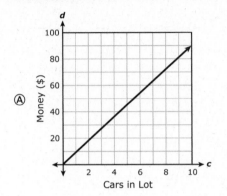

Ⓑ

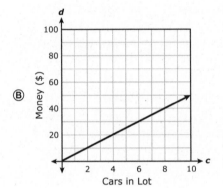

Ⓒ

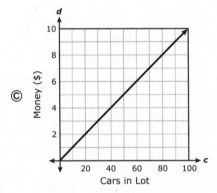

Ⓓ

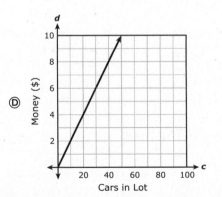

     motivation**math**™LEVEL 8   mentoring**minds**.com

1 Mario works at a movie theater. The graph shows the relationship between the time he works and the amount of money he earns.

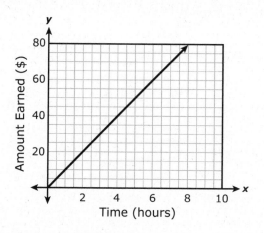

Which of the following is true?

Ⓐ The slope of the line that models the relationship is $\frac{1}{10}$.

Ⓑ Mario earns $10 per hour.

Ⓒ Mario's earnings change at a rate of $1 every ten minutes.

Ⓓ Mario earns $10 per half-hour.

2 Look at the graph shown.

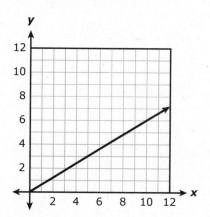

Which unit rate is best represented by the line shown in the graph?

Ⓕ Laci purchases apples for $2.50 per pound.

Ⓖ Melissa purchases 2-liter sodas for $1.50 each.

Ⓗ Jerome purchases bananas for $0.60 per pound.

Ⓙ Wyatt purchases potatoes for $0.80 per pound.

3 Which graph can be used to model a unit rate of $3.50 per gallon?

Ⓐ
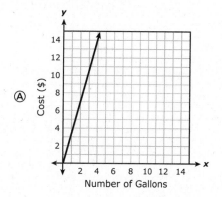

Ⓑ
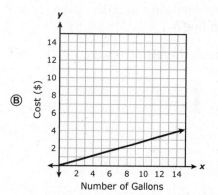

Ⓒ
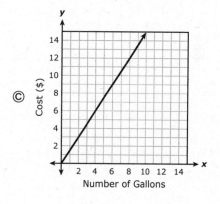

Ⓓ
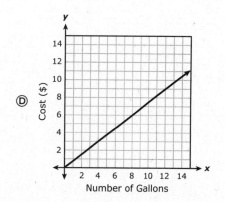

1 Marty purchases cashews. The relationship between cost and the number of pounds he purchases is modeled by the graph.

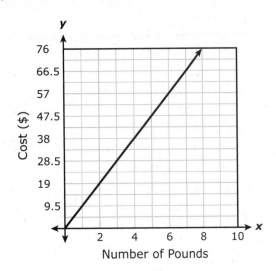

Which of the following best describes the slope of the line graphed?

Ⓐ Cashews cost $19 per pound.

Ⓑ Cashews cost $2 per pound.

Ⓒ Cashews cost $9.50 per pound.

Ⓓ Cashews cost $28.50 per pound.

2 Look at the graph.

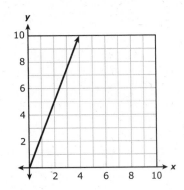

Which unit rate could be represented by the line shown in the graph?

Ⓕ Paul pays $5 per ticket for a movie.

Ⓖ Julia earns $10 per hour babysitting.

Ⓗ The restaurant charges $3 per hot dog.

Ⓙ Xavier reads 2.5 books each month.

3 George opens a savings account and saves $12 each week. Which line can be used to model the relationship between the number of weeks, *w*, and the number of dollars, *d*, George saves?

Ⓐ
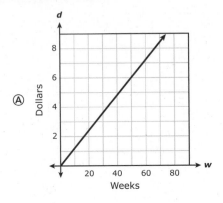

Ⓑ
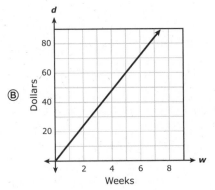

Ⓒ
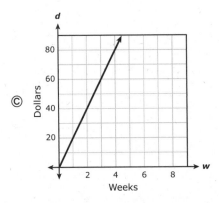

Ⓓ
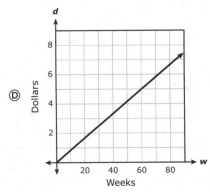

motivation**math**™LEVEL 8
mentoring**minds**.com

1 Mr. and Mrs. Carter leave the house at the same time, driving separate cars. Mr. Carter drives at one rate of speed, while his wife drives at another. The graph shows the rates of the two drivers.

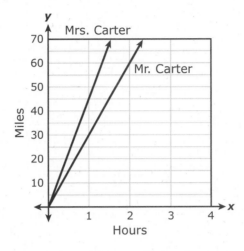

Which person is driving faster? Use the graph and unit rates to explain your answer.

_____

_____

2 Create a scenario to reflect the relationship shown in the graph. Give the graph a title and label the axes.

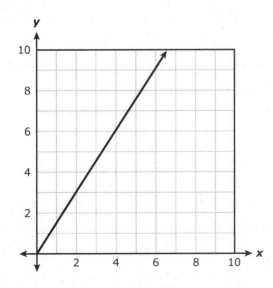

_____

_____

_____

_____

_____

Unit 9 Journal/Vocabulary Activity

Journal

Explain how to use a unit rate in a verbal problem to create a graph of the proportional relationship described in the problem. Give an example.

_____

_____

_____

Vocabulary Activity

For each of the following *proportional* graphs, use the information provided to complete the table. Identify the *slope* of the line, identify the labels for the *x-coordinates* and *y-coordinates*, and record the *unit rate* for the graph.

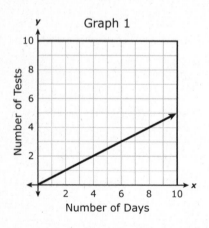

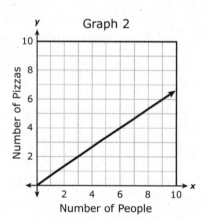

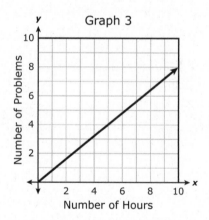

Graph	Slope	Label for *x*-coordinate	Label for *y*-coordinate	Unit Rate
1				
2				
3				

     motivation**math**™LEVEL 8   mentoring**minds**.com

Graph Match

Complete *Graph Match* individually. For each situation given, determine which graphed line has a slope matching the unit rate described. Record the letter of the graph in the blank. Some graphs may be used more than once.

1. ____ Emma takes 5 minutes to run 30 laps.

2. ____ The runners crossed the finish line at a rate of 5 per minute.

3. ____ Daniel loves books and reads 14 pages in 6 minutes.

4. ____ Sarah buys a dozen glazed donuts for $2.88.

5. ____ The cost to play 3 games of miniature golf is $15.

6. ____ Armando buys 8 extra-large pizzas for $36.

7. ____ Martha sells 9 stamps from her collection for $21.

8. ____ Catherine spends $1\frac{1}{2}$ hours baking 6 dozen cookies.

9. ____ James purchases 3 pounds of coffee for $18.

10. ____ Max purchases 3 bags of mixed fruit for $13.50.

A.

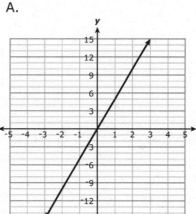

D.

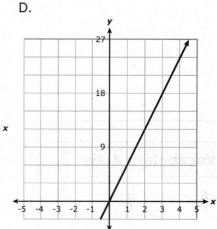

B.

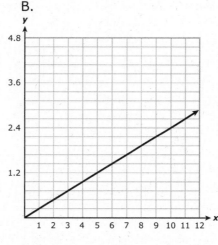

E.

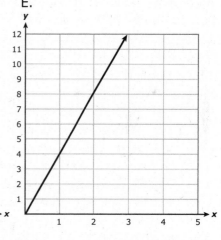

C.

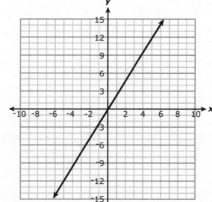

F.

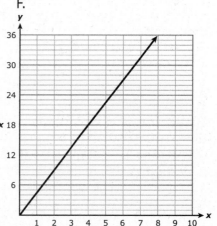

1 A study was conducted to determine the average number of text messages sent by teenagers in a day.

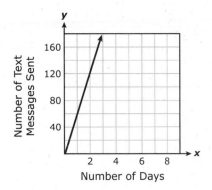

Write a statement describing the unit rate for the average number of text messages sent per day.

2 The graph shows the relationship between the number of hours and the rental cost for a paddle boat.

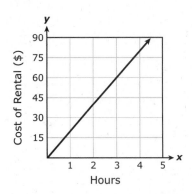

Based on the information in the graph, how much does it cost to rent a paddle boat for one hour?

3 Sonja downloads songs to her phone. The relationship between the cost and the number of songs she downloads is shown.

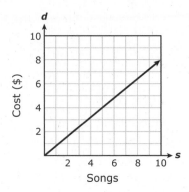

Explain what the slope of the graphed line represents.

4 The graph shows the growth rate, in feet, of sea kelp.

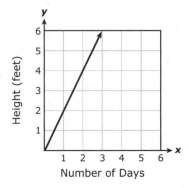

Based on the information in the graph, what is the daily growth rate for sea kelp?

Connections

1. While shopping at the grocery store, look at prices listed on the shelves for several different items. Locate the unit rate information. Discuss with a parent or guardian how understanding unit rates can help save money at the grocery store.

2. Have a friend time you to see how many sit-ups you can do in one minute. Graph a line showing the number of sit-ups per minute. Switch roles and graph your friend's data on the same line. How do the lines compare?

Use the graph to answer questions 1–6.

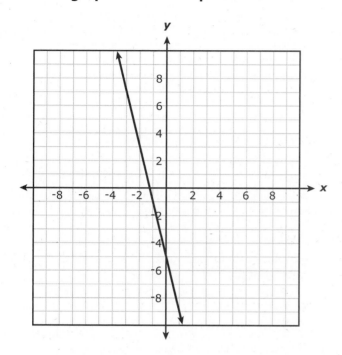

1 Determine the difference in the *x*-values for points (0, -5) and (1, -9). Repeat this process for points (-3, 7) and (-2, 3).

2 Determine the difference in the *y*-values for points (0, -5) and (1, -9). Repeat this process for points (-3, 7) and (-2, 3).

3 Calculate the rate of change or slope of the line. Show your work.

$$\text{slope} = \frac{(y_2 - y_1)}{(x_2 - x_1)}$$

4 At what point does the line cross the *y*-axis?

What is this point called?

5 Complete the following table for the graph.

x	-2	-1	0	1
y				

6 Describe how the slope and *y*-intercept can be determined by looking at data in a table.

_____

_____

_____

_____

Use the information to answer questions 7 and 8.

A video streaming company offers on-demand programming without a monthly contract. The company charges a connection fee plus a charge for each hour of video streaming. The table shows the cost for up to three hours of video streaming for one connection fee.

Cost of Video Streaming

Video Streaming (hours)	0	1	2	3
Cost	$0.75	$1.25	$1.75	$2.25

7 What does the point (0, 0.75) in the table represent?

What is the point called?

8 What is the hourly charge for video streaming?

1 A supermarket advertises a new product by offering samples to customers. The table shows the number of samples distributed each hour.

Samples Distributed

Number of Hours	2	3	4	5	8
Number of Samples	76	114	152	190	304

At what rate does the supermarket distributes samples?

Ⓐ 36 samples per hour

Ⓑ 28 samples per hour

Ⓒ 38 samples per hour

Ⓓ Not here

2 Look at the graph.

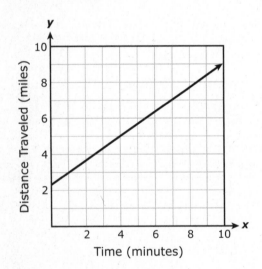

Time (minutes)

Which best describes the slope of the line shown in the graph?

Ⓕ Increasing 3 miles per minute

Ⓖ Decreasing $\frac{3}{2}$ miles per minute

Ⓗ Increasing $\frac{2}{3}$ mile per minute

Ⓙ Decreasing 2 miles per minute

3 What is the rate of change for the data shown?

x	1	3	5	7	9	11
y	6	18	30	42	54	66

Ⓐ 3

Ⓒ 2

Ⓑ 6

Ⓓ $\frac{1}{6}$

4 Claire earns the same pay for each day she works at her new job. She deposits a weekly paycheck into her savings account.

Claire's Savings

Number of Work Days	Savings Account Balance
5	$130
10	$250
15	$370
20	$490

How much money did Claire have in her savings account before starting her new job?

Ⓕ $10

Ⓗ $26

Ⓖ $24

Ⓙ $120

5 Which of the following shows the slope and *y*-intercept of the graph?

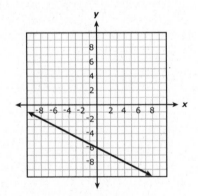

Ⓐ Slope: -2; *y*-intercept: -6

Ⓑ Slope: $\frac{1}{2}$; *y*-intercept: 6

Ⓒ Slope: -2; *y*-intercept: 0

Ⓓ Slope: -$\frac{1}{2}$; *y*-intercept: -6

 motivation**math**™LEVEL 8 mentoring**minds**.com

Use the table to answer questions 1 and 2.

x	y
0	22.0
1	23.5
2	25.0
3	26.5

1 Which description best represents the data?

Ⓐ One American dollar is equivalent to 23.5 Canadian dollars.

Ⓑ A baby measures 22 inches long at birth. The baby grows 1.5 inches each month for three months.

Ⓒ Jenny has $22 in her bank account. She spends $1.50 every day.

Ⓓ A plant grows at a rate of 3 centimeters per month.

2 Where would the graph of a line representing the relationship in the table intersect the y-axis?

Ⓕ (0, 1.5)   Ⓗ (22, 0)

Ⓖ (1.5, 0)   Ⓙ (0, 22)

3 Look at the graph.

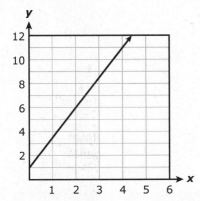

What is the y-intercept represented in the graph?

Ⓐ $b = 0$ Ⓒ $b = 1$

Ⓑ $b = -1$ Ⓓ Not here

4 A mountain bike rider travels 10 miles on the state park bike trail. The graph describes the bike rider's movement along the trail.

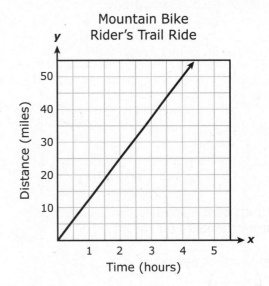

At what rate did the bike rider travel along the trail?

Ⓕ 10 mph   Ⓗ 25 mph

Ⓖ 17.5 mph   Ⓙ 12.5 mph

5 The rotor in a lawn mower engine spins at a constant rate under normal operating conditions.

Rotor Revolutions

Time (minutes)	Revolutions
1	1,750
3	5,250
5	8,750
7	12,250

Under normal conditions, how many revolutions does the rotor spin per minute?

Ⓐ 875 revolutions per minute

Ⓑ 3,500 revolutions per minute

Ⓒ 1,750 revolutions per minute

Ⓓ 750 revolutions per minute

Unit 10 Assessment

1 Jana sells boxes of cookies for a school fundraiser. Each hour, she records the number of boxes sold. Jana's cookie sales are represented by the graph.

Jana's Cookie Sales

Which of the following shows the rate for Jana's cookie sales?

Ⓐ 10 boxes of cookies per hour

Ⓑ 15 boxes of cookies per hour

Ⓒ 20 boxes of cookies per hour

Ⓓ 30 boxes of cookies per hour

2 A discount music store has a one-day sale on all vinyl albums. In order to purchase from the store, each customer must have a yearly membership.

Cost of Vinyl Albums

Number of Vinyl Albums	Total Cost with Membership
4	$35.00
7	$57.50
9	$72.50

How much does the music store charge for a yearly membership?

Ⓕ $5.00   Ⓗ $15.00

Ⓖ $7.50   Ⓙ $22.50

3 Aiden checks out a 300-page book from the library. Before leaving the library, he reads 30 pages. The table shows the hours Aiden spends reading the rest of the book.

Hours	0	1	2	3	4	5	6
Pages Left	270	225	180	135	90	45	0

At what rate does Aiden read the remaining pages of the book?

Ⓐ 70 pages per hour

Ⓑ 30 pages per hour

Ⓒ 25 pages per hour

Ⓓ 45 pages per hour

4 Sophie earns an allowance each week for completing a set of chores. The money is deposited into a savings account that already has money in it. Sophie's savings account balance is shown in the graph.

Sophie's Savings Account Balance

What was the beginning balance of Sophie's savings account?

Ⓕ $25.00   Ⓗ $200.00

Ⓖ $50.00   Ⓙ $75.00

   motivation**math**™LEVEL 8 mentoring**minds**.com

1 Jeff and Jason investigate the distance a toy car travels in 5 seconds during a science lab. The results from the investigation are shown in the graph.

What is the *y*-intercept for this graph? What does this value represent?

What is the rate of change for this investigation? What does this value represent?

Predict the distance the toy car will travel in 6 seconds.

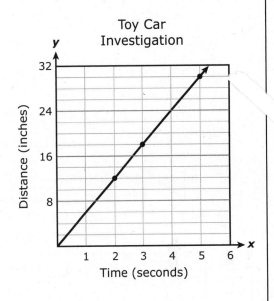

2 Draw a line on the graph and complete the table with 5 points from the line. Find the slope and *y*-intercept of the line drawn. Then, record in words a situation that could be represented by the graph.

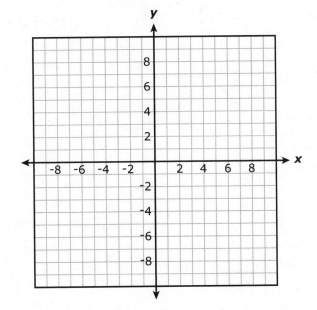

m = _____

b = _____

x	y

Situation: _____

Journal

Describe a real-world situation that can be represented by a linear relationship shown in either a graph or a table. Discuss the slope and *y*-intercept values and how to determine each from the representations.

_____

_____

_____

Vocabulary Activity

Use the terms in the box to correctly label the graph shown. Each term is used only once.

rate of change	*x*-axis	*y*-intercept	slope
y-axis	rise	change in *x* (Δ*x*)	run	change in *y* (Δ*y*)

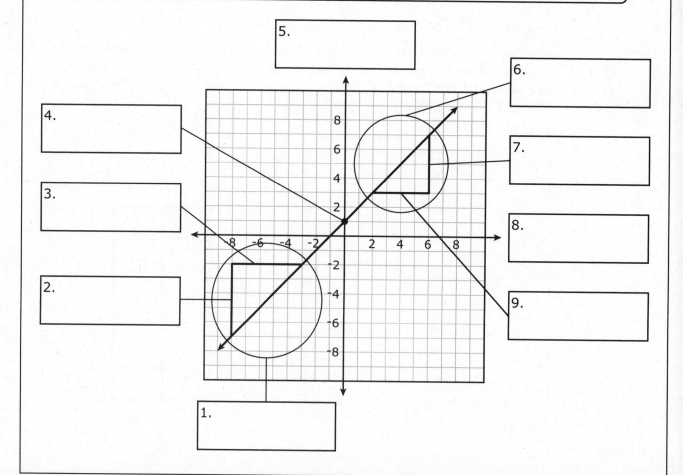

Color by Slope

Using the graph, draw each line segment shown in the geometric design and find the slope of the segment. Then, use the key to color each section of the design. Note: Horizontal lines have a slope of 0 because the change in *y*-values is 0.

Key

Slope	Color
-2	Blue
0	Red
$\frac{1}{2}$	Green
1	Yellow
2	Purple

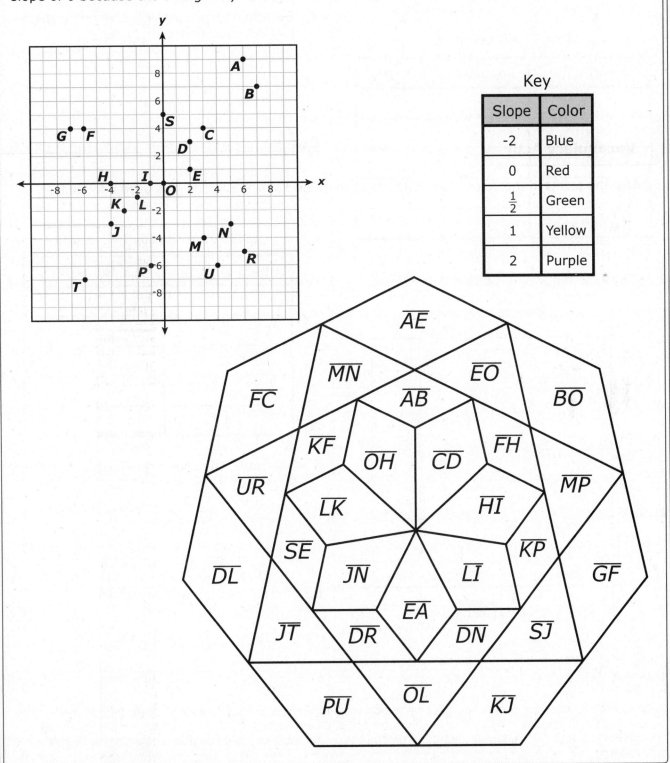

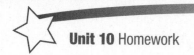

Use the information to answer questions 1–4.

Blood volume is the volume of blood in the circulatory system of an organism. The average blood volume for dogs is 86 milliliters per kilogram.

1 Complete the table to represent the average blood volume for various dog weights.

Dog Blood Volumes

Weight, w (kg)	Blood Volume, b (mL)
5	
10	
20	
30	
40	

2 Graph the data from the completed table.

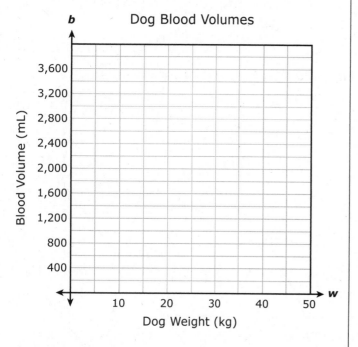

3 Determine the slope from the table. Explain your answer.

4 Determine the y-intercept from the graph. Explain your answer.

Use the table to answer questions 5 and 6.

The Lone Star Plumbing Company specializes in leak repairs. A service call fee and an hourly labor rate is charged for each repair.

Lone Star Plumbing Charges

Hours of Labor	Total Repair Cost
0	$ 25
1	$ 65
2	$105
3	$145
4	$185

5 Determine the Lone Star Plumbing Company's service call fee.

6 What is the hourly labor rate?

Connections

Research foreign currencies and determine how exchange rates are calculated. Choose one foreign currency and develop a table or graph to show the exchange rate for American dollars to the foreign currency. Share the exchange rate or slope and the y-intercept based on the data collected during your research.

 motivation**math**™LEVEL 8 mentoring**minds**.com

Use the information to answer questions 1–3.

As part of an investigation to see how fast plants grow from seeds, Jimmy plants seeds and measures the growth for five weeks.

Plant Growth

Week, w	1	2	3	4	5
Height (cm), h	0.5	1.0	1.5	2.0	2.5

1 Graph the data for the plant growth. Label the axes and provide a title for the graph.

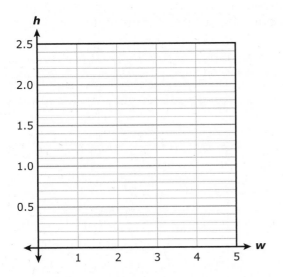

2 Write an equation to determine h, the plant height after w weeks.

3 Is the linear relationship shown in the plant growth data a proportional relationship or a non-proportional relationship? Explain your answer.

Use the information to answer questions 4–6.

Sydney collects aluminum cans for recycling. The number of pounds of cans she collects over several weeks is shown in the graph.

4 Complete the table below to show how many pounds of cans Sydney has collected each week.

Sydney's Can Recycling

Weeks, x	Pounds of Cans, y

5 Write an equation to describe the relationship between x and y.

6 In Sydney's data, is the linear relationship a proportional relationship or a non-proportional relationship? Explain your answer.

1 Which of the following equations represents a linear proportional function?

Ⓐ $y = 2x + 3$

Ⓒ $y = 5x$

Ⓑ $2y = x + 10$

Ⓓ $y = 4x + 2$

2 A graph showing the relationship between time and distance is shown.

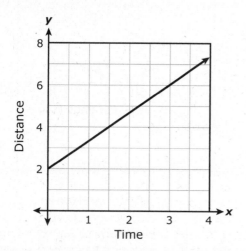

Which equation best represents the line in the graph?

Ⓕ $y = 3x + 2$

Ⓗ $y = 2x + 3$

Ⓖ $y = \frac{3}{4}x + 2$

Ⓙ $y = \frac{4}{3}x + 2$

3 A mail carrier travels at 15 miles per hour through a neighborhood. Which table represents the distance the mail carrier travels in x hours?

Ⓐ
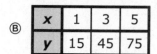

x	0	2	4
y	0	30	55

Ⓑ
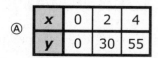

x	1	3	5
y	15	45	75

Ⓒ
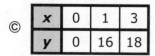

x	0	1	3
y	0	16	18

Ⓓ

x	1	3	4
y	15	40	55

4 Adam trains for the local fun run. As part of a training program, Adam walks one kilometer in 30 minutes. Which graph best represents the relationship between Adam's time and distance traveled?

Ⓕ
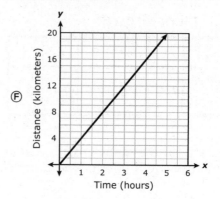

Ⓖ
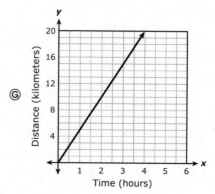

Ⓗ
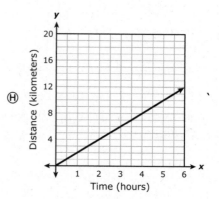

Ⓙ
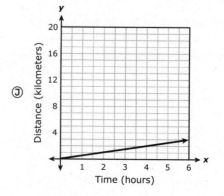

motivation**math**™LEVEL 8

mentoring**minds**.com

1 A local Mexican food restaurant caters parties for 20 or more guests. A set-up/clean-up fee and per person charge applies for all catering services. The table shows the total cost, c, for catering g guests.

g	20	25	40	50
c	$165	$200	$305	$375

Which equation does the Mexican food restaurant use to calculate the total cost for catering a party with 20 or more guests?

Ⓐ $c = \frac{25}{7}g$ Ⓒ $c = 7g + 25$

Ⓑ $c = 25g + 7$ Ⓓ $c = \frac{7}{27}g + 20$

2 Look at the graph.

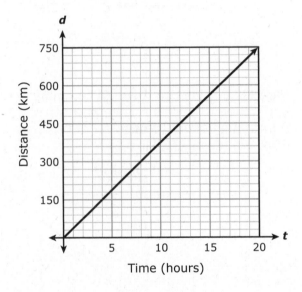

Time (hours)

Which equation best describes the distance versus time data in the graph?

Ⓕ $d = 6t$ Ⓗ $d = 30t$

Ⓖ $d = 37.5t$ Ⓙ $d = 50t$

3 Jackson wants to buy a new video game console. He has saved $50 and earns $20 per lawn that he mows. Which of the following equations can be used to determine the number of lawns Jackson needs to mow, m, in order to buy the video game console, which costs v dollars?

Ⓐ $v = 50m + 20$ Ⓒ $v = 20m + 50$

Ⓑ $m = \frac{2}{5}v + 50$ Ⓓ $m = \frac{5}{2}v + 50$

4 Which of the following best represents a linear proportional relationship?

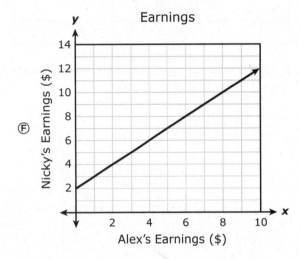

Ⓕ

Ⓖ $y = 3x - 7$

Ⓗ $y = 8x + 25$

Distance (miles)	Gasoline Used (gallons)
24	2
60	5
84	7
108	9

Ⓙ

5 Which table contains values that represent the equation $y = -3x + 2$?

Ⓐ
x	-3	-1	1	3
y	-9	-5	-1	3

Ⓑ
x	-2	0	2	4
y	3	0	-3	-6

Ⓒ
x	-5	-2	2	5
y	-17	-8	4	13

Ⓓ
x	-4	-2	2	4
y	14	8	-4	-10

1 Look at the table.

x	1	2	3	4	5
y	$0.75	$1.50	$2.25	$3.00	$3.75

Which of the following represents the same relationship between x and y?

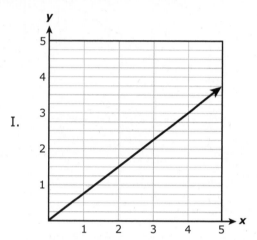

I.

II. $y = \frac{3}{4}x$

III. A karate club earns $0.75 for every candy bar sold during a fundraiser.

Ⓐ I only

Ⓑ II and III only

Ⓒ I and III only

Ⓓ I, II, and III

2 Look at the equation.

$$y = 12x + 1$$

If y represents the total number of cookies, which situation best describes the equation?

Ⓕ After purchasing x dozen cookies, one additional dozen costs $1.

Ⓖ After purchasing x dozen cookies, one cookie is free.

Ⓗ After purchasing x dozen cookies, the next dozen cookies is free.

Ⓙ After purchasing x dozen cookies, one additional cookie costs $1.

3 Cameron works for a car dealership and earns a monthly salary of $1,750 plus a commission for every car he sells.

Cameron's Income

Cars Sold, n	Total Monthly Income, M
1	$2,250
5	$4,250
8	$5,750
13	$8,250

Which equation could be used to find Cameron's total monthly income, M, after selling n cars?

Ⓐ $n = 500M + 1,750$ Ⓒ $M = 500n + 1,750$

Ⓑ $M = 1,750n + 500$ Ⓓ $n = 1,750M + 500$

4 Nickel is a transition metal. A common application for nickel is coin fabrication. Information about the density of nickel is provided in the graph.

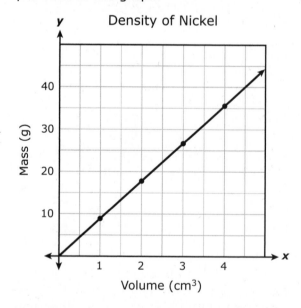

Which material has a density closest in value to nickel?

Ⓕ Iron: $y = 7.9x$ Ⓗ Copper: $y = 9.0x$

Ⓖ Zinc: $y = 7.1x$ Ⓙ Gallium: $y = 6.1x$

Velocity can be described as the rate of motion of an object, as well as the direction of motion. An important graph describing the motion of an object is a velocity versus time graph. A velocity versus time graph provides information about an object's acceleration. An equation representing velocity is:

velocity = acceleration • time

An example of a velocity versus time graph is shown. Use the graph to answer the questions.

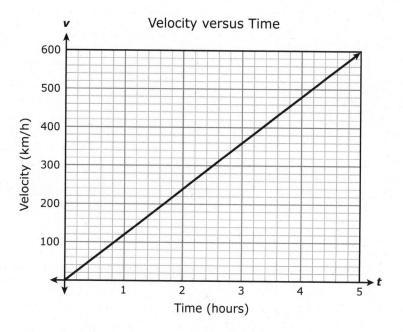

What does the slope of a velocity versus time graph represent?

What equation best represents the line in this velocity versus time graph?

What type of linear relationship does this equation represent? Justify your answer.

If a vehicle continues to move for a total of 6 hours at the constant acceleration shown in the graph, what would the vehicle's velocity be at 6 hours?

If the initial velocity changes to 100 kilometers per hour and the acceleration remains the same, what equation would best represent the new velocity versus time graph?

What type of linear relationship does the new equation represent? Justify your answer.

Unit 11 Journal/Vocabulary Activity

Analysis
i
Analyze

Journal

Compare and contrast linear proportional and linear non-proportional representations. Include similarities and differences in graphs, tables, and equations.

_____

_____

_____

_____

Vocabulary Activity

Describe each vocabulary term by completing the boxes below.

Proportional Relationship	
Equation	Graph
Example	Non-example
Sentence	

Non-proportional Relationship	
Equation	Graph
Example	Non-example
Sentence	

motivation**math**™LEVEL 8

Equal Representation

Play *Equal Representation* with a partner. Each pair of players needs a number cube, a game board, and a paper clip to use with the spinner. Each player needs a pencil. Player 1 rolls the number cube and spins the spinner. Player 1 uses the data from the situation on the spinner to complete a representation based on the number rolled and the instructions. Player 1 initials his/her work when complete, and play passes to player 2. If the selection rolled for the situation has already been completed, the player loses a turn. The game ends when all four representations are complete for all three situations. The winner is the player with more initials on the board.

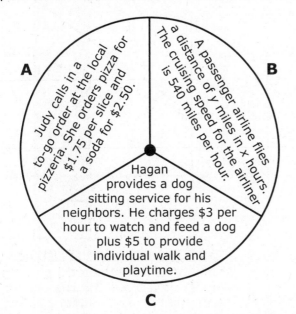

A Judy calls in a to-go order at the local pizzeria. She orders pizza for $1.75 per slice and a soda for $2.50.

B A passenger airline flies a distance of y miles in x hours. The cruising speed for the airliner is 540 miles per hour.

C Hagan provides a dog sitting service for his neighbors. He charges $3 per hour to watch and feed a dog plus $5 to provide individual walk and playtime.

Number Rolled

1: Complete the table.

2: Draw the graph.

3: Write the equation.

4: Determine the type of linear relationship.

5: Player chooses which representation to complete.

6: Partner chooses which representation to complete.

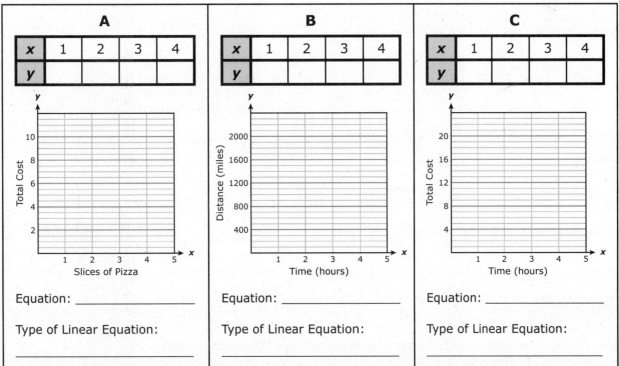

A

x	1	2	3	4
y				

Total Cost / Slices of Pizza

Equation: _____

Type of Linear Equation:

_____

B

x	1	2	3	4
y				

Distance (miles) / Time (hours)

Equation: _____

Type of Linear Equation:

_____

C

x	1	2	3	4
y				

Total Cost / Time (hours)

Equation: _____

Type of Linear Equation:

_____

Use the information to answer questions 1–3.

Students complete an investigation that tests the effect of different forces and accelerations on a toy cart. Data from each trial of the investigation is shown in the table.

Trial	Force (newtons)	Acceleration (m/s²)
1	10	0.5
2	20	1.0
3	30	1.5
4	40	2.0
5	50	2.5

Students use the following equation for all calculations.

Net force = mass • acceleration

1 What is the mass, in kilograms, of the toy cart used in this experiment?

2 What equation best represents the line that contains all the data points from each trial?

3 The line that represents net force shows a linear _____ relationship.

Use the information to answer questions 4–6.

Two students participate in a race. The starting line is one meter in front of the teacher. Data collected during the race for both students is shown in the graph.

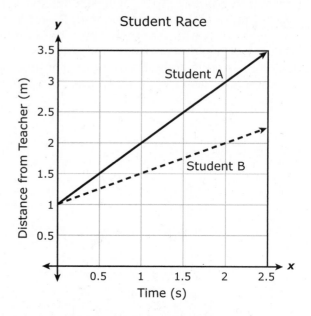

4 What equation best represents the relationship between the distance student A is from the teacher and the number of seconds the student runs?

5 What equation best represents the relationship between the distance student B is from the teacher and the number of seconds the student runs?

6 Each line in the graph represents a linear _____ relationship.

Connections

Look through newspapers and magazines to find examples of linear proportional and linear non-proportional relationships represented as tables, graphs, or equations. Represent each example with two of the three representations. Bring one or two examples to share with the class.

Use the graphs to answer questions 1–6.

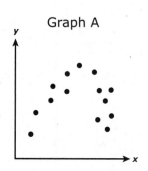
Graph A

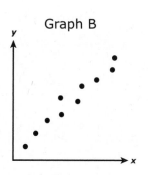
Graph B

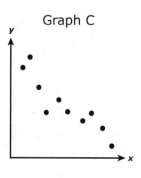
Graph C

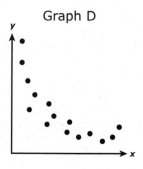
Graph D

1 List characteristics of a graph that suggest a linear relationship.

4 Contrast the relationships represented by x and y for Graph A and Graph C.

2 List characteristics of a graph that suggest a non-linear relationship.

5 Contrast the relationships represented by x and y for Graph C and Graph D.

3 Contrast the relationships represented by x and y for Graph A and Graph B.

6 Contrast the relationships represented by x and y for Graph B and Graph D.

Unit 12 Guided Practice

1 Look at the graphs.

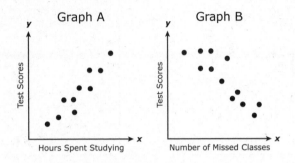

Graph A   Graph B

Which of the following is true for both graphs?

Ⓐ Both graphs suggest non-linear relationships because neither graph contains a line.

Ⓑ Both graphs suggest linear relationships because there appears to be a constant rate of change in each graph.

Ⓒ Both graphs suggest non-linear relationships because there appears to be a constant rate of change in each graph.

Ⓓ There is not enough information given to draw conclusions about the graphs.

2 Which of the following is NOT true about the graph of a linear relationship?

Ⓕ The relationship is represented by the equation $y = mx + b$.

Ⓖ The data appears to be increasing or decreasing at a constant rate.

Ⓗ The relationship may be proportional or non-proportional.

Ⓙ The relationship may be represented by an equation other than $y = mx + b$.

3 Look at the scatterplot.

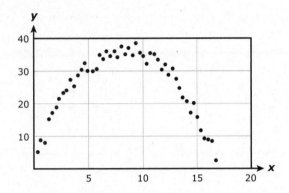

Which of the following is true?

I. The graph suggests a non-linear relationship between x and y because there is not a constant slope.

II. The graph suggests a non-linear relationship between x and y because the line appears to be curved.

III. The graph suggests a non-linear relationship between x and y because the relationship cannot be represented by $y = kx$ or $y = mx + b$.

IV. The graph suggests a non-linear relationship between x and y because it appears to pass through the origin.

Ⓐ II only

Ⓑ II and III only

Ⓒ I, II, and III only

Ⓓ I, II, III, and IV

1 Look at the scatterplot.

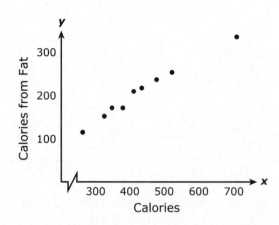

Which of the following is true?

I.   The graph suggests a linear relationship between the number of calories and the number of calories from fat because the graph does not appear to pass through the origin.

II. The graph suggests a linear relationship between the number of calories and the number of calories from fat because the relationship can be represented by the equation $y = mx + b$.

III. The graph suggests a linear relationship between the number of calories and the number of calories from fat because the graph appears to show a constant rate of change.

IV. The graph suggests a linear relationship between the number of calories and the number of calories from fat because the graph appears to show a negative constant of proportionality.

Ⓐ II only

Ⓑ II and III only

Ⓒ I, II, and III only

Ⓓ I, II, III, and IV

2 Look at the graphs.

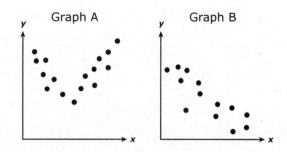

Which statement best describes the relationships in the graphs?

Ⓕ Both Graph A and Graph B suggest linear relationships because Graph A first decreases then increases steadily, and Graph B decreases at a steady rate.

Ⓖ Both Graph A and Graph B suggest non-linear relationships because neither graph crosses the y-axis.

Ⓗ Graph A suggests a linear relationship because it increases steadily for the larger portion of the graph, and Graph B suggests a non-linear relationship because some data points are below the majority of the data.

Ⓙ Graph A suggests a non-linear relationship because it decreases and then increases, and Graph B suggests a linear relationship because it steadily decreases.

1 Look at the graphs shown.

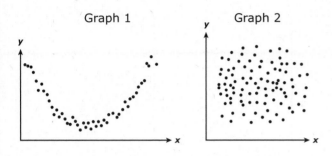

Which statements are true?

I. Graph 1 shows a constant increase in
x-values and a constant increase in
y-values, making the graph linear.

II. Graph 2 shows a constant increase in
x-values and a constant increase in
y-values, making the graph linear.

III. Graph 1 shows that as x-values
increase, y-values decrease to a point
and then begin to increase, making the
graph non-linear.

IV. Graph 2 shows that as x-values
increase, the relationship with the
y-values varies, making the graph
non-linear.

Ⓐ I and II only

Ⓑ II and III only

Ⓒ I and IV only

Ⓓ III and IV only

2 Look at the graphs comparing the distances
of traveling objects over time.

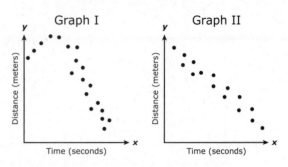

Which statement is true for both graphs?

Ⓕ Both graphs show a linear relationship
because they are both decreasing.

Ⓖ Graph I shows a linear relationship that
increases and then decreases, while
Graph II shows a decreasing linear
relationship.

Ⓗ Graph II shows a decreasing linear
relationship with a constant negative
slope, while Graph I shows a
non-linear relationship that increases then
decreases.

Ⓙ Neither graph shows a linear relationship
because neither passes through (0, 0).

3 Which of the following is NOT true about the
graph of a non-linear relationship?

Ⓐ The graph may increase and then
decrease.

Ⓑ The data appears to be increasing or
decreasing at a constant rate.

Ⓒ The graph of the relationship does not
show a line.

Ⓓ The relationship is represented by an
equation other than $y = mx + b$.

1 The students in Mr. Huck's class are assigned data sets and asked to create scatterplots. Olivia and David each create a plot based on the data provided.

Olivia   David

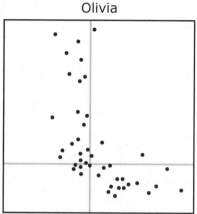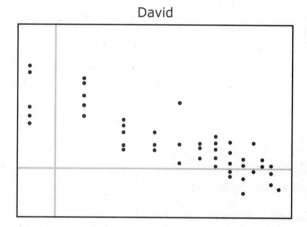

For each student's graph, describe the pattern of the data. Discuss the similarities and differences in the patterns. Use terms such as *linear*, *non-linear*, *increasing*, *decreasing*, *rate*, *constant rate*, and *data* in your discussion.

_____

_____

_____

_____

2 Sketch two graphs using the following descriptions.

As *x* increases, *y* decreases at a constant rate.

As *x* increases, *y* decreases and then increases.

y

x

y

x

motivation**math**™LEVEL 8   ILLEGAL TO COPY   **99**

Unit 12 Journal/Vocabulary Activity

Journal

Explain how to determine whether the graph of a bivariate data set shows a relationship that is linear or non-linear. Are there instances in which the relationship in the graph may not be determined? Explain your answer.

_____

_____

_____

Vocabulary Activity

Use the grids to show examples of linear and non-linear relationships.

Linear Relationship

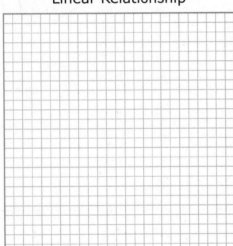

Non-linear Relationship

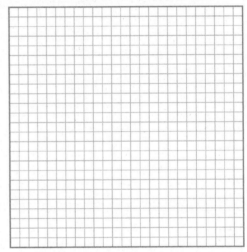

| bivariate data set | contrast | graphical representation |
| linear relationship | non-linear relationship | ordered pair |

Use the terms in the box to write a paragraph explaining the difference between linear and non-linear relationships using bivariate data sets.

_____

_____

_____

motivation**math**™LEVEL 8
mentoring**minds**.com

It's All Linear (NOT)

Play *It's All Linear (NOT)* with a partner. Each pair of players needs a game board and paper clips to use with the spinners. Each player needs a pencil. Player 1 spins both spinners. Using the results of the spin, player 1 looks at the two graphs and fills in the space between them, giving a brief summary of the differences in the two graphs. If correct, player 1 initials the space, and play passes to player 2. If incorrect, player 1 erases his/her work, and play passes to player 2. If values are spun that have already been completed, the player loses a turn. The game ends when all nine spaces are completed. The winner is the player with more initials on the board.

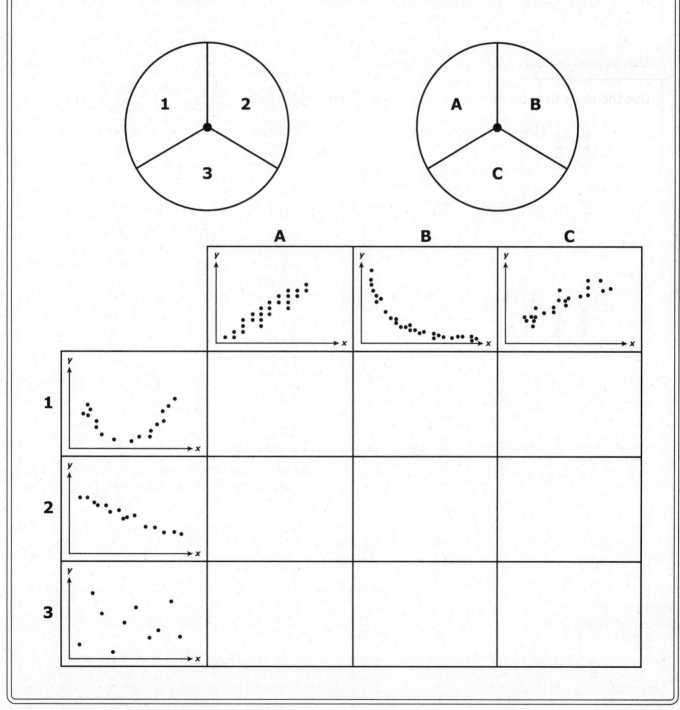

1 The graphs show comparisons between height/shoe size and hat size/shoe size of eighth-grade students.

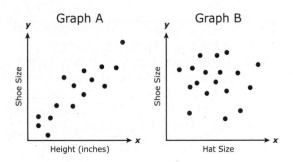

Graph A

Graph B

a. Is the relationship between height and shoe size shown in Graph A linear or non-linear? Explain your answer.

b. Is the relationship between hat size and shoe size shown in Graph B linear or non-linear? Explain your answer.

2 For each graph shown, determine if the relationship is linear or non-linear and explain your reasoning.

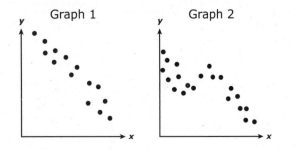

Graph 1

Graph 2

3 A study was conducted to determine what type of relationship, if any, exists between the number of children in a household and the travel time between school and home. The data is shown in the graph.

Is there a relationship between the number of children in a household and the travel time between school and home? Explain your answer.

4 Create scatterplots that show a linear relationship on Graph 1 and a non-linear relationship on Graph 2. Use at least 15 points for each relationship.

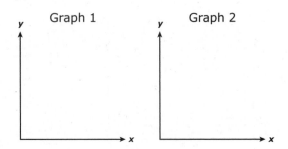

Graph 1

Graph 2

Explain how Graph 1 shows a linear relationship and Graph 2 shows a nonlinear relationship.

Connections

Choose two different categories of data to compare, such as the number of pets and the ages of at least twenty different people. Plot your data as ordered pairs on a graph. Determine if there is a relationship evident and whether the graph shows a linear or non-linear relationship. Present your findings to the class.

 motivation**math**™LEVEL 8 mentoring**minds**.com

Use the graph to answer questions 1–3.

The scatterplot displays the relationship between height and foot length for 25 patients in a doctor's office.

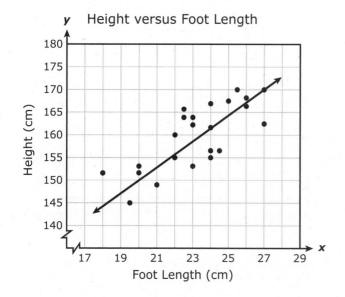

Use the graph to answer questions 4–7.

The scatterplot shows the cost to ship packages of different weights from Northview to Rockland.

1 Based on the graph, what is the approximate length, in centimeters, of a person's foot who is 190 centimeters tall?

4 Using the trend line, estimate the cost of shipping a package that weighs 40 pounds.

5 If the cost to ship a package is $40, what is the approximate weight, in pounds, of the package?

2 Using the trend line, predict the estimated height of a person, in centimeters, whose foot length measures 15 centimeters.

6 Is the following statement true or false? Explain your answer.

According to the graph, a package weighing zero pounds will cost about $5 to ship.

3 What is the slope of the trend line?

If the *y*-intercept is 93, write and solve an expression to predict the height of a person whose foot measures 28 centimeters.

7 Why would the cost to ship zero pounds not be zero dollars?

Use the graph to answer questions 1 and 2.

The scatterplot displays data gathered on the population growth of Jefferson since 2000.

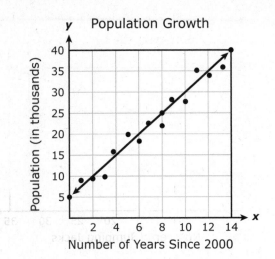

Population Growth

Population (in thousands)

Number of Years Since 2000

Use the graph to answer questions 3 and 4.

Carter owns an ice cream cart and sells various flavors of ice cream cones.

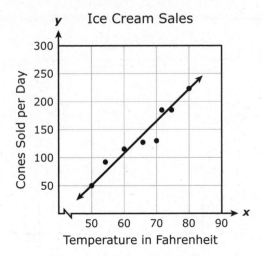

Ice Cream Sales

Cones Sold per Day

Temperature in Fahrenheit

1 Based on the trend line shown, which is the best prediction of the population of Jefferson in 2018?

Ⓐ 43,000 people

Ⓑ 4,500 people

Ⓒ 50,000 people

Ⓓ 5,000 people

2 Based on the data, which of the following could be true?

Ⓕ The population in Jefferson in 2022 will likely be fewer than 55,000.

Ⓖ The population in Jefferson in 2022 will likely have increased to about 60,000.

Ⓗ The population in Jefferson in 2022 will likely be greater than 65,000.

Ⓙ The population in Jefferson in 2022 will likely have increased to about 70,000.

3 Which of the following could be true about Carter's ice cream sales?

Ⓐ When the temperature is 55°F, Carter sells about 55 ice cream cones.

Ⓑ When the temperature is below 40°F, Carter sells a negative number of ice cream cones.

Ⓒ When the temperature is 65°F, Carter sells more than 150 ice cream cones.

Ⓓ When the temperature is 90°F, Carter sells about 275 ice cream cones.

4 Based on the trend line, which is the best prediction of the number of cones sold when the temperature hits 100°F?

Ⓕ 175 cones

Ⓖ 250 cones

Ⓗ 330 cones

Ⓙ 400 cones

motivation**math**™LEVEL 8

mentoring**minds**.com

Use the graph to answer questions 1 and 2.

The scatterplot shows the percent body fat for people who regularly exercise each day.

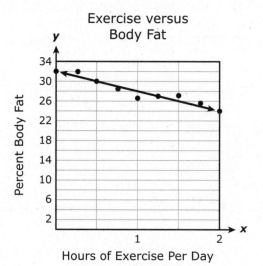

Exercise versus
Body Fat

1 If the scatterplot displayed more data, which shows a possible point that would be included in the graph?

Ⓐ (3, 25)

Ⓑ (3, 20)

Ⓒ (3, 15)

Ⓓ (3, 22)

2 Based on the trend line, which is the best estimate of the number of hours of exercise per day needed to reach a body fat percentage of 16?

Ⓕ 2.5 hours

Ⓖ 3 hours

Ⓗ 4 hours

Ⓙ 5.5 hours

3 The scatterplot displays the results of a student's heart rate after completing different numbers of jumping jacks.

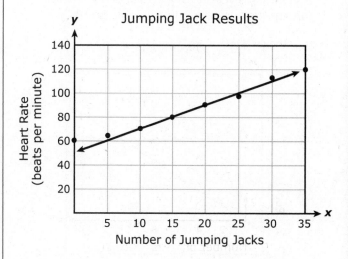

Jumping Jack Results

Based on the trend line, which statement makes the best prediction about a student's heart rate after performing jumping jacks?

Ⓐ After completing 45 jumping jacks, the student's heart rate will increase to over 150 beats per minute.

Ⓑ After completing 45 jumping jacks, the student's heart rate will increase to over 135 beats per minute.

Ⓒ After completing 45 jumping jacks, the student's heart rate will decrease to 125 beats per minute.

Ⓓ After completing 45 jumping jacks, the student's heart rate will decrease to 115 beats per minute.

Use the graph to answer questions 1 and 2.

The value of a certain stock in the stock market is tracked for several days. The information is presented in the graph.

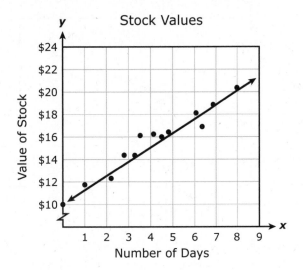

Stock Values

1 Which prediction can be made based on the data?

Ⓐ On day 10, the stock should have a value of approximately $20.

Ⓑ On day 12, the stock should have a value of approximately $23.

Ⓒ On day 10, the stock should have a value of approximately $30.

Ⓓ On day 12, the stock should have a value of approximately $36.

2 According to the trend shown in the graph, how many days will it take the stock value to reach $40?

Ⓕ The stock value will reach $40 in about 10 to 14 days.

Ⓖ The stock value will reach $40 in about 15 to 20 days.

Ⓗ The stock value will reach $40 in more than 20 days.

Ⓙ The stock value will never reach $40.

3 Scientists tracked the traveling distance of a blue whale named Beauregard over several days. Based on their findings, the scientists predict that after 80 days, the blue whale will be 2,400 meters away. Which set of data produces a trend line that models this prediction?

Ⓐ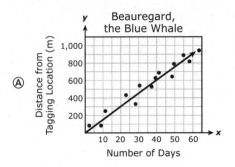

Ⓑ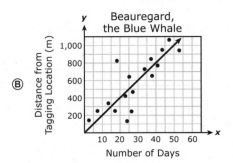

Ⓒ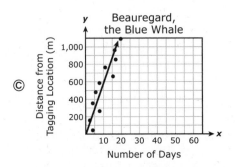

Ⓓ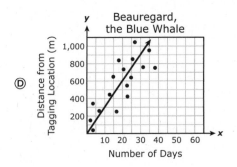

The distance needed to stop a car is relative to the speed the car is traveling. A study is done on stopping distances, in feet, when a car travels between 10 and 45 miles per hour.

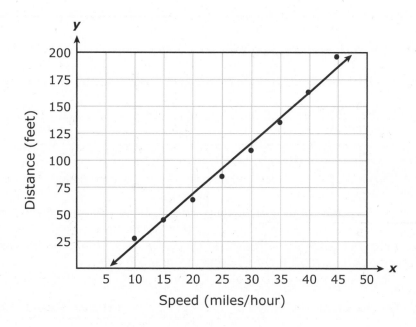

Based on the graph, what is the approximate slope and *y*-intercept of the trend line shown? Are these values reasonable for the given scenario? Explain your answer.

_____

_____

_____

Another study is conducted at higher speeds. The study shows that the actual stopping distance for a car traveling at 85 miles per hour is 543 feet. How do these results compare to the value predicted by the graph above? What do you think accounts for the differences in the values?

_____

_____

_____

_____

Unit 13 Journal/Vocabulary Activity

Journal

Application
i
Apply

Explain how to use a trend line to predict values beyond the scope of a scatterplot.

_____

_____

_____

_____

Vocabulary Activity

Complete a vocabulary round robin activity with three other students. In five minutes, complete each space with a definition and illustration of the vocabulary term. Then, visit three students for three minutes each to discuss and compare definitions and illustrations. Record any additional information learned from the discussions.

Trend Line

Linear Relationship

Scatterplot

Prediction

motivation**math**™LEVEL 8

What's My Color?

Each graph shown represents a bivariate data set and shows a trend line approximating the linear relationship in the graph. Read the description in each box and color the box according to the key for each graph.

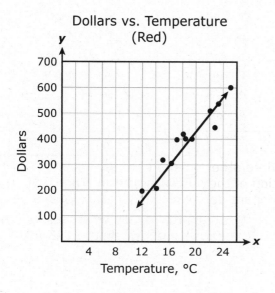

Dollars vs. Temperature
(Red)

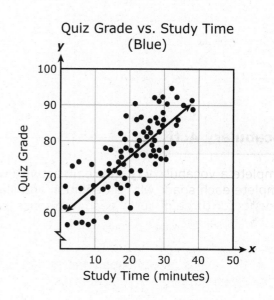

Quiz Grade vs. Study Time
(Blue)

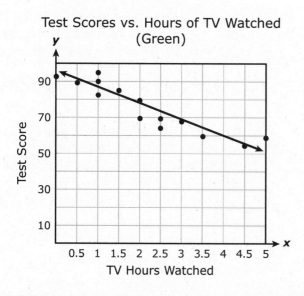

Test Scores vs. Hours of TV Watched
(Green)

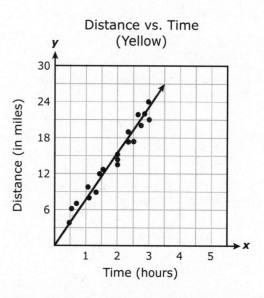

Distance vs. Time
(Yellow)

The point (8, 40) is likely on the line in this graph.	The point $\left(6, 41\frac{2}{3}\right)$ is likely on the line in this graph.	When $x = 60$ on this graph, y is about 110.
The y-intercept for this graph is a negative value.	This graph shows the most proportional relationship.	This graph will cross the x-axis at about $x = 8$.
As the y values decrease in this graph, the x value increase.	When $x = 50$ on this graph, y is about 1,400.	The y-intercept for this graph is about 59.

1 Mrs. Davis has a system for tracking pencils she loans to students. Students may take a pencil as long as they return it or replace it. Mrs. Davis keeps track of the total number of pencils she currently has using a graph such as the one shown.

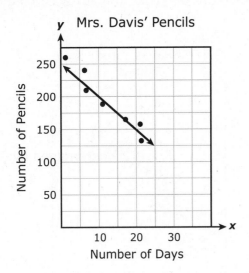

Mrs. Davis' Pencils

Number of Pencils

Number of Days

a. Is Mrs. Davis' pencil supply increasing or decreasing? Explain your answer.

b. Approximately how many pencils will Mrs. Davis have in her supply after 35 days?

c. Predict how many days it will take for the pencil supply to run out.

2 The graph shows the profit history for Fantastic Furniture since it opened in 1995.

Fantastic Furniture

Profit (thousands of dollars)

Number of Years Since 1995

a. In approximately what year will the store earn a profit of about $125,000?

b. Based on the trend in profit, about how much money will Fantastic Furniture profit in 2018? Justify your reasoning.

c. The equation of the trend line is $y = 5x - 10$. Write and solve an expression to predict the company's profit in the year 2030.

Connections

Search newspapers, magazines, and online resources to find examples of scatterplots with trend lines shown. Attach the plots to a sheet of paper. Write a brief synopsis for each graph, describing the trend shown and any predictions that might be made based on the data. Share your findings with the class.

1 For each situation, the earnings, y, vary directly with x, the number of hours worked.

   a. Michael earns $28.50 for three hours of tutoring. How much money will Michael earn for 8 hours of tutoring?

   b. The table shows the relationship between the number of hours Stacey works and her earnings.

Stacey's Earnings

Number of Hours	Earnings ($)
4	140
7	245
11	385

What is k, the constant of variation?

What is the meaning of the constant of variation?

Liam earns $300 for 9 hours of work, and Caryn earns $525 for 15 hours of work. Whose earnings show the same proportional relationship as shown in the table?

   c. Mr. Boyd's earnings can be represented by the equation $y = 23.75x$. What type of relationship is modeled by the graph of this equation?

2 Circle each statement that is true about a direct variation relationship.

The constant of variation is the same as the slope of the line.

In the equation $y = kx$, y is directly proportional to x.

The y-intercept will always be zero.

The value of k can be determined by $\frac{x}{y}$.

3 In the graph, y is directly proportional to x.

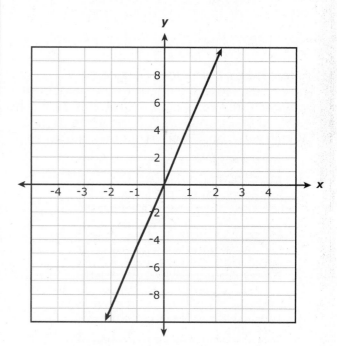

Complete the sentence.

The _____ of the line or the

_____ of variation is 4.5.

Based on the relationship shown in the graph, what is the value of y when $x = 10$?

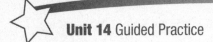
1 The amount Ricky charges for his lawn service varies directly with the number of hours it takes to complete the job. If Ricky charges $112.50 for a 3-hour job, how much money will he charge for a job that takes 5 hours?

Record your answer and fill in the bubbles on the grid below. Be sure to use the correct place value.

2 The number of inches a bungee cord stretches varies directly with the number of pounds it holds. One cord stretches 12 inches when a 30-pound object is attached to it. Which table best represents this relationship?

Ⓕ
Inches	2	4	6	8
Pounds	0.8	1.6	2.4	3.2

Ⓖ
Inches	2	4	6	8
Pounds	5	10	15	20

Ⓗ
Inches	2	4	6	8
Pounds	2	4	6	8

Ⓙ
Inches	2	4	6	8
Pounds	2.5	5	7.5	10

3 While traveling to Florida, June records the number of miles traveled for different time intervals.

Miles Traveled

Time (minutes)	Distance (miles)
30	35
60	70
90	105
120	140

Which best describes the constant of proportionality for the data?

Ⓐ $\frac{7}{6}$ miles per hour

Ⓑ $\frac{7}{6}$ miles per minute

Ⓒ $\frac{6}{7}$ mile per hour

Ⓓ $\frac{6}{7}$ mile per minute

4 If y is directly proportional to x, and $y = 84$ when $x = 7$, what is the value of x when $y = 156$?

Ⓕ 7   Ⓗ 13

Ⓖ 12   Ⓙ 22

5 Jimmy sells cookies in bags of $\frac{1}{2}$ dozen cookies for $4.50. If the cost varies directly to the number of cookies, which packaging and price is equivalent to Jimmy's pricing?

Ⓐ 12 cookies for $8.50

Ⓑ 15 cookies for $11.50

Ⓒ 20 cookies for $15.50

Ⓓ 30 cookies for $22.50

1 It takes Kendrick 20 minutes to travel 5 miles to school on his bicycle. Which correctly shows the relationship between the distance Kendrick travels and time?

Ⓐ Kendrick travels 15 miles per minute.

Ⓑ Kendrick travels 4 miles per minute.

Ⓒ Kendrick travels 0.25 mile per minute.

Ⓓ Kendrick travels 1.25 miles per minute.

2 The number of donuts produced by a machine is directly proportional to the time the machine runs. The machine produces 380 donuts in 20 minutes. How many donuts can the machine produce after running for 45 minutes?

Ⓕ 675 donuts

Ⓖ 855 donuts

Ⓗ 920 donuts

Ⓙ Not here

3 Two quantities, x and y, are related such that y varies directly with x. If the graph of this relationship contains the point (-3, 2), which ordered pair also belongs on the graph?

Ⓐ (9, -6)

Ⓑ (0, -1)

Ⓒ (-12, 11)

Ⓓ (21, -10)

4 An auto mechanic's pay varies directly with the number of hours worked. The mechanic makes $765 for 9 hours of work. Which table best represents this relationship?

Ⓕ
Mechanic's Pay

Hours	3	5	7
Pay ($)	240	400	560

Ⓖ
Mechanic's Pay

Hours	3	5	7
Pay ($)	255	425	680

Ⓗ
Mechanic's Pay

Hours	3	5	7
Pay ($)	240	255	595

Ⓙ
Mechanic's Pay

Hours	3	5	7
Pay ($)	255	425	595

5 Chad sells 3 pounds of barbeque for $28.74. If the cost of the barbeque varies directly with the number of pounds sold, which of the following does NOT reflect the same relationship?

Ⓐ 6 pounds of barbeque for $57.48

Ⓑ 9 pounds of barbeque for $82.26

Ⓒ 12 pounds of barbeque for $114.96

Ⓓ 15 pounds of barbeque for $143.70

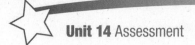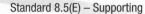
1 When swimming underwater, ear pressure varies directly with depth. The pressure in the ears is 8.6 pounds per square inch at a depth of 20 feet. What is the pressure, in pounds per square inch, at a depth of 40 feet?

Ⓐ 93.0 lb/in.^{2}

Ⓑ 46.5 lb/in.^{2}

Ⓒ 33.8 lb/in.^{2}

Ⓓ 17.2 lb/in.^{2}

2 In Mrs. Smith's pie recipe, the amount of blueberries used is directly proportional to the number of pies. If 4 pies requires 6.8 pounds of blueberries, how many blueberries are needed to bake 13 pies?

Ⓕ 0.65 pound of blueberries

Ⓖ 15.8 pounds of blueberries

Ⓗ 22.1 pounds of blueberries

Ⓙ 24.7 pounds of blueberries

3 If y varies directly with x at a constant rate of -0.2, which of the following shows possible values for x and y?

Ⓐ $x = -15$ and $y = 3$

Ⓑ $x = 2$ and $y = -10$

Ⓒ $x = -25$ and $y = -5$

Ⓓ $x = 3$ and $y = 0.6$

4 The total profit from the Spanish club fundraiser varies directly with the number of dinner tickets sold. If the sale of 22 tickets results in a profit of $253, how many tickets must be sold to reach the fundraising goal of $700?

Ⓕ 21 tickets

Ⓖ 55 tickets

Ⓗ 61 tickets

Ⓙ 46 tickets

5 The amount of energy contained in a falling object varies directly with the height of the object. An object has 56 joules of energy when it falls from a height of 3.5 meters. Which table best represents this relationship?

Ⓐ

Height (meters)	2.2	2.5	2.8	3.1	3.4
Energy (joules)	7.7	8.75	9.8	10.9	11.9

Ⓑ

Height (meters)	2.2	2.5	2.8	3.1	3.4
Energy (joules)	18.2	18.5	18.8	19.1	19.4

Ⓒ

Height (meters)	2.2	2.5	2.8	3.1	3.4
Energy (joules)	33	37.5	42	46.5	51

Ⓓ

Height (meters)	2.2	2.5	2.8	3.1	3.4
Energy (joules)	35.2	40	44.8	49.6	54.4

1 A job search website conducts research on the hourly wage students earn working after-school jobs. The results of the study are shown in the table.

Job	Hours Worked	Weekly Pay
A	20	$154.40
B	15	$120.00
C	25	$175.00
D	18	$153.00
E	10	$77.20

The research finds that the weekly pay, before taxes, that a student earns at an after-school job, *P*, varies directly with *h*, the number of hours worked. Express each job in the table as a direct variation equation.

Job A _____   Job D _____

Job B _____   Job E _____

Job C _____

Which two jobs paid the same hourly wage? Explain your answer.

_____

How many hours will it take to earn $256 working at Job B?

_____

2 Bridgette creates a table of data as shown.

x	1	2	3	4	5
y	80	150	220	290	360

Bridgette makes the observation that for every increase of 1 in the *x*-values, the corresponding *y*-values increase by 70. She concludes that the relationship shown in the table shows that *y* varies directly with *x*. Is Bridgette's conclusion correct? Justify your answer using the table.

Journal

Write a direct variation equation. _____

If the *x*-value is quadrupled, explain how to determine the change in the corresponding *y*-value, providing an example in your explanation.

_____

_____

Vocabulary Activity

Complete the graphic organizer.

Definition

Example

Equation

Direct Variation

Non-example

Related terms

Use the term in a sentence.

On a Roll

Play *On a Roll* with a partner. Each pair of players needs a number cube and a game board. Each player needs a pencil. Player 1 begins by rolling the number cube and solving the corresponding problem. If correct, player 1 is awarded the number of points in the banner next to the problem. If incorrect, player 2 can claim the points by working the problem correctly. If a player rolls the number of a problem that has already been solved, play passes to the next player. The winner is the player with more points after all problems have been solved.

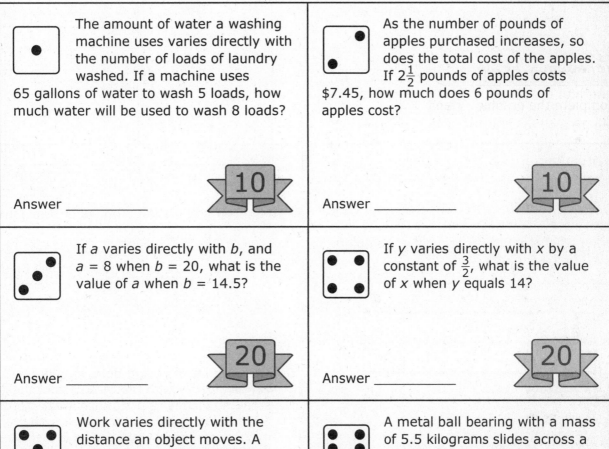

The amount of water a washing machine uses varies directly with the number of loads of laundry washed. If a machine uses 65 gallons of water to wash 5 loads, how much water will be used to wash 8 loads?

Answer _____   10

As the number of pounds of apples purchased increases, so does the total cost of the apples. If $2\frac{1}{2}$ pounds of apples costs $7.45, how much does 6 pounds of apples cost?

Answer _____   10

If *a* varies directly with *b*, and *a* = 8 when *b* = 20, what is the value of *a* when *b* = 14.5?

Answer _____   20

If *y* varies directly with *x* by a constant of $\frac{3}{2}$, what is the value of *x* when *y* equals 14?

Answer _____   20

Work varies directly with the distance an object moves. A man uses a 32-kilogram push lawn mower to mow his yard. If the man pushes the lawn mower a distance of 400 meters, how much work, in joules, does the man do while mowing his yard? (Hint: The weight of the lawn mower is constant.)

Answer _____

A metal ball bearing with a mass of 5.5 kilograms slides across a smooth surface with an acceleration of 3.1 meters per second squared. According to Newton's second law, force varies directly with acceleration. If the mass of the ball is the constant of variation, what force, in newtons, is being applied to the ball bearing?

Answer _____

1 The table shows a relationship between x and y.

x	-4	-3	-2	-1	0
y	10	7.5	5	2.5	0

What value of x will result in a y-value of -13? Justify your answer.

2 The cost of a pizza varies directly with the length of the diameter. If a pizza with a 12-inch diameter costs $8.64, how much should a pizza with a 16-inch diameter cost?

3 Using a constant of variation of $\frac{6}{7}$, complete the table of values for the relationship between x and y.

x	0		14		
y		6		18	24

4 The graph of a direct variation relationship is shown.

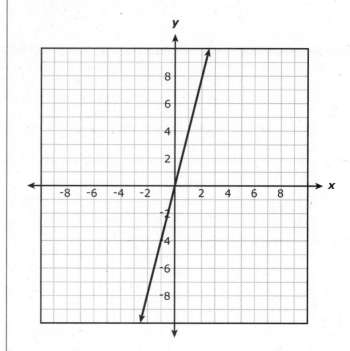

a. The graph shows that when x is equal to 2, y is equal to _____.

b. If the value of x is 17, what will be the value of y?

5 The amount of grilling time, in minutes, varies directly with the thickness of the steak, in inches. If a 1.5-inch steak needs 12 minutes of grilling time, how many minutes of grilling time does a 2-inch steak need?

Connections

Locate at least five examples of direct variation equations, tables, or graphs on the Internet, in newspapers, or in magazines. Attach the examples to a large sheet of paper. For each example, explain the relationship shown and record a statement: *In the (equation/table/graph), the _____ varies directly with the _____.* Use the information from the example to fill in the blanks. Share your work with the class.

1 Explain why each relationship is proportional.

a. $y = -\frac{2}{3}x$

b.
x	-3	-1	1	3	5
y	-9	-3	3	9	15

c. Jacob spends $60 every 7 days on gas for his vehicle.

d.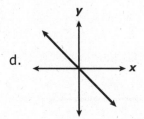

2 Explain why each relationship is non-proportional.

a. $y = 2x - 3$

b.
x	-3	-1	1	3	5
y	11	5	-1	-7	-13

c. Aliyah rents a cabin for $45 per day plus a non-refundable deposit of $15.

d.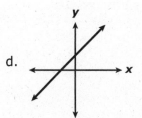

3 Classify each representation as proportional or non-proportional.

a. $y = \frac{1}{2}x$

b. After a $0.50 per hour raise, Zana now earns $11.75 per hour.

c.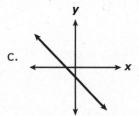

d.
x	3	4	5	6	7
y	-7	-9	-11	-13	-15

e. $y = (12 + 1.25)x$

f. The height of a shrub when it is first planted is 1 foot, and it grows at a rate of 2 inches per year. The shrub is y inches tall after x years.

g.
x	-25	-20	-15	-10	-5
y	-10	-8	-6	-4	-2

h.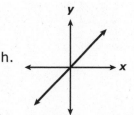

i. $y = -\frac{2}{3}x + 4$

1 A five-minute overseas phone call costs $5.91 and a ten-minute call costs $10.86. Which statement best describes the relationship between the cost and length of an overseas phone call?

Ⓐ The relationship is non-proportional because phone calls cost $4.95 each minute plus a fee of $0.96.

Ⓑ The relationship is proportional because phone calls cost $0.99 per minute.

Ⓒ The relationship is non-proportional because phone calls cost $0.99 each minute plus a fee of $0.96.

Ⓓ The relationship is proportional because phone calls cost $0.96 per minute.

2 Which of the following represents a proportional relationship?

Ⓕ
x	2	5	6	10
y	4	13	16	28

Ⓖ
x	2	5	6	10
y	1	-2	-3	-7

Ⓗ
x	2	5	6	10
y	10	25	30	50

Ⓙ
x	2	5	6	10
y	3	6	7	11

3 Which of the following describes a situation that is non-proportional?

Ⓐ Each light bulb costs $0.10 per hour in electricity cost when turned on.

Ⓑ Each light bulb at a wholesale purchase club costs $3.79 plus the membership fee of $4.95.

Ⓒ Each light bulb in a house contains 25 milligrams of tungsten.

Ⓓ Each light bulb in a light fixture uses 40 watts of electricity per hour.

4 The table shows a relationship between x and y.

x	-6	-2	4	10
y	9	3	-6	-15

Which of the following is NOT true about the relationship in the table?

Ⓕ The table shows a proportional relationship because the relationship can be represented by the equation $y = -\frac{3}{2}x$.

Ⓖ The table shows a proportional relationship because the line that models this relationship passes through the point (0, 0).

Ⓗ The table shows a proportional relationship because $-\frac{9}{6} = -\frac{3}{2} = \frac{-6}{4} = \frac{-15}{10}$.

Ⓙ The table shows a proportional relationship because there is no y-intercept shown in the table.

1 Mr. Mobley plans to have granite countertops installed in his kitchen. Granite Guys charges $75 per square foot of granite with an additional $200 service fee. Stoneworks charges $75 per square foot of granite. Which of the following statements is true?

Ⓐ The pricing at Granite Guys is proportional because it is the more expensive option.

Ⓑ The pricing at Granite Guys is non-proportional because of the additional service fee.

Ⓒ The pricing at Stoneworks is non-proportional because the y-intercept is 0.

Ⓓ The pricing at both stores is proportional because they both charge the same price per square foot.

2 The table shows the costs for various packages of Taffy Treats.

Size (ounces)	4	8	16	32
Cost ($)	0.76	1.52	3.04	6.08

What is true about the equation that can be used to find c, the cost of n ounces?

Ⓕ The equation is proportional because the number of ounces is multiplied by $0.76 to determine the cost.

Ⓖ The equation is non-proportional because $0.76 is added to the number of ounces to determine the cost.

Ⓗ The equation is proportional because the number of ounces is multiplied by $0.19 to determine the cost.

Ⓙ The equation is non-proportional because $0.19 is added to the number of ounces to determine the cost.

3 Look at the graph of the lines.

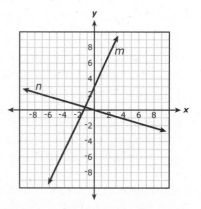

Which of the following is true?

Ⓐ Line m shows a proportional relationship because the y-intercept is not zero.

Ⓑ Line m shows a non-proportional relationship because the equation for the line can be represented by $y = mx + b$, where $b \neq 0$.

Ⓒ Line n shows a proportional relationship because the slope is negative.

Ⓓ Line n shows a non-proportional relationship because the equation of the line can be represented by $y = kx$.

4 Which of the following situations best represents a proportional relationship?

Ⓕ A tree expert earns $35 per hour plus $25 for each service call.

Ⓖ A cell phone company charges $50 per month plus $0.10 per text.

Ⓗ A bakery makes 6 loaves of bread every $\frac{1}{2}$ hour or 12 loaves every hour.

Ⓙ A clothing store sells 10 skirts online each day plus 8 skirts per hour in the store.

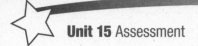
1 Haley collects music boxes. She currently has 7 and plans to collect 3 more each year. Which statement best describes Haley's situation?

Ⓐ Haley's situation is proportional because she will be collecting music boxes at a constant rate.

Ⓑ Haley's situation is proportional because she has already collected 7 music boxes and plans to collect 3 more each year.

Ⓒ Haley's situation is non-proportional because she has already collected 7 music boxes and plans to collect 3 more each year.

Ⓓ Haley's situation is non-proportional because she will be collecting music boxes at a constant rate.

2 Which situation describes a proportional relationship?

Ⓕ Henry saves $45.50 every month to contribute to his college fund.

Ⓖ Alisha bakes 3 dozen cookies every hour to add to the one dozen cookies she has already baked.

Ⓗ Roger begins with 15 canned food items and collects 30 canned food items from each class to donate to the food bank.

Ⓙ Ella paints 18 square feet of fence. To finish the job, she paints 42 square feet of fence every hour.

3 Which table shows a relationship that is proportional?

Ⓐ
x	-2	-1	3	5	7
y	-4	-3	6	8	14

Ⓑ
x	-10	-5	-2	2	5
y	-2	-1	-0.4	0.4	1

Ⓒ
x	-4	-3	-1	1	2
y	-3	-2	0	2	3

Ⓓ
x	6	12	15	18	20
y	1	2	3	4	5

4 The graph shows a relationship between x and y.

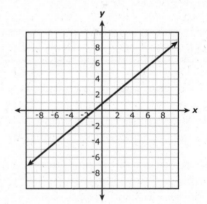

Which of the statements is true?

Ⓕ The relationship is proportional because the line has a constant, positive slope.

Ⓖ The relationship is non-proportional because the slope of the line is increasing.

Ⓗ The relationship is proportional because the line crosses the y-axis once.

Ⓙ The relationship is non-proportional because the line crosses the y-axis at (0, 1).

Mrs. Gardner is curious to know the number of hours her students spend preparing for a major test. On Monday, Mrs. Gardner asks her students to keep track of the total number of hours they study for a major unit test to be given on Friday. Each student submits a graph of his/her results with the test on Friday.

Brennan begins studying Monday night and studies 3 hours each night from Monday to Thursday. Sarah began studying over the weekend and has already studied 4 hours when Mrs. Gardner gives the assignment. She then studies 1 hour per day each day from Monday to Thursday. The graphs for the study times of Brennan and Sarah are shown.

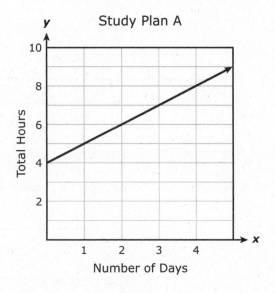

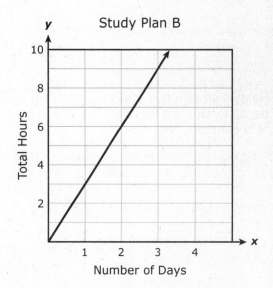

Determine which graph represents a proportional relationship and which represents a non-proportional relationship. Use both the situation and the graphs to explain your answer. Identify which graph was created by each student.

_____

_____

_____

_____

_____

_____

Journal

Comprehension Understand

Write a summary of the processes used to distinguish between proportional and non-proportional situations in a table, a graph, a verbal description, and an equation.

_____

_____

_____

_____

Vocabulary Activity

Complete the activity with a partner. Each pair of players needs a game board. Each player needs a sheet of paper and a pencil. Player 1 begins by choosing any space on the board and completing the task given on his/her sheet of paper. If correct, player 1 records his/her initials in the space, and play passes to player 2. If incorrect, player 1 loses a turn, and play passes to player 2. The first player to initial 3 spaces in a row vertically, horizontally, or diagonally wins the game.

Draw a visual representation that explains the meaning of the term *y-intercept*.	Define *constant of proportionality (k)*.	Write a real-world scenario that demonstrates a *non-proportional relationship*.
Create a graph that shows a *proportional relationship*.	Create a graph that shows a *non-proportional relationship*.	Write the general equations used for *proportional* and *non-proportional relationships*.
Draw a graph that shows the location of the *origin*.	Write a real-world scenario that demonstrates a *proportional relationship*.	Create a table that could be used to graph a *proportional relationship*.

motivation**math**™LEVEL 8

mentoring**minds**.com

What Makes You So Proportional?

Play *What Makes You So Proportional?* with a partner. Each pair of players needs a game board and paper clips to use with the spinners. Each player needs a pencil. Player 1 spins the spinners and uses the values to identify a row and a column. Player 1 identifies the representation in the space as either proportional or non-proportional and provides a verbal justification for his/her choice. If correct, player 1 records his/her answer and initials the space. If incorrect, play passes to player 2. If the values spun have already been initialed, the player loses a turn. The game ends when all spaces are initialed. The winner is the player with more spaces initialed.

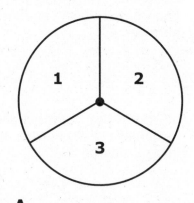
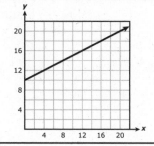

	A	B	C
1	<table><tr><td>**x**</td><td>-1</td><td>2</td><td>4</td><td>7</td></tr><tr><td>**y**</td><td>-1</td><td>8</td><td>14</td><td>23</td></tr></table>	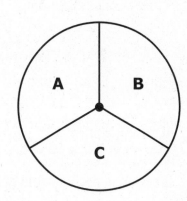	$y = \frac{8}{3}x$
2	$y = 9.8x - 7$	A painter charges $45 per hour to paint the exterior of a house.	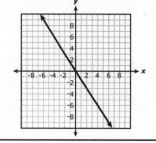
3	A test prep center charges $25 per hour to tutor students taking the SAT. One student uses a coupon for $100 off his sessions.	<table><tr><td>**x**</td><td>**y**</td></tr><tr><td>7.12</td><td>18</td></tr><tr><td>10.68</td><td>27</td></tr><tr><td>14.24</td><td>36</td></tr><tr><td>17.8</td><td>45</td></tr></table>	Judy leaves a 20% tip on the total cost of her meal, not including tax.

1 Read the two scenarios. For each, state whether the scenario represents a proportional or a non-proportional situation. Justify your answers.

A bird weighs 4.0 ounces. It gains 0.01 ounce each month. The bird weighs y ounces after x months.

The track team fundraiser raises $55 per member.

2 Nathan joins a gym during a special promotion. The registration fee is waived, and membership costs $16 each week. Determine if this situation is proportional or non-proportional.

Write an equation that models this situation.

3 Does the table represent a proportional or non-proportional situation? Explain your answer.

x	-2	-1	0	1	2
y	-21	-9	3	15	27

4 Look at the graph.

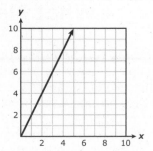

Does the graph represent a proportional or non-proportional relationship? Explain your answer.

Circle the part of the graph that determines whether the relationship is proportional or non-proportional.

5 Determine if each representation shown is proportional or non-proportional.

a. $c = 0.25m + 44$

b.
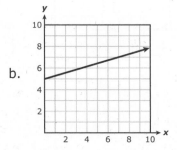

c.

x	-2	-1	0	1	2
y	-1	$-\frac{1}{2}$	0	$\frac{1}{2}$	1

Connections

Plan a savings account using two different methods. In the first method, plan to save a certain amount of money each month. In the second method, plan to save the same amount monthly, but begin with an initial deposit of $50. Create graphs and tables of values for each method. Explain which method is proportional and which is non-proportional. Use your graphs, tables, and explanations to create a poster or multimedia presentation for the class.

1 The mapping shows a relation of *x*- and *y*-coordinates.

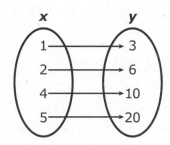

Does the relation represent a function? Explain your answer.

2 Plot the points from the relation shown.

x	-5	-3	0	1	4
y	3	5	-1	2	5

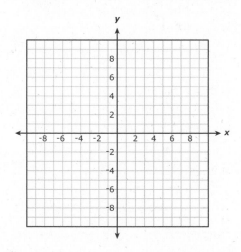

Use the vertical line test to determine if the graph represents a function. Explain your reasoning.

_____

_____

_____

3 Is the relation shown a function? Explain your answer.

{(-1, 7), (3, 8), (4, 7), (6, 13), (10, 8)}

_____

_____

4 Create a mapping of the relation shown.

{(-3, 1), (-2, 2), (-1, 0), (0, -1), (-1, -2)}

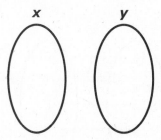

Does the mapping represent a function? Explain your reasoning.

_____

_____

5 Determine whether the following relations are functions. If the relation is a function, write *function*. If not, change one or more numbers in the table to make the relation a function.

x	*y*
-14	7
-10	5
-6	3
-2	1
2	-1

x	*y*
5	2
3	3
1	4
3	5
7	6

1 Which of the following does NOT represent a function?

I.

x	-6	-3	-2	0	1
y	-1	2	3	5	6

II.

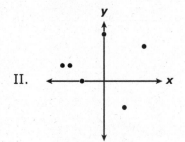

III.

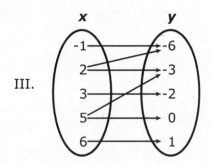

IV. {(-1, 3), (1, 1), (2, 3), (-1, 4), (1, 2)}

Ⓐ I and II only

Ⓑ II and III only

Ⓒ III only

Ⓓ III and IV only

2 Which relation represents a function?

Ⓕ {(5, -9), (3, -11), (0, -13), (5, -15)}

Ⓖ {(-4, -13), (-1, -7), (2, -1), (2, 5), (6, 7)}

Ⓗ {(-8.1, 2), (-7.6, 2), (-7.1, 2), (-6.6, 2)}

Ⓙ {$\left(-1, \frac{1}{2}\right)$, (-1, 1), (1, 2), (1, 4), (3, 8)}

3 Which of the following statements is true?

Ⓐ A function is a relation in which each *y*-value is paired with exactly one *x*-value.

Ⓑ A function is a relation in which each input is paired with only one value from the output.

Ⓒ A function is a relation in which each *x*-value is paired with more than one *y*-value.

Ⓓ A function is a relation in which each dependent variable is paired with only one independent variable.

4 Which graph does NOT represent a function?

Ⓕ

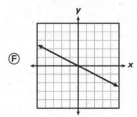

Ⓖ

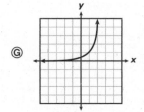

Ⓗ

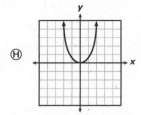

Ⓙ

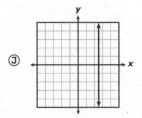

motivation**math**™LEVEL 8   mentoring**minds**.com

1 Which graph represents a function?

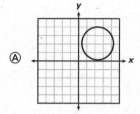

Ⓐ

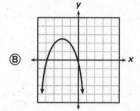

Ⓑ

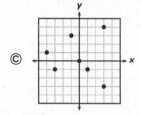

Ⓒ

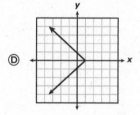

Ⓓ

2 Which statement about functions is true?

Ⓕ The values of the independent quantities may repeat, but the values of the dependent quantities do not.

Ⓖ The x-values are dependent on the y-values.

Ⓗ The output values determine the input values.

Ⓙ Any vertical line intersects the graph only once.

3 Which relation shown is NOT a function?

Ⓐ

x	0	4	9	8	9
y	-1	-2	-3	-4	-5

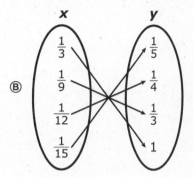

Ⓑ

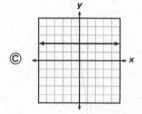

Ⓒ

Ⓓ {(-4, 3), (-3, 4), (-2, 2), (3, -2), (4, 3)}

4 A relation between x- and y-values is shown.

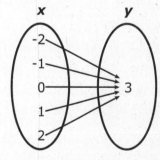

Does the relation represent a function?

Ⓕ No, each independent quantity is mapped to more than one dependent quantity.

Ⓖ Yes, each dependent quantity is mapped to only one independent quantity.

Ⓗ No, each y-value is mapped to more than one x-value.

Ⓙ Yes, each x-value is mapped to only one y-value.

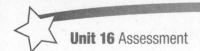

Unit 16 Assessment

1 Which of the following relations is a function?

    I. {(-2, 3), (2, -3), (4, -2), (-3, 4)}

    II. {(-2, 2), (4, 3), (-3, 3), (-2, 4)}

    III. {(2, -3), (3, -4), (3, -3), (-4, 4)}

    IV. {(-4, 3), (-3, -3), (2, -3), (-2, -4)}

Ⓐ I, III, and IV only

Ⓑ I and IV only

Ⓒ II and III only

Ⓓ I only

2 The table shows a relation between *x* and *y*.

x	y
-6	5
-2	2
0	5
1	-1
3	-2

Does the relation in the table represent a function?

Ⓕ Yes, because for each output value there is exactly one input value

Ⓖ No, because for every input value there is more than one output value

Ⓗ Yes, because each *x*-value is paired with exactly one *y*-value

Ⓙ No, because each *y*-value is paired with exactly one *x*-value

3 Which of the following does NOT represent a function?

I.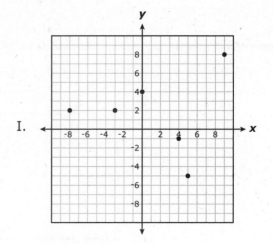

II.

x	y
-4	7
-2	1
0	-1
2	1
4	7

III.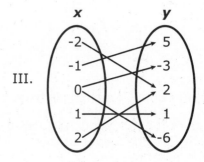

IV. {(-2, 5), (-1, -3), (6, 3), (-2, 8), (1, 3)}

Ⓐ III and IV only

Ⓑ I and II only

Ⓒ II, III, and IV only

Ⓓ I, II, III, and IV

 motivation**math**™LEVEL 8   mentoring**minds**.com

For each situation, determine if the resulting relation will always, sometimes, or never be a function. Provide an example set of data using the representation given, and provide a justification for your answer.

a. The cost of a small cheese pizza is $8. Additional toppings cost $1.35 each.

Always/Sometimes/Never a function

Number of Toppings	Total Cost of Pizza

Justification _____

_____

b. The students in Mr. Genaro's class measure their heights in inches. The heights are paired with the students' corresponding shoe sizes.

Always/Sometimes/Never a function

{(____, ____), (____, ____), (____, ____), (____, ____), (____, ____)}

Justification _____

_____

c. Kelly makes key chains by braiding colored cording. The cost of the key chains depends on the colors used. Three key chains using purple cording cost a total of $6. Two key chains using red cording cost a total of $3. Three key chains using yellow cording cost a total of $5. Four key chains using blue cording cost a total of $8.

Always/Sometimes/Never a function

Justification _____

_____

_____

_____

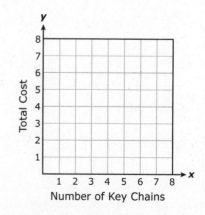

Journal

Mr. Tacoma displays the following statement for his students to consider.

All functions are relations, but all relations are not functions.

Is the statement true or false? Justify your response.

_____

_____

_____

Vocabulary Activity

Complete the graphic organizers by providing examples and non-examples of functions, including ordered pairs, tables, mappings, and graphs.

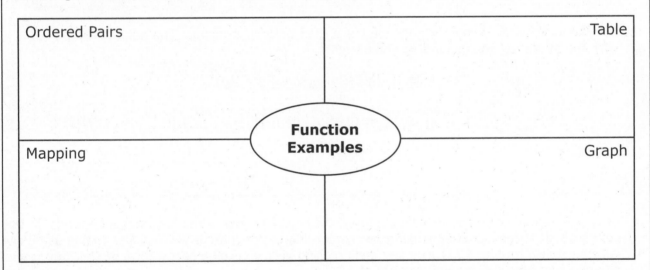

FUNctions Maze

Beginning at *START* on the maze, determine whether the model shows a function or not, and use the choice to shade a path to follow. The correct path leads to the *FINISH* of the maze.

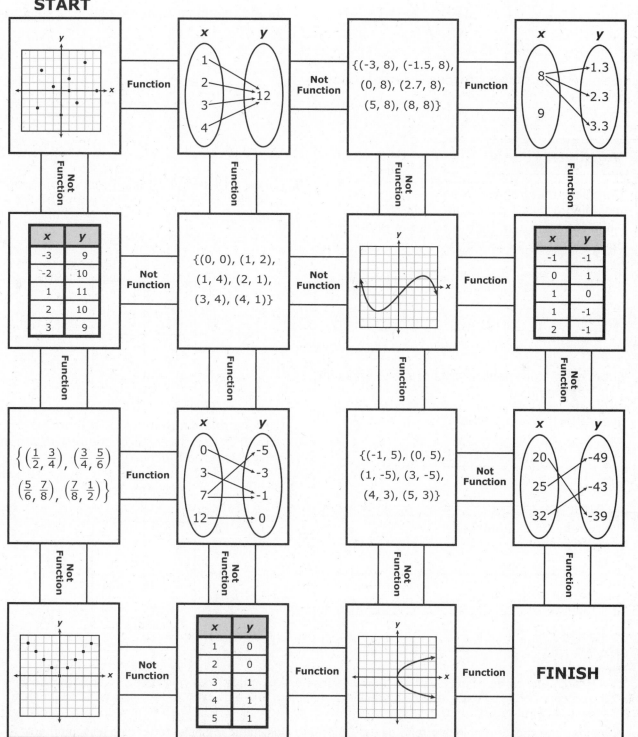

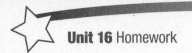
1 Look at the relation.

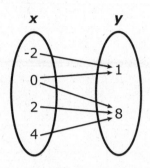

Is the relation shown a function? Justify your answer.

_____

_____

2 Fill in the blanks so that each set of ordered pairs represents a function.

{(-6, ___), (-3, ___), (-1, ___), (2, ___)}

{(___, 11), (___, 12), (___, 13), (___, 14)}

3 Label each statement as *true* or *false*. Explain your reasoning.

Every function is a relation.

_____

_____

Every relation is a function.

_____

_____

4 The table shows a relation between *x*- and *y*-values.

x	-1	0	1	2	3
y	-2	1	4	7	10

Is the relation shown a function? Explain your answer.

_____

_____

5 Draw a relation that is a function on Graph 1. Use the vertical line test to prove that it is a function.

Graph 1

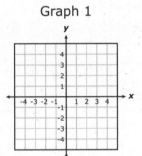

Draw a relation that is NOT a function on Graph 2. Use the vertical line test to prove that it is not a function.

Graph 2

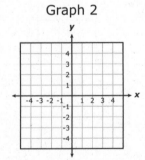

Connections

1. Research real-world examples of functions. Choose one example from your research and represent it as a set of ordered pairs, a table of values, a mapping, and a graph. Create a poster or multimedia presentation to present to the class.

2. You are the substitute teacher for a day in your math class, and you have to teach a lesson on how to identify functions. Write a script to use in teaching the lesson.

1 A video store charges $3.00 to rent a movie. The store also offers a membership that costs $15. Members are allowed to rent movies for $1.50 each. Write an equation to represent each rental plan. Let c represent the total cost and m represent the number of movies rented.

2 Mr. Reeves buys concert tickets online. The ticket provider charges a one-time convenience fee with each online purchase. The table shows the total cost for purchasing different numbers of tickets.

Number of Tickets	Total Cost ($)
3	127.50
5	202.50
8	315.00
12	465.00

Write an equation to determine c, the total cost for n tickets.

3 The Pine Tree UIL team holds a car wash to raise money. The team spends $12.50 for supplies and charges a fee of $5.00 per car. Write an equation to model the relationship between y, the total earnings for washing x cars.

4 Mr. Martin receives a gift card to Coffee Express. Mr. Martin purchases a coffee each morning with the gift card, as shown in the table.

Day	Remaining Gift Card Balance ($)
2	35.50
4	31.00
7	24.25
10	17.50

Write an equation to determine b, the gift card balance after d days.

5 Look at the graph of a line.

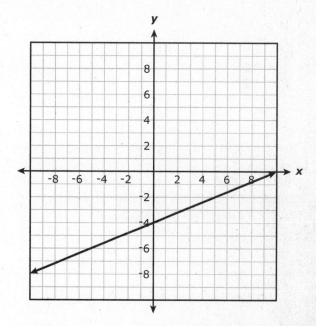

Write an equation that best represents the function.

1 A balloon is released from the top of a 75-foot building. The balloon rises at a rate of 2 feet per second. Which equation describes the height of the balloon, h, after s seconds?

Ⓐ $h = 75s$

Ⓑ $h = 2s$

Ⓒ $h = 2s + 75$

Ⓓ $h = 75s + 2$

2 Look at the set of ordered pairs.

$\{(-8, 3), (-6, 2), (-4, 1), (-2, 0)\}$

Which of the following shows the correct equation for the function represented by the ordered pairs?

Ⓕ $y = -0.5x - 1$

Ⓖ $y = -2x - 1$

Ⓗ $y = -\frac{1}{4}x + 1$

Ⓙ $y = -2x - 2$

3 An art studio charges $65 per month for art lessons. There is also an additional supply fee of $25 at the time of registration. Which equation best describes the total cost, c, given the number of months, m?

Ⓐ $c = 65m - 25$

Ⓑ $c = 90m$

Ⓒ $c = 25m + 65$

Ⓓ $c = 65m + 25$

4 Natasha graphs line m on the coordinate plane.

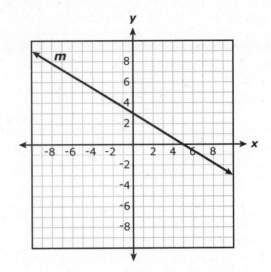

Which of the following equations best represents the line Natasha graphs?

Ⓕ $y = -\frac{1}{2}x + 3$

Ⓖ $y = \frac{5}{3}x + 5$

Ⓗ $y = -\frac{3}{5}x + 3$

Ⓙ $y = -\frac{2}{3}x + 5$

5 Marcy receives a coupon from Outdoor Experts and decides to purchase new chairs for her outdoor patio. The table shows the costs for different numbers of chairs from Outdoor Experts.

Number of Chairs	3	4	5	6
Total Cost ($)	312	441	570	699

Which equation best shows the relationship between t, the total cost, and c, the number of chairs purchased?

Ⓐ $t = 129c - 75$

Ⓑ $t = 104c - 75$

Ⓒ $t = 129c + 75$

Ⓓ $t = 116.5c + 75$

 motivation**math**™LEVEL 8 mentoring**minds**.com

1 Mrs. Lugar makes and ships personalized baseball caps. The table shows the relationship between the cost, *y*, and the number of baseball caps sold, *x*.

Number of Caps	1	2	3	4
Total Cost ($)	31.50	58.00	84.50	111.00

Which equation best represents the relationship?

Ⓐ $y = 26.50x$

Ⓑ $y = 26.50x + 5$

Ⓒ $y = 31.50x$

Ⓓ $y = 5x + 26.50$

2 The graph shows a relationship between temperature and time.

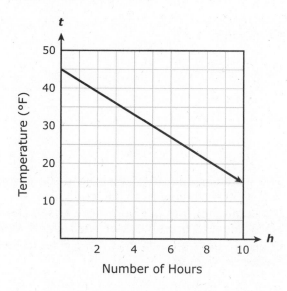

Which best represents the equation that shows the temperature, *t*, after *h* hours?

Ⓕ $t = -45h$

Ⓖ $t = -5h + 45$

Ⓗ $t = -3h + 45$

Ⓙ $t = -\frac{2}{3}h + 45$

3 A local theater group sells individual tickets to performances for $10 each. There are 25 season ticket holders who pay for the performances in advance. Which equation represents the amount of money, *M*, brought in during one month through the sale of individual tickets?

Ⓐ $M = 25t + 10$

Ⓑ $M = 10t + 25$

Ⓒ $M = 10t + 250$

Ⓓ $M = 250t + 10$

4 Look at the table.

x	-2	1	3	6
y	-2	7	13	22

Which equation best represents the data?

Ⓕ $y = x + 4$

Ⓖ $y = 4x + 1$

Ⓗ $y = 5x – 4$

Ⓙ $y = 3x + 4$

5 Mrs. Fuller plants a 4-inch tomato plant in her garden. The tomato plant grows at a rate of 2 inches each week. Which equation can be used to determine *h*, the height of the tomato plant in inches after *w* weeks?

Ⓐ $h = 2w + 4$

Ⓑ $h = \frac{1}{2}w + 4$

Ⓒ $h = 4w + 2$

Ⓓ $h = 2w + \frac{1}{4}$

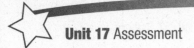

1 A function is represented by the following set of ordered pairs.

$$\{(-3, -13), (0, -7), (3, -1), (6, 5)\}$$

Which equation represents the function?

Ⓐ $y = 3x - 7$

Ⓑ $y = 6x - 7$

Ⓒ $y = 2x - 7$

Ⓓ $y = \frac{1}{2}x - 7$

2 Mrs. Durham purchases turkey from the deli counter for $3.25 per pound. She also purchases a loaf of bread from the bakery for $4.50. Which equation can be used to represent the total cost, c, of Mrs. Durham's purchase of bread and t pounds of turkey?

Ⓕ $c = 4.50t + 3.25$

Ⓖ $c = (4.50 + 3.25)t$

Ⓗ $c = 3.25t$

Ⓙ $c = 3.25t + 4.50$

3 Look at the table.

x	-3	-1	2	4	7
y	13	5	-7	-15	-27

Which equation best models the data?

Ⓐ $y = -4x + 1$

Ⓑ $y = 2x - 8$

Ⓒ $y = -12x + 3$

Ⓓ $y = 3x + 2$

4 The monthly cost of renting a trumpet is modeled in the graph.

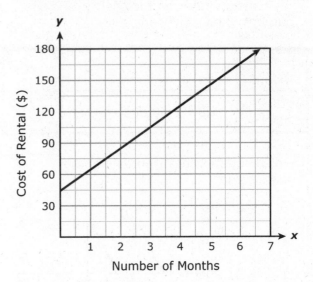

Which equation best represents the cost, y, of renting a trumpet for x months?

Ⓕ $y = 45x$

Ⓖ $y = 35x + 45$

Ⓗ $y = 65x + 45$

Ⓙ $y = 20x + 45$

5 The water level in the lake during the spring was 1.5 feet below the spill level. The unusually hot and dry summer caused the water level to drop 0.6 foot each week. Which equation best models the water level in feet, f, after w weeks?

Ⓐ $f = -1.5w + 0.6$

Ⓑ $f = -0.6w + 1.5$

Ⓒ $f = -1.5w - 0.6$

Ⓓ $f = -0.6w - 1.5$

1 Lines *m* and *n* are shown.

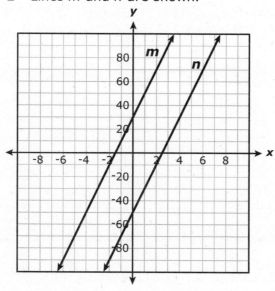

Use the equations of the lines to describe the similarities and differences in the graphs.

_____

_____

_____

_____

_____

2 Consider the following table.

x	-3	-1.5	2	2.5
y		-2		

Record an equation that could be used to represent a linear relationship between *x* and *y* containing the ordered pair given in the table.

At *x* = 2.5, add *y* = -14 to the table. Record an equation that could be used to represent the linear relationship between *x* and *y* in the table, given the additional information.

Does the first equation you wrote match the second? If the equations are different, explain why they are different. If they are the same, explain why.

_____

_____

_____

Journal

Select one of the following representations and explain how to determine the values of m and b when writing an equation in the form $y = mx + b$ to represent a linear relationship for the representation.

table   graph   verbal

_____

_____

_____

Vocabulary Activity

The representations model linear relationships. Add the missing representations to complete the boxes. Then, label each representation using as many of the terms listed as possible.

dependent quantity, independent quantity, ordered pair, slope, y-intercept

Table	Equation	Graph
<table><tr><th>x</th><th>y</th></tr><tr><td>-2</td><td></td></tr><tr><td>-1</td><td></td></tr><tr><td>0</td><td></td></tr><tr><td>1</td><td></td></tr><tr><td>2</td><td></td></tr></table>		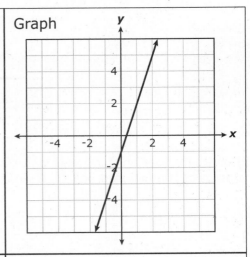
<table><tr><th>x</th><th>y</th></tr><tr><td>-2</td><td></td></tr><tr><td>-1</td><td></td></tr><tr><td>0</td><td></td></tr><tr><td>1</td><td></td></tr><tr><td>2</td><td></td></tr></table>	$y = \frac{1}{2}x - 4$	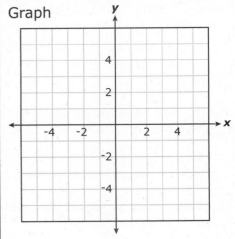

motivation**math**™LEVEL 8
mentoring**minds**.com

Three in a Line

Play *Three in a Line* with a partner. Each pair of players needs a game board. Each player needs a pencil. Player 1 selects a space on the board and determines an equation to represent the relationship. Player 1 states his/her equation aloud. If correct, player 1 records the equation in the space and marks the space with an X. If incorrect, player 1 loses a turn, and play passes to player 2. Player 2 repeats the process, marking his/her space with an O when correct. The first player to mark three spaces in a row vertically, horizontally, or diagonally wins.

Jumel's cell phone plan costs $0.35 per text plus a monthly fee of $45. What is the total monthly cost, *y*, for *x* texts? y = _____	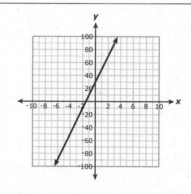 y = _____	<table><tr><td>**x**</td><td>**y**</td></tr><tr><td>-1</td><td>-2</td></tr><tr><td>1</td><td>-0.5</td></tr><tr><td>3</td><td>1</td></tr><tr><td>5</td><td>2.5</td></tr><tr><td>7</td><td>4</td></tr></table> y = _____
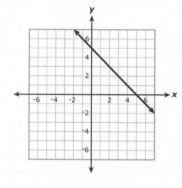 y = _____	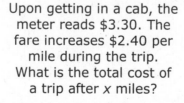 y = _____	A swimming pool containing 5,000 gallons of water drains at a rate of 12 gallons per minute. How many gallons remain, *y*, after *x* minutes? y = _____
<table><tr><td>**x**</td><td>**y**</td></tr><tr><td>0</td><td>-1</td></tr><tr><td>2</td><td>5</td></tr><tr><td>4</td><td>11</td></tr><tr><td>6</td><td>17</td></tr><tr><td>8</td><td>23</td></tr></table> y = _____	Upon getting in a cab, the meter reads $3.30. The fare increases $2.40 per mile during the trip. What is the total cost of a trip after *x* miles? y = _____	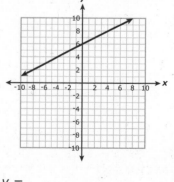 y = _____

For the table in the middle:

x	-2	-1	0	1	2
y	14	8	2	-4	-10

1 Sebastian plans to sell his paintings to raise money for a summer art trip. He purchases supplies for $80 and sells his paintings for $35 each. Write an equation that models the total profit, *P*, Sebastian will earn from selling *x* paintings.

2 The cost of renting a jet ski for various numbers of hours is shown in the table.

Jet Ski Rental

Number of Hours	2	3	4	5	6
Rental Cost ($)	90	105	120	135	150

Write an equation that models the total cost, *C*, in dollars, of renting a jet ski for *h* hours.

3 A set of ordered pairs is shown.

{(-3, 21), (-1, 13), (0, 9), (2, 1), (5, -11)}

Write an equation to represent the relationship between *x* and *y* in the set of ordered pairs.

4 Celia and Destiny each write an equation to represent the line shown in the graph.

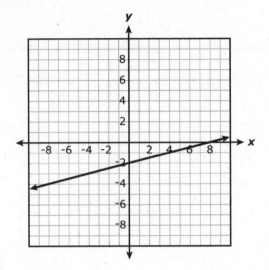

Celia writes $y = 4x - 2$ for the graph shown, and Destiny writes $y = \frac{1}{2}x - 2$. Which student is correct? Explain your answer.

5 At the time of the weather forecast on the evening news, the temperature was 3 degrees below zero. The temperatures continued to fall at a rate of 1.5 degrees each hour due to a winter storm. Write an equation to determine the temperature, *t*, in degrees, after *h* hours.

Connections

Companies use equations, graphs, and tables to chart profits and losses. Use the Internet to locate three examples of profit and loss data represented by an equation, a graph, or a table. For each example, describe the relationship in the data. Is it linear or non-linear? Present the information to the class.

1 A rectangular prism and a cylinder are shown.

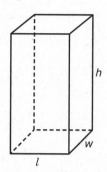 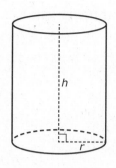

Explain how to find the volume of the rectangular prism.

Explain how to find the volume of the cylinder.

How is finding the volume of a rectangular prism and a cylinder similar? How is it different?

What is the formula for finding the volume of a cylinder?

2 Chyna purchases a new pencil bag.

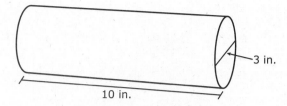

10 in.

3 in.

Shade the base of the pencil bag. What shape is the base of the pencil bag?

What formula is used to determine the area of the base?

Using the formula for volume of a cylinder, explain how to determine the volume of the pencil bag, in cubic inches.

Write an expression to determine the volume of the pencil bag, in cubic inches.

3 A cylindrical trash can has a diameter of 15 inches.

25 in.

Cyrus calculates the volume of the trash can using the expression $(15^2)(\pi)(25)$. Is the expression Cyrus used correct? Explain your answer.

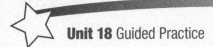

1 A rainwater collection barrel has the dimensions shown.

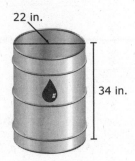

22 in.

34 in.

Which explanation describes how to determine the number of cubic inches the barrel holds when at capacity?

Ⓐ $(11\pi)(34)(34)$, because the area of the base, 11π, is multiplied by the height squared

Ⓑ $(121\pi)(34)$, because the area of the base, 121π, is multiplied by the height

Ⓒ $(22)(1,156)$, because the diameter of the base is multiplied by the height squared

Ⓓ $(484)(34)$, because the diameter of the base squared is multiplied by the height

2 Darius is asked to determine the volume of a cylindrical pipe for his father's plumbing business. The pipe has a diameter of 6 inches and a length of 34 inches. Which best explains how Darius can determine B, the area of the base of the pipe, in square inches?

Ⓕ Multiply the square of $\frac{34}{2}$ by 3.14

Ⓖ Multiply 34 and 34

Ⓗ Multiply the square of $\frac{6}{2}$ by 3.14

Ⓙ Multiply 6 and 6

3 A container of yogurt is shaped like a cylinder. The radius of the container is $\frac{7}{8}$ inch, and the height is 3 inches. Which expression can be used to find the volume of the yogurt container, in cubic inches?

Ⓐ $\left(\frac{7}{8}\right)(3)$

Ⓒ $\left(\frac{22}{7} \cdot \frac{7}{8} \cdot \frac{7}{8}\right)(3)$

Ⓑ $\left(2 \cdot \frac{22}{7} \cdot \frac{7}{8}\right)(3)$

Ⓓ $\left(2 \cdot \frac{7}{8}\right)(3)$

4 Myra purchases a can of chips.

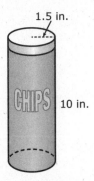

1.5 in.

10 in.

The formula for finding the volume of a cylinder is $V = Bh$. Which best represents B?

Ⓕ $\pi(1.5)^2$, because B is the area of the circular base

Ⓖ $\pi(3)$, because B is the circumference of the circular base

Ⓗ 3, because B is the diameter of the circular base

Ⓙ $2\pi(1.5)$, because B is the distance around the circular base

5 The volume of a cylindrical container is 17.6 cubic centimeters. A disc has an area of 4.4 square centimeters, equivalent to the area of the base of the container. If each disc is 1 centimeter tall, how many discs will the container hold?

Ⓐ 1.27

Ⓒ 22

Ⓑ 4

Ⓓ 77.44

1 Corbin begins calculating the volume of a cylinder, in cubic meters, using the following steps.

$V = Bh$

$V = (113.04) \times 20$

Which model could represent Corbin's cylinder?

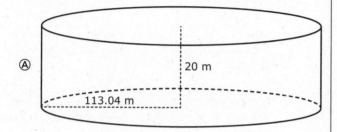

Ⓐ 20 m
113.04 m

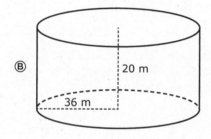

Ⓑ 20 m
36 m

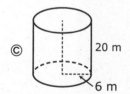

Ⓒ 20 m
6 m

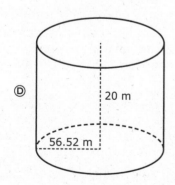

Ⓓ 20 m
56.52 m

2 The base of a cylinder that is 30 centimeters tall is shown.

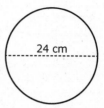

24 cm

Which expression can be used to find the volume of the cylinder, in cubic centimeters?

Ⓕ (24)(30), because the diameter of the circular base is multiplied by the height of the cylinder to find the volume

Ⓖ (144π)(30), because the area of the circular base is multiplied by the height of the cylinder to find the volume

Ⓗ (12)(30), because the radius of the circular base is multiplied by the height of the cylinder to find the volume

Ⓙ (24π)(30), because the circumference of the circular base is multiplied by the height of the cylinder to find the volume

3 Leann determines the volume of the cylinder shown using the formula $V = Bh$.

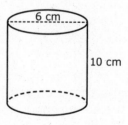

6 cm
10 cm

Which expression does Leann use to determine B, the area of the base of the cylinder, in square centimeters?

Ⓐ (3.14)(6)(6)

Ⓑ $(3.14)\left(\frac{6}{2}\right)$

Ⓒ (3.14)(8)(2)(10)

Ⓓ (3.14)(3)(3)

1 Look at the cylinder.

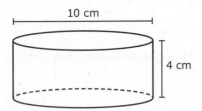

10 cm

4 cm

Which best demonstrates how to determine the volume of the cylinder?

Ⓐ (10)(4), because $V = Bh$

Ⓑ $\pi(100)(4)$, because $V = \pi d^2 h$

Ⓒ $\pi(20)(4)$, because $V = 2\pi rh$

Ⓓ $\pi(25)(4)$, because $V = \pi r^2 h$

2 Matthew makes a cardboard box shaped like a cylinder.

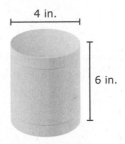

4 in.

6 in.

If the volume of the box can be found using $V = Bh$, which expression can be used to find the area of the lid in square inches?

Ⓕ $\frac{22}{7}(4)(4)$

Ⓖ $\frac{22}{7}(2)(4)$

Ⓗ $\frac{22}{7}(2)(2)$

Ⓙ $\frac{22}{7}(4)(6)$

3 Tabitha explains to her classmate how to find the volume of a cylinder. Which shows a correct explanation?

Ⓐ Multiply pi times the diameter to find the area of the base, then multiply by the height.

Ⓑ Multiply pi by twice the diameter to find the area of the base, then multiply by the height.

Ⓒ Multiply pi by the radius squared to find the area of the base, then multiply by the height.

Ⓓ Multiply pi by the height squared to find the area of the base, then multiply by the radius.

4 In the weight room, the weights are stored in vertical stacks. When stacked, the weights form a cylinder as shown.

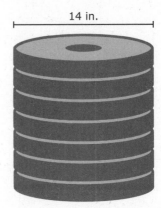

14 in.

If each weight is 1 inch high, which equation can be used to find the volume, in cubic inches, of the cylinder formed by the stacked weights?

Ⓕ $V = (3.14)(2)(7)(7)$

Ⓖ $V = (3.14)(7)(7)(7)$

Ⓗ $V = (3.14)(14)(7)(7)$

Ⓙ $V = (3.14)(14)(14)(7)$

1   Look at the cylinder.

Write an expression that can be used to determine the volume, in cubic centimeters, of the cylinder. Leave your answer in terms of π.

_____

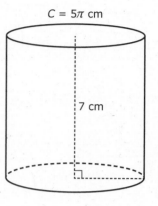

$C = 5\pi$ cm

7 cm

Explain your answer.

_____

_____

_____

_____

2   Mrs. Anderson's math class studies a unit on volume. Students have learned that the formula for finding the volume of a prism is $V = Bh$, where B is the area of the base of the prism. Mrs. Anderson introduces the formula for finding the volume of a cylinder as $V = Bh$. Dominique states that since the formulas are the same for both prisms and cylinders, the volumes will also be the same if the dimensions of the figures are congruent. Explain the error in Dominique's reasoning. Provide examples to justify your explanation.

_____

_____

_____

Journal

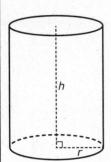

Using the diagram, explain to a sixth-grade student how the dimensions shown relate to the formula for finding the volume of a cylinder, $V = Bh$. Make your explanation clear so that he/she could find the volume of the cylinder.

_____

_____

_____

_____

Vocabulary Activity

Complete this activity with a partner. Each pair of students needs one six-sided number cube. Each student needs a sheet of paper and a pencil. Take turns rolling the number cube and following the directions that match the number rolled.

Sketch a *cylinder* and give an example of one located in the classroom.

Explain how to find the *height* of any cylinder.

Describe how to find the *area of the base* (B) of any cylinder.

Sketch a cylinder with a *radius* of 2 centimeters and highlight the radius.

Explain verbally how to find the *volume* of any cylinder.

Define *volume* and *area*. Give a real-world example of each.

Can It

Play *Can It* with a partner. Each pair of players needs a game board, a number cube, and a paper clip to use with the spinner. Each player needs a pencil and a sheet of paper. Player 1 spins the spinner and rolls the number cube. If the spinner lands on a space marked $B = ?$, player 1 determines the area of the base of a cylinder with the volume shown and a height equal to the number rolled. If the spinner lands on a space marked $V = ?$, player 1 determines an expression to find the volume of a cylinder with a base area shown and a height equal to the number rolled. If correct, player 1 initials the can with the matching base area or volume expression. If incorrect, play passes to player 2, who repeats the process. The game ends when all cans are initialed, or the teacher calls time. The winner is the player with more cans initialed.

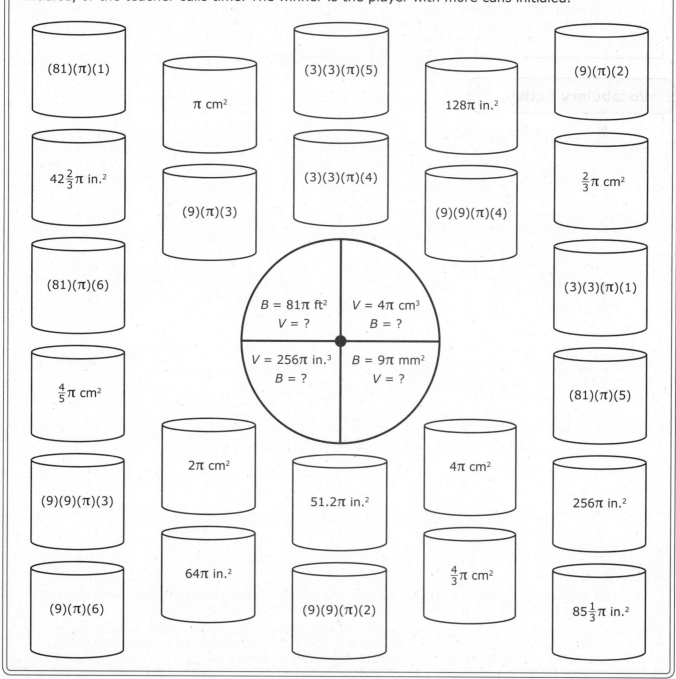

The cans are labeled:

- $(81)(\pi)(1)$
- π cm²
- $(3)(3)(\pi)(5)$
- 128π in.²
- $(9)(\pi)(2)$
- $42\frac{2}{3}\pi$ in.²
- $(9)(\pi)(3)$
- $(3)(3)(\pi)(4)$
- $(9)(9)(\pi)(4)$
- $\frac{2}{3}\pi$ cm²
- $(81)(\pi)(6)$
- $(3)(3)(\pi)(1)$
- $\frac{4}{5}\pi$ cm²
- 2π cm²
- 4π cm²
- $(81)(\pi)(5)$
- $(9)(9)(\pi)(3)$
- 51.2π in.²
- 256π in.²
- 64π in.²
- $\frac{4}{3}\pi$ cm²
- $(9)(\pi)(6)$
- $(9)(9)(\pi)(2)$
- $85\frac{1}{3}\pi$ in.²

Spinner:
- $B = 81\pi$ ft² $V = ?$
- $V = 4\pi$ cm³ $B = ?$
- $V = 256\pi$ in.³ $B = ?$
- $B = 9\pi$ mm² $V = ?$

1   An aboveground pool is in the shape of a cylinder as shown.

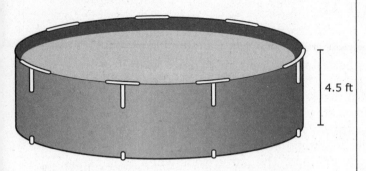

4.5 ft

If the diameter of the swimming pool is 16 feet, write an expression to determine the capacity of the swimming pool in cubic feet. Write your answer in terms of π.

2   Look at the cylinder.

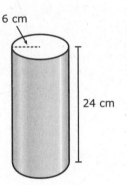

6 cm

24 cm

Write an expression that can be used to find the area of the base, *B*, in square centimeters. Use π ≈ 3.14.

3   Sketch and label a cylinder in which the volume can be found using the expression $\pi(3^2)(13)$.

4   Look at the cylinder.

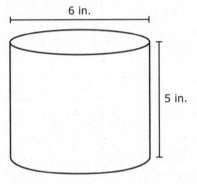

6 in.

5 in.

Give a written explanation about how to find the volume of the cylinder, in cubic inches.

_____

_____

_____

_____

Connections

1. Locate at least five examples of cylinders around your house. Take pictures of the different items you find. Share the photos with the class to see who found the most interesting cylinder.

2. Select a cylindrical drinking cup. Measure the diameter of the base of the cup, and write an expression to find the area of the base of the cup. Fill the cup with water, and measure the height of the water level. Write an expression to find the volume of the water in the cup.

1   Jesse scoops sand using a hollow plastic toy in the shape of a cone. He is able to pour three full scoops of sand to exactly fill a cylinder-shaped sand bucket.

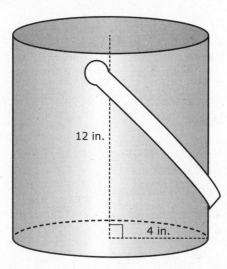

12 in.

4 in.

Sketch and label the dimensions of the cone-shaped scoop Jesse uses, if the base and height are congruent to the base and height of the cylindrical sand bucket.

Explain how to determine the volume of the cone if given the volume of the cylinder. Justify your explanation using information from the problem.

2   A cone and a cylinder each have congruent bases with areas of 28.26 units^2. The shapes have congruent heights that measure 10 units. Sketch and label a possible cone and cylinder that meet this criteria.

Write two statements that describe how the volumes of the cone and cylinder are related.

3   A cylinder has a base area of 25π square inches and a volume of 300π cubic inches. A cone has a base congruent to the cylinder and a volume of 100π cubic inches. What are the heights of the cylinder and cone? Explain your answer.

Write an expression to determine the volume of the cone given the volume of the cylinder.

Write an expression to determine the volume of the cylinder given the volume of the cone.

1 Look at the figure.

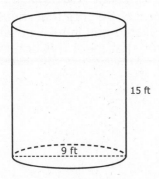

15 ft

9 ft

Which of the following has a volume that is one-third the volume of the cylinder?

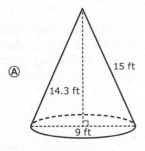

Ⓐ   15 ft
14.3 ft
9 ft

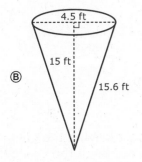

4.5 ft
15 ft
Ⓑ
15.6 ft

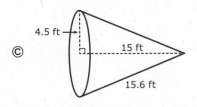

4.5 ft
15 ft
Ⓒ
15.6 ft

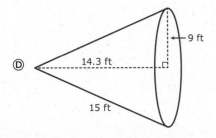

9 ft
14.3 ft
Ⓓ
15 ft

2 Look at figure A and figure B.

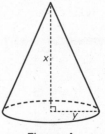 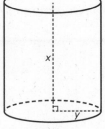

x   y   x   y

Figure A   Figure B

Which of the following does NOT describe the relationship between the volumes of figure A and figure B?

Ⓕ The volume of figure B is one-third the volume of figure A.

Ⓖ The volume of figure B can be found by tripling the volume of figure A.

Ⓗ The volume of figure A can be found by dividing the volume of figure B by three.

Ⓙ The volume of figure A is one-third the volume of figure B.

3 Which statement correctly describes the relationship between a cylinder and a cone?

Ⓐ If the cylinder and the cone have congruent bases, then the volume of the cylinder is one-third the volume of the cone.

Ⓑ If the cone and the cylinder have congruent bases and congruent heights, then the volume of the cone is three times the volume of the cylinder.

Ⓒ If the cylinder and the cone have congruent bases and congruent heights, then the volume of the cylinder is three times the volume of the cone.

Ⓓ If the cone and the cylinder have congruent bases, then the volume of the cone is one-third the volume of the cylinder.

motivation**math**™LEVEL 8

1 A cylinder has a base that is congruent to the base of a cone. The heights, h, of the two figures are also congruent. If the volume of the cone is 250π inches^3, which expression can be used to find the volume of the cylinder?

Ⓐ $3 \times 250\pi \times h$

Ⓑ $\frac{1}{3} \times 250\pi$

Ⓒ $3 \times 250\pi$

Ⓓ $\frac{1}{3} \times 250\pi \times h$

2 Look at the figures.

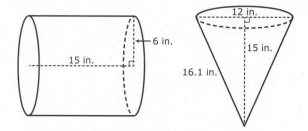

Which statement correctly describes the volumes of the two figures?

Ⓕ The volume of the cone is $\frac{1}{3}$ the volume of the cylinder.

Ⓖ The volumes are the same because the base areas are the same.

Ⓗ The volumes are the same because the dimensions are the same.

Ⓙ The volume of the cone is $\frac{1}{3}$ greater than the volume of the cylinder.

3 A movie theater has two different sizes of popcorn containers. Annalise chooses the container shown.

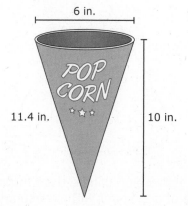

The second container is a cylinder and holds three times as much popcorn as the container Annalise chose. Which of the following best represents the dimensions of the cylindrical container?

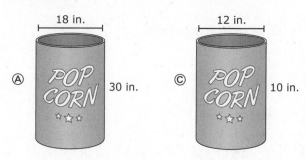

Unit 19 Assessment

1 Look at the cone.

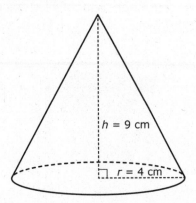

$h = 9$ cm

$r = 4$ cm

Which expression can be used to find the volume of a cylinder with a base and height that are congruent to the corresponding measures in the cone?

Ⓐ $V = \left(\frac{1}{2}\right)(4\pi)(9)$

Ⓑ $V = (\pi)(4^2)(9)$

Ⓒ $V = \left(\frac{1}{3}\right)(\pi)(4^2)(9)$

Ⓓ $V = (3)(\pi)(4^2)(9)$

2 The can of paint shown has a volume of 200π inches^3.

What is the volume of a cone with a base and height that are congruent to the corresponding measures of the paint can?

Ⓕ 600π inches^3

Ⓖ $\frac{200}{6}\pi$ inches^3

Ⓗ 100π inches^3

Ⓙ $\frac{200}{3}\pi$ inches^3

3 Which statement best describes the relationship between the volume of a cone and a cylinder that have congruent bases and heights?

Ⓐ The cone has a volume that is equal to the volume of the cylinder.

Ⓑ The cone has a volume that is three times greater than the volume of the cylinder.

Ⓒ The cone has a volume that is $\frac{1}{2}$ the volume of the cylinder.

Ⓓ The cone has a volume that is $\frac{1}{3}$ the volume of the cylinder.

4 Which cylinder and cone have a volume ratio of 3 to 1?

Ⓕ
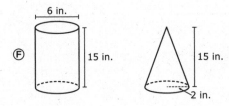
6 in. / 15 in. / 15 in. / 2 in.

Ⓖ
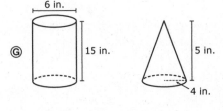
6 in. / 15 in. / 5 in. / 4 in.

Ⓗ
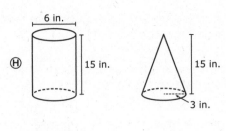
6 in. / 15 in. / 15 in. / 3 in.

Ⓙ
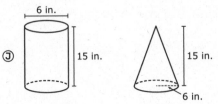
6 in. / 15 in. / 15 in. / 6 in.

motivation**math**™LEVEL 8

mentoring**minds**.com

1 Trisha and Maggie gather data on the dimensions and volumes of several different cylinders and cones. They record the data in two different tables as shown.

Table 1

B	h	V
10π	4	40π
18.84	9	169.56
66	14	924
18π	25	450π
1.099	1.2	1.3188
$\frac{44}{7}$	$\frac{1}{2}$	$\frac{22}{7}$

Table 2

B	h	V
10π	4	$\frac{40}{3}\pi$
18.84	27	169.56
198	14	924
18π	25	150π
1.099	1.2	0.4392
$\frac{44}{7}$	$\frac{3}{2}$	$\frac{22}{7}$

Write an equation to find V given B and h for each table of data.

Table 1: _____   Table 2: _____

Using the data in the table and the equations, write a statement generalizing the relationship between the volume of a cylinder and the volume of a cone.

_____

_____

2 Label the length of the radius of the base and the height of the cone with numbers of your choosing.

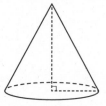

Sketch a cylinder with the same dimensions next to the cone. Write two statements comparing the volumes of the two figures.

_____

_____

Unit 19 Journal/Vocabulary Activity

Journal

Julianna sketches a cylinder and a cone that have congruent bases. The cylinder has a height that is $\frac{1}{3}$ the height of the cone. Julianna claims the volumes of the two figures are equivalent. Do you agree with her statement? Justify your answer.

_____

_____

_____

Vocabulary Activity

Follow the instructions to complete the vocabulary activity.

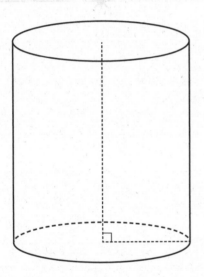
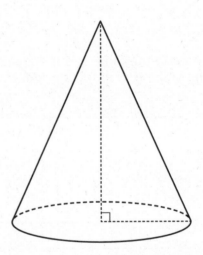

1. Shade the *base(s)* of each figure.

2. Draw an arrow pointing to the *height* of each figure.

3. Draw a rectangle around the *cylinder*.

4. Draw a circle around the *cone*.

5. Trace the *radius* of each figure.

       motivation**math**™LEVEL 8   mentoring**minds**.com

Turn Up the Volume

Play *Turn Up the Volume* with a partner. Each pair of players needs a game board and a paper clip to use with the spinners. Each player needs a pencil. Player 1 begins by spinning both spinners and recording the figure spun and the volume spun in any space on the table. Player 1 then writes an expression that can be used to find the volume of the figure not spun that has a congruent base and equal height. If correct, player 1 initials the space, and play passes to player 2 who repeats the process. If incorrect, player 1 erases his/her work, and play passes to player 2. The first player to initial 3 spaces in a row horizontally, vertically, or diagonally wins.

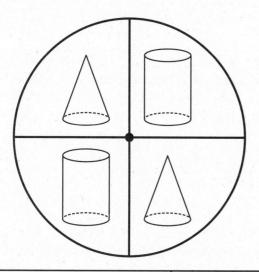

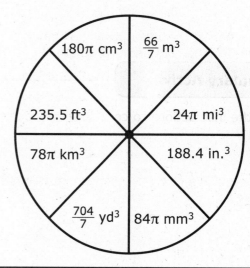

Figure:	Figure:	Figure:
Volume:	Volume:	Volume:
Expression:	Expression:	Expression:
Player initials:	Player initials:	Player initials:
Figure:	Figure:	Figure:
Volume:	Volume:	Volume:
Expression:	Expression:	Expression:
Player initials:	Player initials:	Player initials:
Figure:	Figure:	Figure:
Volume:	Volume:	Volume:
Expression:	Expression:	Expression:
Player initials:	Player initials:	Player initials:

1 Joshua fills container X with water. He wants to pour the water into container Y until it is full.

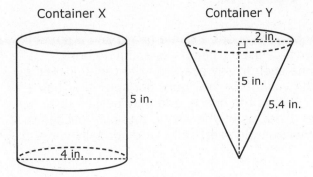

Container X   Container Y

What fraction of container X will still have water after filling container Y one time? Explain your answer.

2 Figure A and figure B have congruent heights and bases.

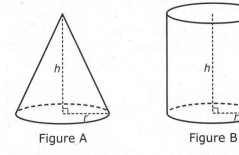

Figure A   Figure B

If the volume of figure B is $\pi r^2 h$, write an expression to find the volume of figure A.

3 Molly and Brendan make 3-D figures out of clay. Molly makes a cone like the one shown, using 49π cubic inches of clay.

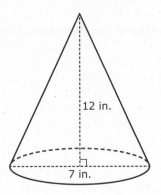

If Brendan makes a cylinder with a congruent base and height to Molly's cone, how many cubic inches of clay will he use? Explain your answer.

4 The volume of the cylinder is 280π cubic units. The volume of the cone is $93\frac{1}{3}\pi$ cubic units.

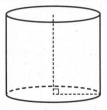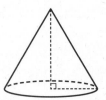

Write the ratio of the volume of the cone to the volume of the cylinder as a fraction.

Connections

Find an example of a cylinder in your house, such as a can of soup. Measure the dimensions of the cylinder. Draw and label a cone with a congruent base area and height to the cylinder. Write a statement comparing the volume of the cylinder to the volume of the cone.

Use the information to answer questions 1–3.

Three squares are joined at the vertices to form a right triangle as shown.

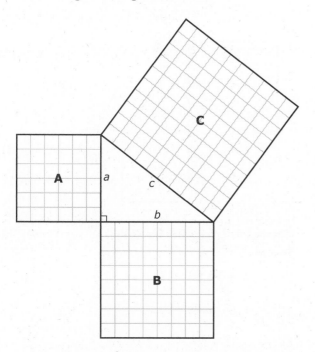

Use the diagram to answer questions 4 and 5.

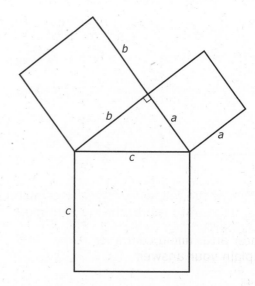

4 How does the area of each square relate to the corresponding side length of the triangle?

_____

_____

_____

1 What is the relationship between the area of each square and the length of each side of the triangle?

5 If a = 5 units, b = 12 units, and c = 13 units, explain the relationship between the areas of the three squares.

2 Determine the area of each square.

A = _____   B = _____   C = _____

What is the sum of the areas of square A and

square B? _____

How does the sum of the areas of A and B compare to the area of square C?

6 Fill in the blanks to complete the sentence.

According to the _____

_____, the sum of the _____ of

two legs of a _____ triangle is equal to

the square of the _____.

3 The Pythagorean Theorem states that, for any right triangle, $a^2 + b^2 = c^2$. How can the model be used to explain this equation?

1 Look at the figure.

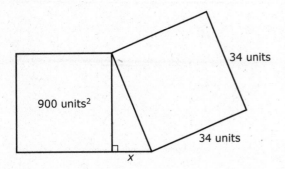

Which of the following correctly completes the diagram to represent the Pythagorean Theorem?

Ⓐ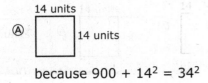

because $900 + 14^2 = 34^2$

Ⓑ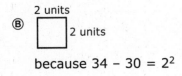

because $34 - 30 = 2^2$

Ⓒ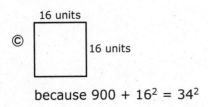

because $900 + 16^2 = 34^2$

Ⓓ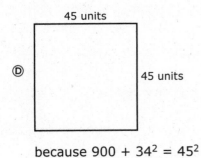

because $900 + 34^2 = 45^2$

2 Consider the diagram.

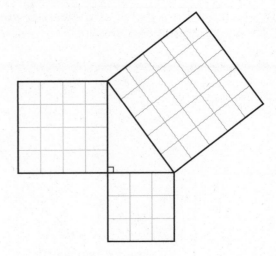

Based on the diagram, which of the following is NOT true?

Ⓕ $3^2 + 4^2 = 5^2$

Ⓖ $3^2 + 5^2 = 4^2$

Ⓗ $5^2 - 4^2 = 3^2$

Ⓙ $5^2 - 3^2 = 4^2$

3 Which of the following is true about all right triangles?

Ⓐ The sum of the measures of the legs of a right triangle is equal to the measure of the hypotenuse.

Ⓑ The product of the measures of the legs of a right triangle is equal to the measure of the hypotenuse.

Ⓒ The sum of the measures of the legs of a right triangle squared is equal to the square of the hypotenuse.

Ⓓ The sum of the squares of each leg of a right triangle is equal to the square of the hypotenuse.

motivation**math**™LEVEL 8   mentoring**minds**.com

1 A right triangle is formed by joining three squares at their vertices.

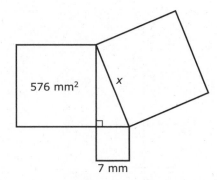

576 mm²   x   7 mm

Which equation can be used to find the length of x?

Ⓐ $x = 576 + 7$

Ⓑ $x = 576 + 7^2$

Ⓒ $x^2 = 576 - 7$

Ⓓ $x^2 = 576 + 7^2$

2 A right triangle is formed by line segments KM, MP, and KP.

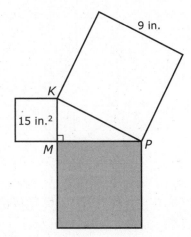

9 in.   K   15 in.²   M   P

Based on the diagram, which describes the best method to determine the area of the shaded region?

Ⓕ The area of the shaded region is equal to the sum of the areas of the two unshaded regions.

Ⓖ The area of the shaded region is equal to the difference in the areas of the unshaded regions.

Ⓗ The area of the shaded region is equal to the sum of the side lengths of the unshaded regions.

Ⓙ The area of the shaded region is equal to the difference in the side lengths of the unshaded regions.

3 Which of the following is true about the Pythagorean Theorem?

Ⓐ The Pythagorean Theorem can be used to determine the side lengths of any right triangle.

Ⓑ The Pythagorean Theorem can be used to determine the side lengths of any triangle.

Ⓒ The Pythagorean Theorem can be used to determine the angle measures of any right triangle.

Ⓓ The Pythagorean Theorem can be used to determine the angle measures of any triangle.

4 Look at the diagram.

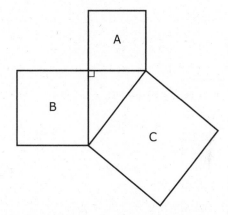

A   B   C

Using the Pythagorean Theorem, which of the following is true?

Ⓕ The sum of the areas of squares B and C is equal to the area of square A.

Ⓖ The difference of the areas of squares A and B is equal to the area of square C.

Ⓗ The sum of the areas of squares A and B is equal to the area of square C.

Ⓙ The sum of the areas of squares A and C is equal to the area of square B.

1 Look at the figure.

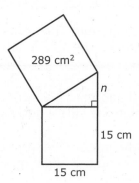

Which of the following correctly completes the diagram to represent the Pythagorean Theorem?

Ⓐ
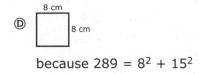

because $289 - 15^2 = 2^2$

Ⓑ
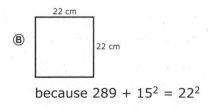

because $289 + 15^2 = 22^2$

Ⓒ
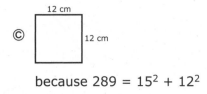

because $289 = 15^2 + 12^2$

Ⓓ
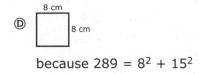

because $289 = 8^2 + 15^2$

2 Based on the Pythagorean Theorem, which of the following is NOT true?

Ⓕ $b^2 + a^2 = c^2$

Ⓖ $b^2 + c^2 = a^2$

Ⓗ $c^2 - a^2 = b^2$

Ⓙ $c^2 - b^2 = a^2$

3 Consider the diagram.

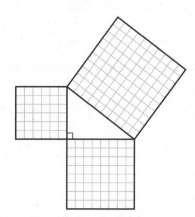

Which of the following is true?

Ⓐ $8^2 + 10^2 = 6^2$ Ⓒ $8^2 - 6^2 = 10^2$

Ⓑ $6^2 + 8^2 = 10^2$ Ⓓ $10^2 + 6^2 = 8^2$

4 Triangle *PQR* is shown.

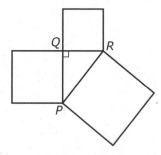

According to the Pythagorean Theorem, which of the following statements is supported by the diagram?

Ⓕ The square of the length of $\overline{RP}$ plus the square of the length of $\overline{QR}$ equals the square of the length of $\overline{PQ}$.

Ⓖ The length of $\overline{PQ}$ plus the length of $\overline{QR}$ equals the length of $\overline{RP}$.

Ⓗ The square of the length of $\overline{PQ}$ plus the square of the length of $\overline{QR}$ equals the square of the length of $\overline{RP}$.

Ⓙ The length of $\overline{PQ}$ plus the length of $\overline{RP}$ equals the length of $\overline{QR}$.

The Pythagorean Theorem may be proven using different models and diagrams. One diagram used to justify the Pythagorean Theorem is shown.

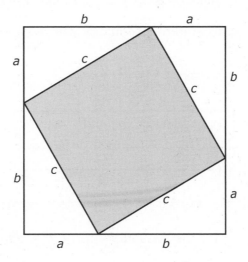

Use the diagram to answer the following questions.

(a) Write an expression that can be used to find the area of the large square.

(b) Write an expression that can be used to find the area of the smaller, tilted square.

(c) Write an expression that can be used to find the area of one of the triangles.

(d) Use your responses from parts (b) and (c) to write another expression to find the area of the large square.

So, the sum of the areas of the parts is equal to the area of the large square

$$(a + b)(a + b) = c^2 + 2ab$$

Suppose $a = 5$, $b = 12$, and $c = 13$. Use the equation and the values given to justify the Pythagorean Theorem, $a^2 + b^2 = c^2$.

Journal

Comprehension — Understand

Rylie states the Pythagorean Theorem in his own words.

The sum of the legs of a right triangle squared is equal to the square of the hypotenuse.

Do you agree or disagree with his statement? Justify your answer.

_____

_____

_____

Vocabulary Activity

Complete the graphic organizer for the vocabulary term, *Pythagorean Theorem*.

Pythagorean Theorem

Formula	Definition

Model/Diagram

Example	Non-example

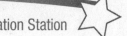

Pythago-What?

Play *Pythago-What?* with a partner. Each pair of players needs a game board and one two-color counter. Each player needs a pencil. Player 1 begins by placing the counter on the space at the bottom of the game board and using his/her finger to flick the counter across the board. Using the model the counter lands on or closest to, player 1 writes an equation that can be used to show the relationship between the side lengths of the triangle based on the Pythagorean Theorem. If the equation is written correctly, player 1 records his/her initials on the model, and play passes to player 2. If the equation is written incorrectly, player 1 erases the equation, and play passes to player 2. The game ends when all the models have equations written under them. The winner is the player with more initials on the board.

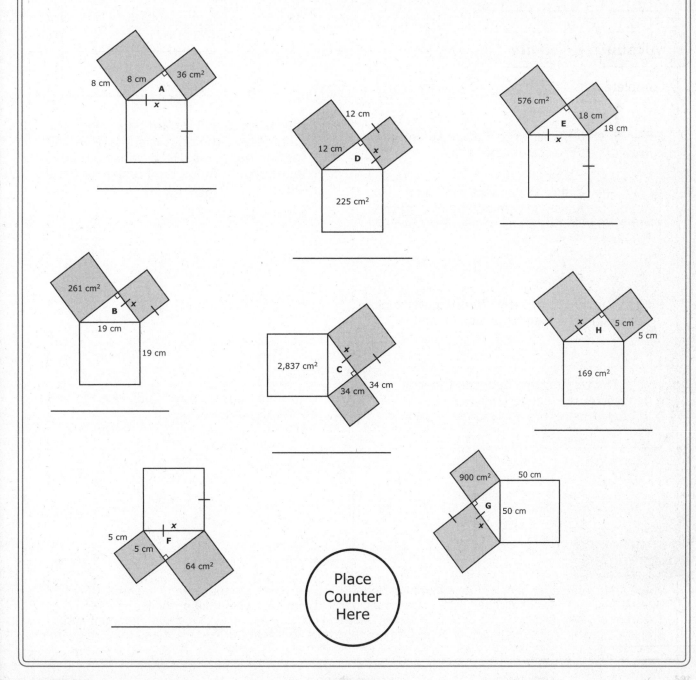

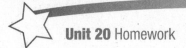
1 A triangle is formed by joining the vertices of three squares as shown.

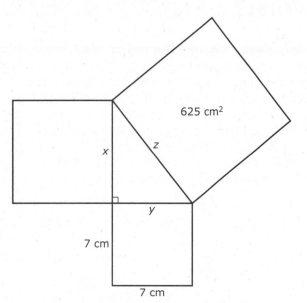

625 cm²

x

z

y

7 cm

7 cm

For each statement, write *T* if the statement is true or *F* if the statement is false.

a. ____ The area of the square with side length *x* can be determined by finding the difference in the areas of the other two squares.

b. ____ The length of side *z* can be determined by adding the lengths of sides *x* and *y*.

c. ____ The relationship between the side lengths of the right triangle can be modeled using the equation $x^2 + y^2 = z^2$.

2 Cody has a garden area in his yard in the shape of a right triangle. The diagram shows two patios that he has created using 1-foot by 1-foot pavers.

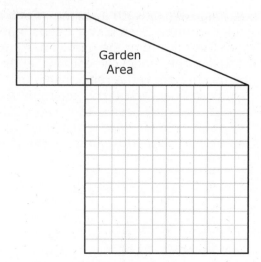

Garden Area

Cody wants to add a third patio along the hypotenuse of the right triangle. How can Cody use the areas of the patios already created to determine the number of pavers needed for the third patio?

How many pavers does Cody need to build the third patio?

Connections

There are a number of people throughout history that have proven the Pythagorean Theorem. The twentieth president of the United States, President Garfield, provided one proof of the Pythagorean Theorem in 1876. Research the work of President Garfield concerning the Pythagorean Theorem, and prepare a poster, research paper, or speech to describe how President Garfield explained the Pythagorean Theorem.

motivation**math**™LEVEL 8

mentoring**minds**.com

1 Georgia receives a snow globe for her birthday. The globe has a diameter of 4 inches.

Write an equation Georgia can use to find the volume, in cubic inches, of the spherical part of her snow globe. Use π ≈ 3.14.

To the nearest hundredth, what is the volume of the spherical part of the snow globe?

2 A cylindrical trash can has a height of 15 inches and a diameter of 10 inches.

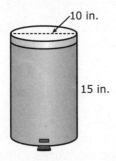

10 in.

15 in.

Write an equation that can be used to find the volume of the trash can, in cubic inches.

What is the volume of the trash can? Leave your answer in terms of π.

3 The circular opening of an ice cream cone has a diameter of 7 centimeters. The height of the cone is 10 centimeters.

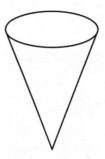

Write an equation that can be used to find the volume, in cubic centimeters, of the ice cream cone. Use π ≈ $\frac{22}{7}$.

What is the volume of the ice cream cone?

4 A cylindrical silo can store approximately 600 cubic yards of grain. The radius of the silo is 5 yards. To the nearest tenth of a yard, what is the height of the silo? Use π ≈ 3.14.

Unit 21 Guided Practice

1 A water tower has a spherical tank with a diameter of 6 meters.

Which of the following is closest to the volume of the water tower tank?

Ⓐ 288π m^3

Ⓑ 12π m^3

Ⓒ 48π m^3

Ⓓ 36π m^3

2 The top of a tower, the turret, is cone-shaped. The turret has a volume of $471\frac{3}{7}$ cubic feet and a radius of 7.5 feet. To the nearest foot, what is the height of the turret? Use $\pi \approx \frac{22}{7}$.

Ⓕ 2 ft

Ⓖ 5 ft

Ⓗ 8 ft

Ⓙ 10 ft

3 The diagram shows the dimensions of a vegetable juice can.

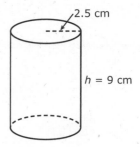

2.5 cm

h = 9 cm

If Max purchases a carton with 6 cans of juice, what is the number of cubic centimeters of juice he purchases? Round the volume to the nearest hundredth. Use $\pi \approx 3.14$.

Record your answer and fill in the bubbles on the grid below. Be sure to use the correct place value.

4 In her college sculpture class, Miranda has a marble rectangular prism that measures 3 meters high by 3.5 meters long by 2 meters wide. She chisels the marble into a cylinder that measures 2 meters high with a diameter of 3 meters. Approximately how much marble does Miranda chisel away from the original rectangular prism in order to form the cylinder? Use $\pi \approx 3.14$.

Ⓕ 14.13 m^3

Ⓖ 6.87 m^3

Ⓗ 21 m^3

Ⓙ 35.55 m^3

motivation**math**™LEVEL 8
mentoring**minds**.com

1 George spends 20 minutes inflating a beach ball. When completely inflated, the ball has a diameter of 18 inches. To the nearest hundredth cubic inch, what is the volume of the fully inflated beach ball? Use $\pi \approx 3.14$.

Record your answer and fill in the bubbles on the grid below. Be sure to use the correct place value.

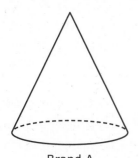

2 Tim chooses a disposable cup for the water cooler in his building. He narrows the selection to two brands with the dimensions shown in the diagram.

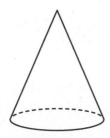

Brand A
Radius = 4 cm
Height = 9 cm

Brand B
Radius = 3 cm
Height = 8 cm

How many more cubic centimeters does Brand A hold than Brand B? Use $\pi \approx 3.14$.

Ⓕ 226.08 cm³

Ⓖ 75.36 cm³

Ⓗ 25.12 cm³

Ⓙ 678.24 cm³

3 A storage tank has a height of 10 feet and a diameter of 6 feet. The tank is half filled with oil.

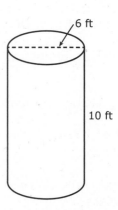

6 ft

10 ft

Approximately how much oil, in cubic feet, is currently in the cylindrical tank?

Ⓐ 90π ft³

Ⓒ 45π ft³

Ⓑ 360π ft³

Ⓓ 180π ft³

4 A plastic candy container and its dimensions are shown in the diagram.

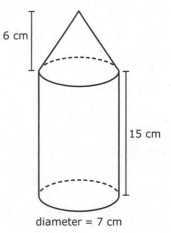

6 cm

15 cm

diameter = 7 cm

Which best shows the volume of the candy container? Use $\pi \approx \frac{22}{7}$.

Ⓕ $654\frac{1}{2}$ cm³

Ⓖ $808\frac{1}{2}$ cm³

Ⓗ $577\frac{1}{2}$ cm³

Ⓙ 2,618 cm³

Unit 21 Assessment

1 Robyn, Greg, and Doug each drink punch from differently shaped drinking glasses. Robyn has a sphere with a radius of 2 inches. Greg has a cylinder with a radius of 2 inches and a height of 4 inches. Doug has a cone with a radius of 3 inches and a height of 5 inches. Which statement about the volumes is NOT true?

Ⓐ Robyn's glass has the least volume.

Ⓑ Greg's glass has a greater volume than Doug's glass.

Ⓒ Doug's glass has a greater volume than Robyn's glass.

Ⓓ Greg's glass and Doug's glass have equal volumes.

2 Zadie makes a holiday decoration from a styrofoam cone with the dimensions shown.

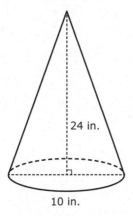

24 in.

10 in.

What is the approximate volume of Zadie's decoration, to the nearest cubic inch? Use $\pi \approx 3.14$.

Record your answer and fill in the bubbles on the grid below. Be sure to use the correct place value.

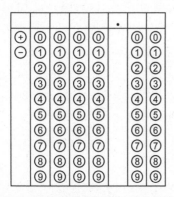

3 A solid brass soccer trophy is composed of a sphere resting on top of a cylinder, as shown in the diagram. The diameter of the cylinder is 6 centimeters, and the height is 8 centimeters. The radius of the sphere is 6 centimeters.

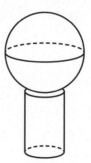

Which is closest to the volume of the trophy? Use $\pi \approx \frac{22}{7}$.

Ⓐ $226\frac{2}{7}$ cm³

Ⓑ $1,131\frac{3}{7}$ cm³

Ⓒ $1,810\frac{2}{7}$ cm³

Ⓓ $377\frac{1}{7}$ cm³

4 A cylindrical juice glass is 8 centimeters tall and has a diameter of 6 centimeters. If the glass is $\frac{3}{4}$ full, which of the following is closest to the volume of juice in the glass?

Ⓕ 9π cm³

Ⓖ 72π cm³

Ⓗ 54π cm³

Ⓙ 31π cm³

motivation**math**™LEVEL 8

1 Marilyn packages her homemade caramel corn to give as gifts to her friends. She will use either a cylindrical canister or a rectangular box for packaging, as shown in the diagram.

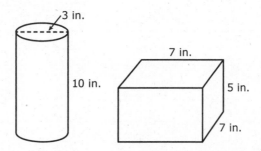

3 in.
10 in.
7 in.
5 in.
7 in.

Marilyn made one batch of caramel corn. She wants to give caramel corn to as many of her friends as possible. Which container should Marilyn use? Justify your answer.

2 Rauf makes and sells candies that are solid milk chocolate cones. He decides to alter his design to create a new candy. The shape of the new candy is a truncated cone made from his original design as shown.

Candy Cone

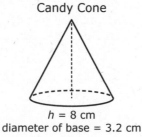

$h = 8$ cm
diameter of base = 3.2 cm

New Candy

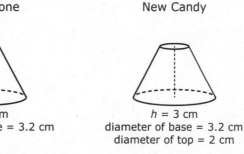

$h = 3$ cm
diameter of base = 3.2 cm
diameter of top = 2 cm

To the nearest hundredth cubic centimeter, how much milk chocolate is used to make each piece of the new candy? Use $\pi \approx 3.14$. Explain your solution process.

Rauf decides to sell each piece of the new candy at a price that is $\frac{1}{2}$ the price of each candy cone. If the candies sell equally well, will Rauf make more profit, less profit, or the same profit from the sale of the new candies when compared with the candy cones? Justify your answer.

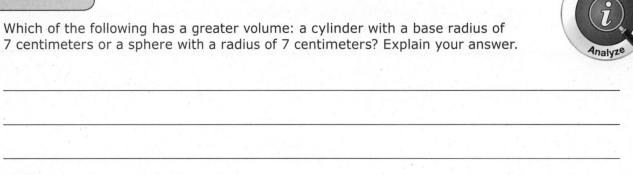

Journal

Which of the following has a greater volume: a cylinder with a base radius of 7 centimeters or a sphere with a radius of 7 centimeters? Explain your answer.

_____

_____

_____

Vocabulary Activity

Etymology is the study of the history of a word by tracing its development from early languages. The word, *volume*, is derived from the Latin words, *volumen*, meaning "something that is rolled up" and *volvere*, meaning "to turn around, to roll." Today, *volume* is a word with multiple meanings. Use a dictionary to find and record three different meanings of the word *volume*.

Meaning 1 (Math meaning): _____

_____

Meaning 2 (Science meaning): _____

_____

Meaning 3 (Library meaning): _____

_____

How do you think these modern meanings relate to the original Latin meanings?

_____

_____

_____

_____

Achieve Volume Victory

Play *Achieve Volume Victory* with the class. The teacher begins the game by signaling start. Each player finds the volume of the figures, to the nearest hundredth, and ranks them from greatest volume to least volume, with the rank of 1 noting the greatest volume and 9 noting the least volume. The first player to correctly rank the volumes of the figures Achieves Volume Victory! (Use $\pi \approx 3.14$.)

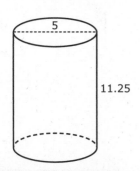

5

11.25

Volume	Rank

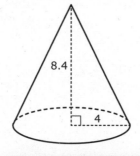

6

Volume	Rank

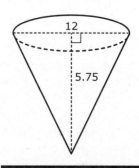

12

5.75

Volume	Rank

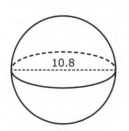

10.8

Volume	Rank

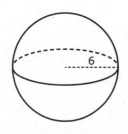

8.4

4

Volume	Rank

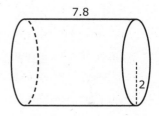

7.8

2

Volume	Rank

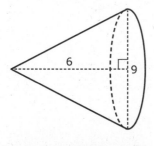

6

9

Volume	Rank

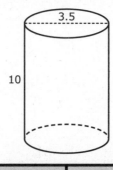

3.5

10

Volume	Rank

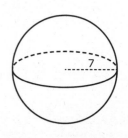

7

Volume	Rank

1 A can of tomato soup holds 33.75 cubic inches of soup. If the radius of the cylindrical can is 1.5 inches, how tall is the can, to the nearest tenth of an inch? Use $\pi \approx 3.14$.

2 For a class project, Connie made a teepee from a large sheet of paper. The teepee was shaped like a cone with a diameter of 12 inches and a height of 15 inches. What is the volume of the cone to the nearest hundredth cubic inch? Use $\pi \approx 3.14$.

3 An aboveground swimming pool is cylindrical in shape. It has a diameter of 12 feet and is 7 feet deep. What is the approximate volume, in cubic feet, of the pool? Use $\pi \approx \frac{22}{7}$.

4 A bowling ball has a radius of $5\frac{1}{4}$ inches. There are 3 holes for fingers that have a combined volume of 4 cubic inches. What is the total volume of the bowling ball, to the nearest cubic inch? Use $\pi \approx 3.14$. Explain your reasoning.

5 Fred purchases a cone filled with cinnamon pecans. The cone is 7 inches tall and has a diameter of 2 inches. How many cubic inches does the cone hold? Leave your answer in terms of π.

Connections

1. Use the Internet to research the dimensions, in centimeters, of regulation soccer balls, basketballs, and volleyballs. Using the dimensions, calculate the volume of each, and compare the balls based on the number of cubic centimeters of air each holds.

2. Locate three cylinders in your house and measure the dimensions of each, to the nearest inch. Calculate the volumes of the cylinders and explain to a family member how you found the volumes.

1 A rectangular prism and its net are shown with the bases shaded.

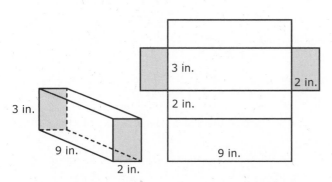

(a) Write an expression inside each face of the net that can be used to find the area of that face. What is the lateral surface area of the prism?

(b) The formula to find the lateral surface area of a prism is $S = Ph$. Write and solve an expression to find the perimeter of the base, P.

(c) Multiply the perimeter of the base by the height of the prism. How does the value compare to your response in part (a)?

(d) The formula to find the total surface area of a prism is $S = Ph + 2B$. Write and solve an expression to find the area of the base, B.

(e) Using the formula, write and solve an expression to find the total surface area of the prism.

2 Look at the triangular prism and its net.

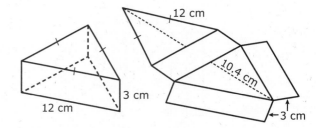

Write and solve an expression to find the lateral surface area of the prism.

Write and solve an expression to find the total surface area of the prism.

3 A cylinder with radius r and height h is shown.

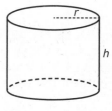

The formula for finding the lateral surface area of a cylinder is $S = 2\pi rh$. Define each part of the formula.

S _____

$2\pi r$ _____

h _____

The formula for finding the total surface area of a cylinder is $S = 2\pi rh + 2\pi r^2$. Explain each part of the formula as shown.

S _____

$2\pi r$ _____

h _____

2 _____

πr^2 _____

Unit 22 Guided Practice

1 A rectangular prism is shown.

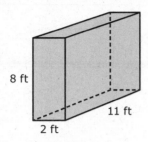

8 ft

11 ft

2 ft

Which expression can be used to find the lateral surface area of the prism?

Ⓐ (8 + 2) • 11

Ⓑ (8 + 2 + 11) • 11

Ⓒ (8 + 2 + 8 + 2) • 11

Ⓓ (8 + 2 + 8 + 2) 11 + 2(8 • 2)

2 Candace bought a poster of Paris to give to her mother as a birthday gift. She rolled the poster, placed it in a storage tube, and wrapped the entire tube with wrapping paper.

36 in.

2 in.

To the nearest inch, how many square inches of wrapping paper did Candace use to wrap her mother's gift? Use π ≈ 3.14.

Ⓕ 72 in.^{2}

Ⓖ 226 in.^{2}

Ⓗ 229 in.^{2}

Ⓙ 232 in.^{2}

3 A skateboard ramp at the skate park is in the shape of a right triangular prism as shown.

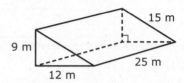

15 m

9 m

12 m

25 m

What is the lateral surface area of the ramp?

Ⓐ 1,008 m^2 Ⓒ 900 m^2

Ⓑ 954 m^2 Ⓓ 108 m^2

4 A wooden box in the shape of a rectangular prism is stained.

6 in.

3 in.

13.5 in.

What is the surface area of the box?

Ⓕ 279 in.^{2} Ⓗ 198 in.^{2}

Ⓖ 243 in.^{2} Ⓙ 117 in.^{2}

5 The student athletic boosters create noisemakers out of cylindrical canisters as shown.

2.5 in.

6 in.

Which expression can be used to find the lateral surface area of the noisemaker that will be decorated?

Ⓐ 2π(1.25) • 2   Ⓒ π(1.25)^2

Ⓑ 2π(1.25) • 6   Ⓓ 2π(1.25)^2

1 Benjamin wrapped a box in shipping paper to mail to his grandfather.

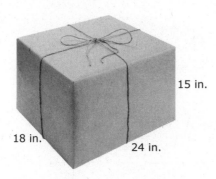

15 in.

18 in.

24 in.

How many square inches of paper did Benjamin use to wrap the box?

Ⓐ 1,260 in.²

Ⓑ 1,404 in.²

Ⓒ 1,584 in.²

Ⓓ 2,124 in.²

2 The tent shown is made of water resistant fabric. The floor of the tent is made of the same material.

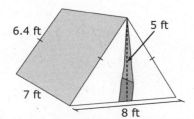

6.4 ft

5 ft

7 ft

8 ft

How much fabric is needed to create the lateral faces of the tent?

Ⓕ 185.6 ft²

Ⓖ 145.6 ft²

Ⓗ 89.6 ft²

Ⓙ 40.0 ft²

3 Look at the cylinder.

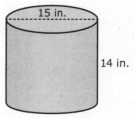

15 in.

14 in.

Which expression can be used to find the surface area of the cylinder?

Ⓐ $2\pi(7.5) \cdot 14$

Ⓑ $2\pi(7.5) \cdot 14 + \pi(7.5)^2$

Ⓒ $2\pi(7.5) \cdot 14 + 2\pi(7.5)^2$

Ⓓ $2\pi(7.5) \cdot 14 + 2\pi(15)^2$

4 Which prism does NOT have a lateral surface area of 240 square centimeters?

Ⓕ
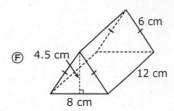
6 cm
4.5 cm
12 cm
8 cm

Ⓖ
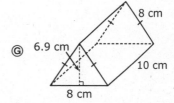
8 cm
6.9 cm
10 cm
8 cm

Ⓗ
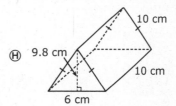
10 cm
9.8 cm
10 cm
6 cm

Ⓙ
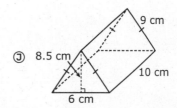
9 cm
8.5 cm
10 cm
6 cm

Unit 22 Assessment

1 A right triangular prism is shown.

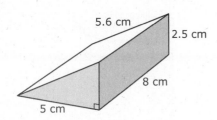

What is the lateral surface area?

- Ⓐ 117.3 cm²
- Ⓑ 104.8 cm²
- Ⓒ 97.3 cm²
- Ⓓ 71.1 cm²

2 A label covers the lateral surface area of a can.

To the nearest tenth square inch, what is the lateral surface area of the can?
Use π ≈ 3.14.

- Ⓕ 16.3 in.² Ⓗ 32.7 in.²
- Ⓖ 21.2 in.² Ⓙ 38.0 in.²

3 Look at the rectangular prism.

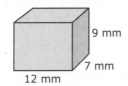

What is the surface area of the prism?

- Ⓐ 294 mm² Ⓒ 510 mm²
- Ⓑ 342 mm² Ⓓ 756 mm²

4 Mindy covers a hat box in decorative fabric for her room.

How many square inches of fabric does Mindy use to cover the entire box? Use $\pi \approx \frac{22}{7}$.

- Ⓕ $735\frac{3}{7}$ in.²
- Ⓖ $622\frac{2}{7}$ in.²
- Ⓗ $1,131\frac{3}{7}$ in.²
- Ⓙ $3,281\frac{1}{7}$ in.²

5 A triangular prism is shown.

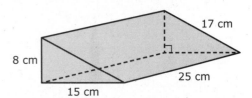

Which expression can be used to find the surface area of the triangular prism?

- Ⓐ $(8 + 15 + 25)(17) + 2\left(\frac{1}{2}\right)(15)(25)$
- Ⓑ $(8 + 15 + 17)(25) + 2\left(\frac{1}{2}\right)(15)(8)$
- Ⓒ $(8 + 17 + 25)(15) + 2\left(\frac{1}{2}\right)(15)(17)$
- Ⓓ $(15 + 17 + 25)(8) + 2\left(\frac{1}{2}\right)(17)(8)$

motivation**math**™LEVEL 8

mentoring**minds**.com

1 Jessa bakes cookies for the band fundraiser bake sale. The cookies are circular with a circular hole in the middle. Each cookie is dipped in chocolate.

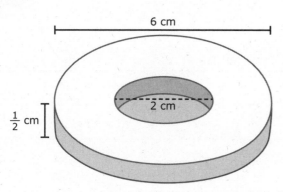

How many square centimeters of cookie is covered by chocolate? Explain your solution process.

2 Frederick and Frances build a small climbing tower for their cat, Farley. A sketch of the tower is shown.

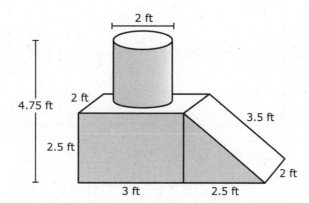

The tower is covered using one piece of carpet. The tower is placed on the floor so the bottom is not carpeted. How many square feet of the tower will be covered with carpet? Use π ≈ 3.14.

Name ______________________________

Unit 22 Journal/Vocabulary Activity

Standard 8.7(B) – Readiness

Journal

In a prism, explain why the formula for finding the lateral surface area uses the perimeter of the base times the height. Use a sketch to aid in your explanation if necessary.

____

____

____

Vocabulary Activity

Use the Grade 8 Mathematics Reference Materials to complete the table.

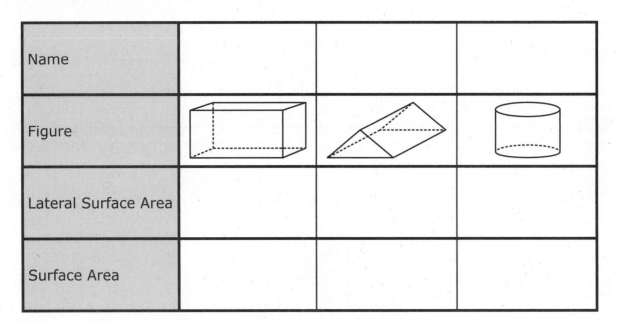

Name			
Figure	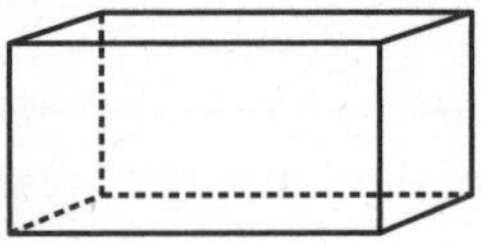	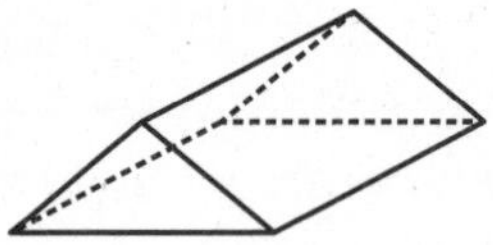	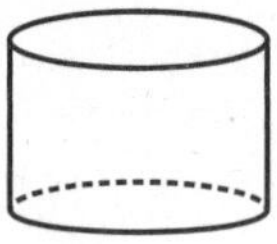
Lateral Surface Area			
Surface Area			

Shade the lateral surface area on each figure.

Highlight the perimeter or circumference of the base of each figure.

Trace the height of each figure.

What does *P* stand for in the formula? ______________________________

What does *h* stand for in the formula? ______________________________

What does *r* stand for in the formula? ______________________________

Connect Four Squares

Play *Connect Four Squares* with a partner. Each pair of players needs a game board. Each player needs a different color highlighter and a sheet of paper. Player 1 selects a square and works the problem stated. If correct, player 1 highlights the square with his/her color. If incorrect, the square is not highlighted. Play passes to player 2, who repeats the process. Players may select only one square per turn. The first player to highlight four squares in a row horizontally, vertically, or diagonally wins. Use $\pi \approx 3.14$.

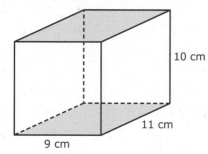

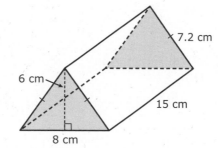

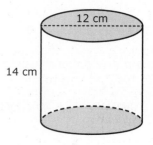

Find *B* for the rectangular prism.	What is *P* for the triangular prism?	Determine $2\pi rh$ for the cylinder.	What is the surface area of the rectangular prism and the cylinder combined?
Determine the lateral surface area of the triangular prism.	What is the surface area of the rectangular prism and the triangular prism combined?	Find *B* for the cylinder.	Determine *P* for the rectangular prism?
What is the surface area of the cylinder and the triangular prism combined?	Find $2\pi rh + 2\pi r^2$ for the cylinder.	Determine $Ph + 2B$ for the triangular prism.	What is *Ph* for the rectangular prism?
Find $Ph + 2B$ for the rectangular prism.	Determine *B* for the triangular prism.	What is the circumference of the base of the cylinder?	Find the surface area for all three figures combined.

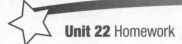

1 Marius and his dad build a lamp in the shape of a triangular prism, open on the top and bottom.

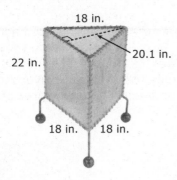

How many square inches of canvas did Marius and his dad use to make the lamp?

2 Eliza packs a treat for after school. She completely wraps her stack of cookies using plastic wrap.

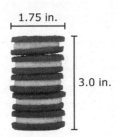

To the nearest tenth square inch, what is the surface area Eliza covers? Use π ≈ 3.14.

3 Jessi paints wooden cubes for her brother's building set. The cubes each have a side length of 7.5 centimeters. If Jessi paints 4 cubes, how many square centimeters of surface does she paint?

4 Hugo has a slice of cake. He wants to cover the top and lateral sides in chocolate icing.

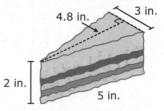

How many square inches of cake will be covered by icing?

Connections

Look around your house for items that are shaped like rectangular prisms, triangular prisms, and cylinders. Measure their dimensions. Determine the lateral and total surface area for each item. For each item, explain the method or methods you used to determine the lateral and total surface areas. Share your work with the class.

       motivation**math**™LEVEL 8   mentoring**minds**.com

1 Mr. Montgomery builds a ramp to a doorway for his mother's wheelchair. The ramp begins 22 inches from the house, and is 10 inches from the ground at its highest point.

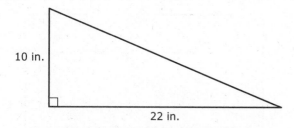

10 in.

22 in.

To the nearest tenth of an inch, how long is the ramp that Mr. Montgomery builds?

2 A slide and its ladder are designed to form a right triangle with the ground, as shown in the figure.

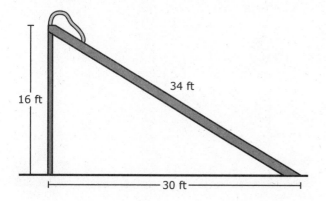

34 ft

16 ft

30 ft

Do the dimensions shown in the figure create a right triangle? Justify your answer.

3 Mrs. Berry's class studies the countries of the Caribbean. Ellen writes a report about Jamaica and makes a replica of the country's flag. Ellen's rectangular flag is 32 inches long and 24 inches wide. She purchases wide yellow ribbon to create the X design on the flag as shown.

How many inches of ribbon does Ellen use to create the design?

4 Lillian purchases a rectangular mirror with a diagonal measure of 25 centimeters and a height of 15 centimeters. What is the perimeter of the mirror?

1 An 11-foot ladder is leaning against a building. The vertical distance from the ground to the top of the ladder is 10 feet.

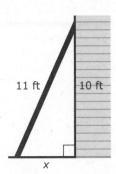

Which is closest to x, the horizontal distance between the base of the ladder and the building?

Ⓐ 1 ft   Ⓒ 5 ft

Ⓑ 3 ft   Ⓓ 7 ft

2 Manuel purchases a rectangular picture frame that has a diagonal measure of 17 inches and a height of 8 inches. What is the width of the picture frame?

Ⓕ 9 in.   Ⓗ 12 in.

Ⓖ 10 in.   Ⓙ 15 in.

3 Xavier sketches several designs for a math club pin. The math club voted for the pin shape to be a right triangle. Which of the following triangles could NOT be the shape used for the math club pin?

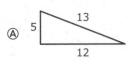
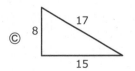

4 Josiah builds a room that has a 9-foot ceiling height. One wall has a 15-foot diagonal.

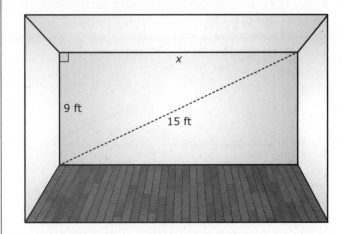

Which expression can be used to determine the length of the wall?

Ⓕ $\sqrt{225 + 81}$ Ⓗ $\sqrt{225 \div 81}$

Ⓖ $\sqrt{225 - 81}$ Ⓙ Not here

5 To go to school each day, Zane walks 24 yards due south to the bank then 45 yards east.

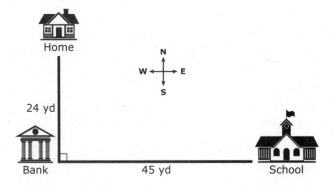

If Zane were able to walk a straight line from home to school, how many yards shorter would his walk be?

Ⓐ 11 yards

Ⓑ 18 yards

Ⓒ 33 yards

Ⓓ 51 yards

1 James paints the outside of his house. He leans a 13-foot ladder against the house. The base of the ladder is 5 feet away from the house.

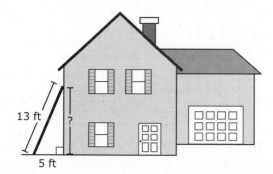

13 ft ? 5 ft

Which expression can be used to determine the distance from the base of the house to the top of the ladder?

Ⓐ $\sqrt{169 + 25}$

Ⓑ $\sqrt{169 - 25}$

Ⓒ $\sqrt{13^2 + 5^2}$

Ⓓ $\sqrt{169}$

2 A diagram of home plate is shown.

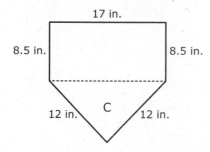

17 in.

8.5 in.   8.5 in.

12 in.   C   12 in.

Home plate is composed of a rectangle and a triangle. Is triangle C a right triangle?

Ⓕ Yes, triangle C is a right triangle because $a^2 + b^2 = c^2$.

Ⓖ Yes, triangle C is a right triangle because the legs of the triangle are congruent.

Ⓗ No, triangle C is not a right triangle because $a^2 + b^2 \neq c^2$.

Ⓙ No, triangle C is not a right triangle because the legs of the triangle are congruent.

3 While training for a marathon, Ladona runs 8 miles north from her house. Then, she runs 5 miles east and returns home by the shortest route.

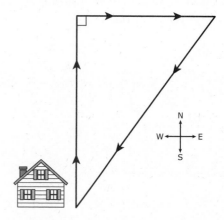

N
W ←→ E
S

To the nearest tenth mile, what is the total distance Ladona runs?

Ⓐ 9.4 miles

Ⓑ 16.6 miles

Ⓒ 24.5 miles

Ⓓ 22.4 miles

4 Elijah uses light-weight wooden rods to build the frame for a kite. The design of his kite is shown.

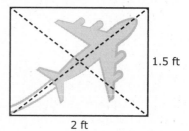

1.5 ft

2 ft

What is the length of one of the wooden rods on the diagonal of the kite?

Ⓕ 2.5 ft

Ⓖ 3.5 ft

Ⓗ 5 ft

Ⓙ 7 ft

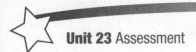
1 A running back and a linebacker are 9 yards apart when the running back begins running with the ball. The running back runs straight ahead for 40 yards to the end zone, while the linebacker runs 41 yards along a diagonal to reach the running back.

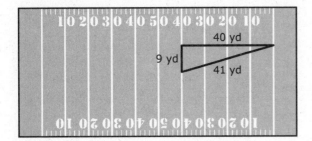

Does the triangle that results from the players' positions form a right triangle?

Ⓐ No, the sum of the length of each leg is greater than the length of the hypotenuse.

Ⓑ Yes, the sum of the length of each leg doubled is equal to the length of the hypotenuse doubled.

Ⓒ No, the sum of the length of each leg squared is not equal to the length of the hypotenuse squared.

Ⓓ Yes, the sum of the length of each leg squared is equal to the length of the hypotenuse squared.

2 If the area of a square sandbox is 64 square meters, which is closest to the length of the diagonal of the sandbox?

Ⓕ 8 m

Ⓖ 9 m

Ⓗ 10 m

Ⓙ 11 m

3 Jeremy draws a line to divide a trapezoid into a square and a right triangle as shown.

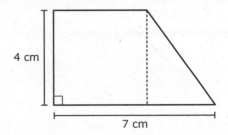

Which expression can be used to determine the length of the hypotenuse?

Ⓐ $\sqrt{4^2 + 3^2}$

Ⓑ $\sqrt{4^2 + 7^2}$

Ⓒ $\sqrt{4^2 - 3^2}$

Ⓓ $\sqrt{11^2}$

4 A sketch of a staircase is shown.

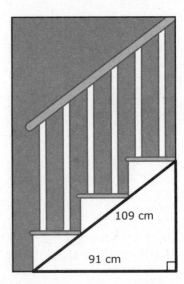

What is the vertical distance from the floor to the third step?

Ⓕ 14.1 cm

Ⓖ 60 cm

Ⓗ 200 cm

Ⓙ 80.6 cm

Standard 8.7(C) – Readiness

1 A baseball diamond is formed by placing bases at the vertices of a square with a distance of 90 feet between them. The average catcher throws from home plate to second base in 2.0 seconds. What is the estimated speed, in feet per second, an average catcher throws from home plate to second base?

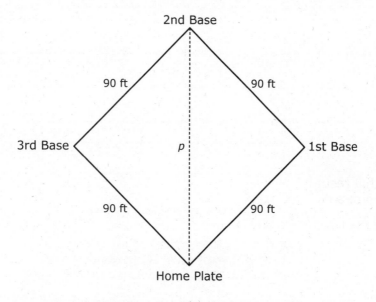

2nd Base

90 ft   90 ft

3rd Base   p   1st Base

90 ft   90 ft

Home Plate

2 Consider a rectangular prism with dimensions as shown.

What is the length of a diagonal, *x*, from the top, back corner to the bottom, front corner of the prism?

Explain the steps used to determine the value of *x*.

_____

_____

_____

_____

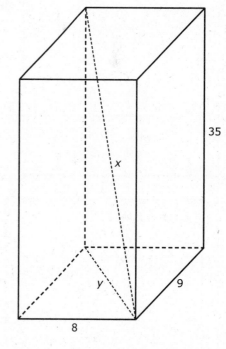

35

x

y

9

8

motivation**math**™ LEVEL 8   ILLEGAL TO COPY

Journal

Why is the Pythagorean Theorem an important mathematical discovery? Use specific examples about the Pythagorean Theorem or its converse.

_____

_____

_____

_____

Vocabulary Activity

Complete the graphic organizer for the vocabulary term shown.

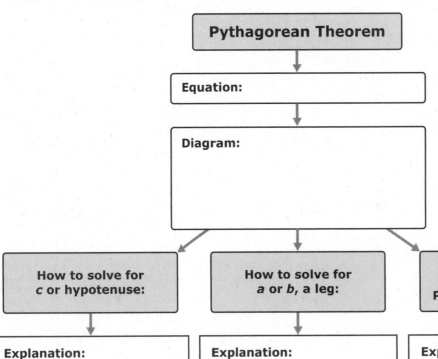

Pythagorean Theorem

Equation:

Diagram:

How to solve for c or hypotenuse:

How to solve for a or b, a leg:

How to solve for the converse of the Pythagorean Theorem:

Explanation:

Explanation:

Explanation:

motivation**math**™LEVEL 8   mentoring**minds**.com

Pythagorean Puzzler

In each square, a set of three numbers is given. Determine whether the three values form a right triangle. If the values do form a right triangle, shade the square using a red pencil. If the values do not form a right triangle, shade the square using a blue pencil.

1, 2, 3	9, 6, 5	6, 9, 3	6, 4, 5	6, 10, 12	3, 1, 3	8, 12, 7	37, 35, 12
6, 2, 5	6, 3, 8	5, 9, 12	9, 6, 12	3, 9, 10	11, 10, 6	12, 15, 9	10, 11, 12
9, 3, 11	13, 12, 4	5, 10, 12	16, 10, 12	8, 12, 16	24, 25, 7	14, 11, 16	3, 5, 6
4, 3, 5	7, 5, 11	6, 7, 2	9, 11, 12	10, 6, 8	9, 7, 11	40, 30, 20	17, 7, 11
4, 8, 9	17, 8, 15	10, 5, 11	40, 41, 9	20, 14, 10	12, 24, 30	10, 15, 6	22, 21, 9
8, 3, 10	17, 9, 10	5, 12, 13	20, 6, 15	25, 23, 21	12, 23, 20	30, 15, 16	16, 20, 25

What design is formed by the shaded boxes that confirms your shading is correct?

Unit 23 Homework

1 Lisa's parents purchase a flat screen television. The screen measures 45 inches on the diagonal. The base of the screen is 36 inches long. What is the height, in inches, of the television screen?

2 A helicopter rises vertically 3 kilometers and then flies due west 4 kilometers.

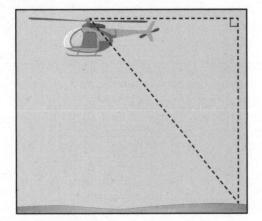

How many kilometers is the helicopter from its starting point?

3 Determine whether each of the triangles shown are right triangles. Justify your response.

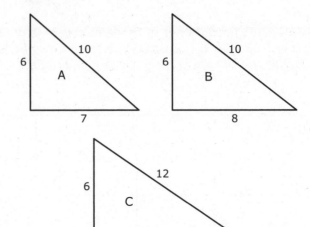

Triangle A

Triangle B

Triangle C

Connections

Find an example of a triangle that appears to be a right triangle in a magazine, a newspaper, at home, at school, etc. Sketch the triangle and measure the dimensions. Determine whether or not the example is a right triangle using the Pythagorean Theorem. Share your findings with the class.

motivation**math** ™ LEVEL 8

Use the graph to answer questions 1–11.

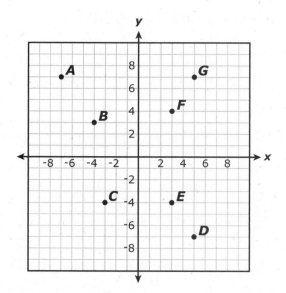

1 What is the distance from point *C* to point *E*?

2 What is the distance from point *E* to point *F*?

3 Is it possible to count the distance from point *F* to point *C*? Explain your answer.

4 Use a ruler to form a triangle with vertices at points *C*, *E*, and *F*. What type of triangle is triangle *CEF*?

5 Explain how to find the distance from point *C* to point *F*.

6 What is the length of side *CF*?

7 Write an equation to determine the distance from point *A* to point *E*.

8 What is the distance from point *A* to point *B*?

9 Between what two whole numbers on the number line does the distance from point *F* to point *G* lie?

10 Can the expression $\sqrt{3^2 + 8^2}$ be used to determine the distance between point *C* and point *D*? Explain your answer.

11 For each of the following, write *true* if the statement is true or *false* if the statement is false.

a. The approximate distance from point *B* to point *D* is 14.1 units.

b. The distance from point *F* to point *G* is equal to the distance from point *D* to point *E*.

c. The distance from point *A* to point *F* measures approximately 10.4 units.

d. The equation $11^2 + 3^2 = c^2$ can be used to determine *c*, the distance from point *A* to point *C*.

1   Points *N* and *P* are graphed on the coordinate plane as shown.

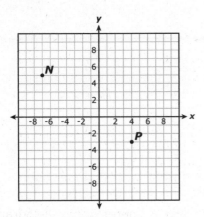

Which of the following best approximates the distance from point *N* to point *P*?

Ⓐ 11 units

Ⓑ 12.8 units

Ⓒ 13.6 units

Ⓓ 14.2 units

2   Look at quadrilateral *PQRS*.

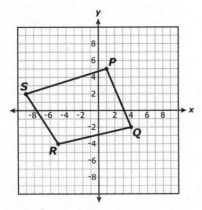

Which of the following is NOT true?

Ⓕ The length of $\overline{QR}$ is approximately 9.2 units.

Ⓖ Side *PQ* measures approximately 7.6 units.

Ⓗ The length of $\overline{SP}$ is approximately 9.8 units.

Ⓙ Side *RS* measures approximately 7.2 units.

Use the graph to answer questions 3–5.

Look at isosceles triangle *QRS*.

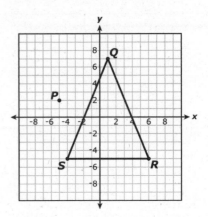

3   What is the perimeter of triangle *QRS*?

Ⓐ 36 units

Ⓑ 169 units

Ⓒ 39 units

Ⓓ 45 units

4   If point *T* is located at (6, 3), which expression can be used to find the distance from point *T* to point *S*?

Ⓕ $10^2 - 8^2$

Ⓖ $\sqrt{8^2 + 10^2}$

Ⓗ $\sqrt{10^2 - 8^2}$

Ⓙ $10^2 + 8^2$

5   A line is drawn from point *P* to point *Q*. Which best approximates the length of $\overline{PQ}$?

Ⓐ 7.1 units

Ⓑ 6.7 units

Ⓒ 8.2 units

Ⓓ 7.8 units

Use the graph to answer questions 1–3.

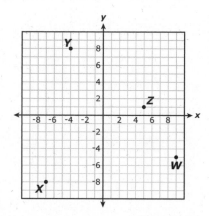

4 Look at parallelogram *LMNO*.

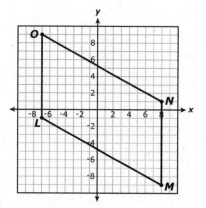

1 Which equation can be used to calculate the distance from point *Z* to point *W*?

Ⓐ $c^2 = 4 + 6$

Ⓑ $c^2 = 3 + 16$

Ⓒ $c^2 = 16 + 36$

Ⓓ $c^2 = 8 + 12$

What is the perimeter of parallelogram *LMNO*?

Record your answer and fill in the bubbles on the grid below. Be sure to use the correct place value.

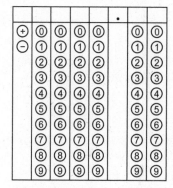

2 Between which two points does the distance measure 15 units?

Ⓕ *Y* and *X*

Ⓖ *X* and *Z*

Ⓗ *Z* and *Y*

Ⓙ *Y* and *W*

5 Look at triangle *JKL*.

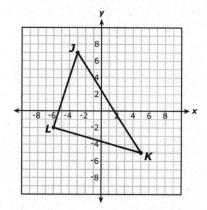

3 Which of the following is true?

Ⓐ The distance from point *W* to point *Z* is between 6 and 7 units.

Ⓑ The distance from point *Y* to point *W* is equal to the distance from point *Y* to point *X*.

Ⓒ The distance from point *Y* to point *Z* is between 12 and 13 units.

Ⓓ The distance from point *X* to point *Y* is equal to the distance from point *X* to point *W*.

What is the approximate measure of side *JK*?

Ⓐ 14.4 units

Ⓒ 13.9 units

Ⓑ 10.4 units

Ⓓ 15.1 units

1 Points *A* and *B* are graphed on the coordinate plane as shown.

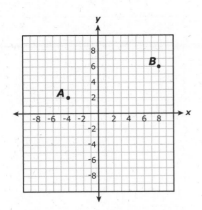

Which expression can be used to find the distance between points *A* and *B*?

Ⓐ $4 + 12 = c^2$

Ⓑ $8 + 24 = c^2$

Ⓒ $36 + 64 = c^2$

Ⓓ $16 + 144 = c^2$

2 Look at points *K* and *J* on the graph.

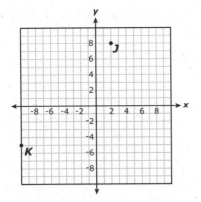

What is the distance from point *K* to point *J*?

Ⓕ 12.5 units

Ⓖ 17.7 units

Ⓗ 18 units

Ⓙ 25 units

3 Look at the graph.

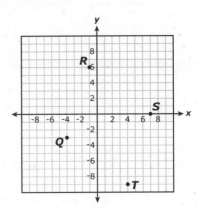

Between which two points on the graph is the distance equal to 10?

Ⓐ *Q* and *S*

Ⓑ *S* and *T*

Ⓒ *T* and *Q*

Ⓓ *R* and *T*

4 Look at triangle *XYZ* on the graph.

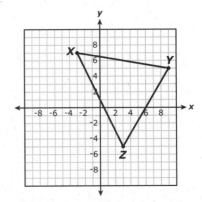

Which statement is true?

Ⓕ All sides of the triangle have the same length.

Ⓖ The length of side *XY* is 12.2 units.

Ⓗ Side *YZ* has a length of 10.7 units.

Ⓙ Side *XZ* has a length of 13 units.

1   A circle is graphed on a coordinate plane. The center of the circle is located at (-5, 4).

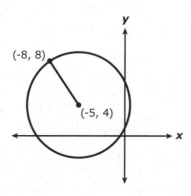

What is the radius of the circle? Explain how you determined your answer.

2   Point *A* is graphed on a coordinate plane.

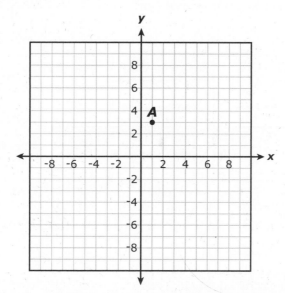

Plot six additional points that are a distance of exactly 5 units from point *A*. No point may lie on a horizontal or vertical line with point *A*. Explain the process used to determine the location of the points.

_____

_____

Journal

Explain how the Pythagorean Theorem is applied when finding the distance between two points on a coordinate plane.

_____

_____

_____

_____

Vocabulary Activity

Use the clues to unscramble the vocabulary terms. Then, unscramble the circled letters to reveal the teacher's response to Lala.

| N | D | C | I | S | E | T | A |
the length of a line segment between two points

| N | I | P | T | O |
an exact location or position

| E | G | L |
either side of a right triangle that forms the right angle

| E | T | R | O | C | N | A | O | D | I | | N | E | L | A | P |
a plane formed by two perpendicular number lines intersecting at 0

| A | N | P | T | H | G | Y | O | A | R | E | | M | E | H | T | O | R | E |
the relationship between the three sides of a right triangle

| U | N | Y | H | E | P | E | O | T | S |
in a right triangle, the side opposite the right angle

| H | T | R | I | G | | E | I | N | T | L | A | R | G |
a triangle with exactly one right angle

Lala: I'm so cold!

Teacher: ___o ___i___ i___ ___h___ c___r___e___ . . . ___t'___
___ ___wa___s 90 ___eg___e___s!

Keep Your Distance

Play *Keep Your Distance* with a partner. Each pair of players needs a game board and a paper clip to use with the spinner. Each player needs a pencil and a sheet of paper. Player 1 spins the spinner two times, recording the result in the table after each spin. Player 1 calculates the distance between the two points and, if correct, records the distance in the table. If the distance is incorrect, player 1 erases the points and play passes to player 2. If a player spins the same point in both spins, a distance of 0 is recorded in the table and play passes to the next player. After each player has taken 10 turns, the players total the points (the distances found). The winner is the player with more points.

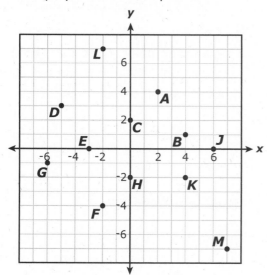

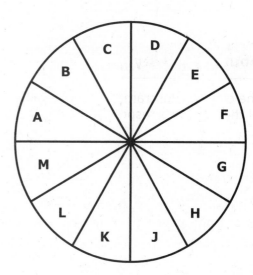

Player 1

	Point 1	Point 2	Distance
1			
2			
3			
4			
5			
6			
7			
8			
9			
10			
		Total	

Player 2

	Point 1	Point 2	Distance
1			
2			
3			
4			
5			
6			
7			
8			
9			
10			
		Total	

Unit 24 Homework

Use the graph to answer questions 1–3.

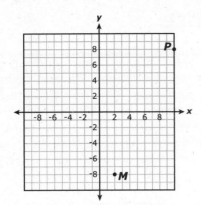

1 What is the approximate distance between points *M* and *P*, to the nearest tenth?

2 Plot a new point, *L*, at (6, 0).

Which distance is longer, from point *M* to point *L* or from point *P* to point *L*? Show your work.

3 If point *N*(-3, 5) is added to the graph, find the perimeter of triangle *MNP*, to the nearest tenth.

4 Point *A* is plotted on the coordinate plane.

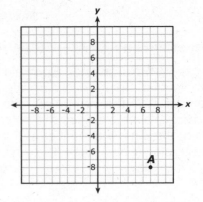

Plot another point, *B*, so that the distance between points *A* and *B* can be found using the expression $\sqrt{49 + 225}$.

5 Look at triangle *DEF*.

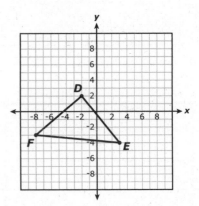

What are the lengths, to the nearest hundredth, of the sides of triangle *DEF*?

DE = _____   *EF* = _____

FD = _____

Connections

Measure the length and width of your room. Using the scale factor of one square on grid paper is equal to one foot, plot the length and width of your room on the grid paper. Use the plot to determine the length of the diagonal of your room. Repeat the process using other objects or rooms. Measure the actual lengths of the diagonals to check your work.

For questions 1–4, represent each word problem using an equation or inequality.

1   Lucy and her sister, Mya, need money for lunch. Their mother gives each of them the same amount of money. Lucy receives two dollar bills and 3 coins, and Mya receives one dollar bill and 7 coins. If the coins each girl receives have the same value, find c, the value of one coin.

2   The temperature in Reklaw is 70°F and is decreasing at a rate of 2° per hour. The temperature in Sacul is 68°F and is decreasing at a rate of 1.5° per hour. Find h, the number of hours until the temperature in Sacul is higher than the temperature in Reklaw.

3   Members of the theater club sold tickets for the spring musical. On Friday night, they made $125 in presales and sold 120 tickets at the door. For the Saturday night show, they earned $180 in presales and sold 110 tickets at the door. If the theater club earned the same amount each night, what is t, the cost per ticket?

4   Mrs. Jimenez makes and sells monogrammed fleece blankets. It costs her $5.95 for the fabric for each blanket and $175 per month to rent the embroidery machine. She sells the blankets for $29.95 each. Find b, the number of blankets Mrs. Jimenez must sell to earn a profit each month.

For problems 5–7, create a real-world problem that corresponds to the equation or inequality provided.

5 $100 + 25x = 35x + 75$

_____

_____

_____

_____

_____

6 $0.25x + 1.6 > 0.3x$

_____

_____

_____

_____

7 $4(x + 5) \geq 6x$

_____

_____

_____

_____

_____

Unit 25 Guided Practice

1 Camie and Jorge each begin saving money for a new computer. Camie saves $5 per week plus $50 she receives for her birthday. Jorge saves $7 per week. Which of the following can be used to find w, the number of weeks until Jorge has saved at least the same amount as Camie?

Ⓐ $7w = 5w + 50$

Ⓑ $50 + 5w < 7w$

Ⓒ $5w + 50 \geq 7w$

Ⓓ $7w \geq 5w + 50$

2 Liam and Harper are racing on a track. Liam runs 4 miles per hour and gets a 0.25 mile head start. Harper runs 0.5 mile per hour faster than Liam. If Harper and Liam run the same distance, how many hours, x, do they run?

Ⓕ $4x + 0.25 = 0.5x$

Ⓖ $4x + 0.25 = 4.5x$

Ⓗ $4x + 0.25 = 3.5x$

Ⓙ $4x - 0.25 = 3.5x$

3 During a garage sale, Mrs. Graham makes change with only 2 types of coins. Two customers need the same amount of change. One customer receives 8 coins, 3 of which are nickels. The second customer receives 11 coins, 7 of which are nickels. Which equation could be used to determine c, the value of the second coin?

Ⓐ $5c + 3 = 4c + 7$

Ⓑ $3c + 5(0.05) = 7c + 4(0.05)$

Ⓒ $5c + 3(0.05) = 4c + 7(0.05)$

Ⓓ $3c + 8 = 11c + 7$

4 Which situation is best represented by the equation $2 + 1.5x = 2x$?

Ⓕ Billy's movie club charges a membership fee of $2 plus $1.50 per rental, while Suzie's movie club has no membership fee but charges $2 per rental. Billy and Suzie find that they each rented the same number of movies last month and paid the same total amount. Find x, the number of movies each person rented.

Ⓖ Betty and Wilma both sell cookies to earn money for a trip. Betty charges $2 per cookie and Wilma charges $1.50 per cookie. If Betty has $1.50 left from her allowance, how many cookies, x, must they each sell before they have the same amount of money?

Ⓗ Charli and Gabe both travel the same distance to school. After school, Charli catches a bus to her grandma's house which is 1.5 miles from the school. After a short visit, Charli walks at a rate of 2 miles per hour to her house. Gabe walks directly to his home from the school at a rate of 2 miles per hour. If Charli and Gabe walk for the same amount of time, x, how many miles does each person walk from school?

Ⓙ Jimmy and Jack stop at separate street vendors on their way to work one day. The stand where Jimmy stops sells a refillable soda for $2 and pretzels for $2 each. Jack stops at a vendor that sells pretzels for $1.50 each. Jimmy purchases the same number of pretzels as Jack and also spends the same amount of money. Find x, the number of pretzels they each purchase.

1 At one point during the summer, Marsha has read 500 pages of her summer reading assignment, and Jan has read 460 pages. Marsha reads 20 pages per week for the remainder of the summer, and Jan reads 30 pages per week for the remainder of the summer. How many weeks, w, will it take before the girls have read the same number of pages?

Ⓐ $500 + 30w = 460 + 2w$

Ⓑ $30 + 500w = 20 + 460w$

Ⓒ $20 + 500w = 30 + 460w$

Ⓓ $500 + 20w = 460 + 30w$

2 Roger and Novak have a hot dog eating contest. After the first 2 minutes, Roger has consumed 8 hot dogs and Novak has consumed only 7 hot dogs. From that point, Roger eats 3 hot dogs each minute while Novak eats 4 hot dogs per minute. After how many minutes, m, will Novak have eaten more hot dogs than Roger?

Ⓕ $8 + 3m > 7 + 4m$

Ⓖ $8 + 3m < 7 + 4m$

Ⓗ $3 + 8m > 4 + 7m$

Ⓙ $3 + 8m < 4 + 7m$

3 Alton and Kyle are asked to write an expression about a mystery number. Alton writes *five less than one-third of the mystery number*. Kyle writes *the sum of negative three and one-sixth of the mystery number*. If Alton and Kyle have the same mystery number, which of the following can be used to find x, the mystery number?

Ⓐ $5 - \frac{1}{3}x = -3 + \frac{1}{6}x$

Ⓑ $\frac{1}{3}x - 5 = \frac{1}{6}(-3 + x)$

Ⓒ $\frac{1}{3}x - 5 = -3 + \frac{1}{6}x$

Ⓓ $-5 + \frac{1}{3}x = -\frac{1}{6}x + 3$

4 Which scenario could be represented by the inequality $40 + 30x < 50x$?

Ⓕ A fitness club offers two membership options. The first option has an initial fee of $50 and then charges $30 per month. The second option has no initial fee but charges $40 per month. After how many months, x, will the first option be a better value than the second?

Ⓖ Lila is looking into alarm systems for her home. Company A offers a plan that has an initial fee of $40 then charges $30 per month. Company B offers a plan that charges $50 per month. After how many months, x, will Company A cost less than Company B?

Ⓗ Regina purchases a new cell phone. Her first option is to purchase a plan that charges $40 per month, and she receives a phone for $30. The second plan charges $50 per month, and she receives the phone for free. After how many months, x, will the first option cost less than the second option?

Ⓙ The local theater charges $40 for each set of 4 adult tickets, or patrons can purchase a membership to the theater for $50 and pay $30 for each set of 4 adult tickets. After how many performances, x, is a membership the better option?

5 Jinger makes soap to sell at craft fairs. The first bar of soap sells for $2, and each additional bar costs $1.25. The cost of making the soap is $0.95 per bar. Jinger pays $50 for renting a booth. How many bars of soap, b, will Jinger need to sell to at least break even?

Ⓐ $2 + 1.25(b - 1) = 0.95b + 50$

Ⓑ $3.25b \geq 0.95b + 50$

Ⓒ $2 + 1.25(b - 1) \geq 0.95b + 50$

Ⓓ $1.25 + 2(b - 1) = 0.95b + 50$

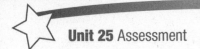

1 Mallory and Aimee save money for summer camp. They both plan to save the same amount of money. Mallory has $35 and plans to save $15 each week. Aimee has $5 and plans to save $50 each week. Which of the following can be used to determine x, the number of weeks it will take Mallory and Aimee to save the same amount of money?

Ⓐ $35x + 5 = 15x + 50$

Ⓑ $35x + 15 = 50x + 5$

Ⓒ $50x + 35 = 15x + 5$

Ⓓ $50x + 5 = 15x + 35$

2 An animal shelter conducts an annual fundraising drive. The animal shelter must raise at least enough money to cover their annual rental of $2,500 and weekly expenses of $450. So far, the shelter has received a one-time donation of $125 and pledged donations of $680 per week. Which inequality can be used to find w, the number of weeks it can take the shelter to meet the goal?

Ⓕ $125w + 680 \leq 2,500w + 450$

Ⓖ $125w + 680 \geq 2,500w + 450$

Ⓗ $680w + 125 \leq 450w + 2,500$

Ⓙ $680w + 125 \geq 450w + 2,500$

3 Amber and Jesse are each given a clue about a mystery number. Amber's clue says *the sum of half a number and eighteen*. Jesse's clue says *the difference of eleven and three times a number*. If Amber and Jesse have the same mystery number, which equation can be used to find p, the mystery number?

Ⓐ $2(p + 18) = (11 - 3)p$

Ⓑ $2p + 18 = 3 - 11p$

Ⓒ $\frac{1}{2}p + 18 = 11 - 3p$

Ⓓ $\frac{1}{2}(p + 18) = (11 - 3)p$

4 Which situation is best represented by the inequality $12x + 70 \geq 10x + 80$?

Ⓕ Cell phone company A charges an $80 deposit and $10 each month for unlimited service. Cell phone company B charges a $70 deposit and $12 each month for unlimited service. After how many months, x, will cell phone company A cost more than cell phone company B?

Ⓖ Caroline receives $80 for her birthday and earns $10 each time she babysits. Addison has saved $70 and earns $12 each time she babysits. How many times must the girls babysit, x, so that Addison has at least as much money as Caroline?

Ⓗ The science club plans a field trip. A trip to an observatory will cost $80 for gas plus a $10 entrance fee per member. A trip to a planetarium will cost $70 for gas plus a $12 entrance fee per member. How many miles, x, can the science club travel so that the observatory trip is less expensive than the trip to the planetarium?

Ⓙ Marco wants to rent a drum set. At Music World, the cost to rent drums is $12 per month plus an $80 deposit. Instrumental Music rents drums for $10 per month with a $70 deposit. How many months, x, can Marco rent drums from Music World and pay less than he will at Instrumental Music?

5 Two shipping companies charge different amounts to ship a package. Company A charges $5.50 for the first pound and $0.40 for each additional pound. Company B charges $6.75 for the first pound and $0.35 for each additional pound. If the cost to ship a package is the same for both companies, what is the weight in pounds, x, of the package?

Ⓐ $5.5 + 0.4x = 6.75 + 0.35x$

Ⓑ $5.5x + 0.4 = 6.75x + 0.35x$

Ⓒ $5.5 + 0.4(x - 1) = 6.75 + 0.35(x - 1)$

Ⓓ $5.5(x - 1) + 0.4 = 6.75(x - 1) + 0.35$

Analysis
i
Analyze

1 Shannon completes the following problem on a math test.

Write a real-world problem to match the inequality 12.5 + 0.4x > 14.75 + 0.25x.

Her response is shown.

Coach Hughes shops for trophies for the end-of-season banquet. Carver's Trophy Shop sells a trophy for $12.50 plus $0.40 per letter for engraving. Haskell's Trophies sells a trophy for $14.75 plus $0.25 per letter for engraving. How much money, x, does Coach Hughes need to spend on engraving before the trophy from Carver's costs less than the trophy from Haskell's?

Shannon's response is marked incorrect. What mistake(s) did she make?

_____

_____

Rewrite Shannon's response correctly.

_____

_____

_____

_____

_____

Synthesis
i
Create

2 Given the following, write one word problem to match the equation and one word problem to match the inequality.

$7 + 0.2(p - 1) = 5 + 0.3(p - 1)$ $7 + 0.2(p - 1) < 5 + 0.3(p - 1)$

_____   _____

_____   _____

_____   _____

_____   _____

_____   _____

Journal

In grade 6, you began writing one-step equations and inequalities to represent situations. In grade 7, the standard involved writing two-step equations and inequalities. In grade 8, the equations and inequalities have variables on both sides of the equal/inequality sign. Describe how writing equations and inequalities in grade 8 is similar to and different from grades 6 and 7. Do you think writing the equations and inequalities is more difficult in grade 8? Explain your answer.

_____

_____

_____

_____

Vocabulary Activity

For each equation or inequality shown, state the meaning of the symbol circled. Then, list words and/or phrases that could be used to represent the symbol in a word problem.

$6s - 11 \circledleq -2s + 5$

Meaning: _____

Words/Phrases: _____

_____

$4n \circledgeq -28n - 3$

Meaning: _____

Words/Phrases: _____

_____

$3(4 + 4x) \circledless 12x + 12$

Meaning: _____

Words/Phrases: _____

_____

$0.4p + 3.8 \circledgreater 1.2p$

Meaning: _____

Words/Phrases: _____

_____

$\frac{1}{2}n - 4 \circledeq 14 - 10n$

Meaning: _____

Words/Phrases: _____

_____

motivation**math**™LEVEL 8   mentoring**minds**.com

Why Should You Never Say 288 To Anyone?

For each problem, write an equation or inequality that could be used to determine a solution. Find the equation or inequality in the box, and record its letter in the space next to the problem. When all the problems have been matched with an equation or inequality, use the letters to fill in the corresponding blanks and reveal the answer to the title question.

$$\frac{}{5} \quad \frac{}{2} \quad \frac{}{4} \quad , \qquad \frac{}{2} \quad \frac{}{1} \quad \frac{}{1} \qquad \frac{}{3} \quad \frac{}{6} \quad \frac{}{1} \quad \frac{}{4} \quad \frac{}{4}$$

1. _____ Betsy considers changing her music download service. Her current service offers downloads at $0.99 each with a monthly fee of $4.95. Betsy receives an offer from another service that offers a monthly fee of $6.75 with downloads at $0.74 each. How many songs, n, will Betsy need to download for the new service to cost less than her current service?

Equation/Inequality: _____

2. _____ Two containers have leaks. Container X begins with 80 ounces and leaks at a rate of 0.6 ounce per minute. Container Y begins with 100 ounces and leaks at a rate of 1 ounce per minute. How many minutes, n, before the containers have the same number of ounces?

Equation/Inequality: _____

3. _____ Two candles are lit at exactly 8 P.M. The 12-inch candle burns 0.5 inch each hour. The 18-inch candle burns 1.5 inches every hour. How many hours, n, will the candles burn before the 18-inch candle is shorter than the 12-inch candle?

Equation/Inequality: _____

4. _____ A video game club charges a rental fee of $5 per game for nonmembers. For a $25 annual fee, members rent games for $3 per game. How many games, n, does a member need to rent in a year to make the cost of the membership fee worth paying?

Equation/Inequality: _____

5. _____ At Rock-n-Bowl, shoe rental costs $2, and each game costs $3.50. At Strikez, each game costs $3, and shoe rental costs $4.50. If the same amount of money is spent at both locations, how many games, n, are bowled?

Equation/Inequality: _____

6. _____ Darla makes pies for a fundraiser. Each pie costs $3 to make, and she spends $20 on equipment. Darla plans to sell the pies for $5 each. How many pies, n, must Darla sell before she at least begins making a profit?

Equation/Inequality: _____

T: $80 - 0.6n = 100 - n$	S: $5n > 25 + 3n$
R: $3n + 20 < 5n$	I: $3.5n + 2 = 3n + 4.5$
O: $0.99n + 4.95 > 0.74n + 6.75$	G: $12 - 0.5n > 18 - 1.5n$
M: $5n < 3n - 20$	L: $0.99n + 4.95 \leq 0.74n + 6.75$

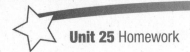
For problems 1 and 2, write a real-world problem that corresponds to the equation or inequality given.

1

$$20 + 10x > 28 + 8x$$

_____

_____

_____

_____

_____

2

$$\frac{3}{4}x = 18 - \frac{1}{2}x$$

_____

_____

_____

_____

3 Two hikers start at different points on a hiking trail. The first hiker starts at 300 yards from the trailhead and hikes at a rate of 150 yards per minute. The second hiker starts at 50 yards from the trailhead and hikes at a rate of 180 yards per minute. Write an equation or inequality to find m, the number of minutes the hikers walk until the second hiker is walking ahead of the first hiker.

4 Jocelyn and Hannah shop for jeans and T-shirts. Jocelyn buys one pair of jeans for $39 and eight T-shirts. Hannah buys one pair of jeans for $45 and six T-shirts. If each girl spends the same total amount for her purchases, write an equation to find p, the price of one T-shirt.

5 The concession stand keeps track of sales each night. On the first night, the stand began with $272 and sold 87 hamburgers. On the second night, the concession stand began with $251 and sold 93 hamburgers. If the total amount of money the concession stand has at the end of each night is the same, find the price of one hamburger, h.

6 Albert and Makayla are each renting a car for one day. Albert's rental agreement states that the car costs $35 per day and $0.15 per mile driven. Makayla's agreement states that the car she is renting costs $45 per day and $0.10 per mile driven. How many miles will Albert and Makayla drive if they spend the same amount of money on their rentals?

Connections

Search in a newspaper or online to find advertisements showing the costs of purchasing the same major appliance on payment plans from two different locations. Write an equation that could be used to find the number of monthly payments it would require for the total cost from both locations to be the same. Create a poster presentation with your advertisements and equation. Share your poster with the class.

Use the information to answer questions 1–4.

Cameron earns $4 each day walking his neighbor's dog. He spends $8 purchasing treats for the dog. Jackson spends $3 each day at the local coffee shop. He has $13 saved from a birthday gift.

1   Write an equation that can be used to determine the number of days, x, until the boys have an equal amount of money.

2   Sketch a model of the equation.

3   Explain how to use the model to determine the value of x.

4   How many days until the boys have an equal amount of money?

5   Explain, in words, the mistake made in solving the equation.

$$\frac{11}{2}x + 26 = 5x - 10$$

$$5x + \frac{11}{2}x + 26 = 5x - 10 - 5x$$

$$\frac{21}{2}x + 26 - 26 = -10 - 26$$

$$\frac{21}{2}x = -36$$

$$\frac{21}{2}x \cdot \frac{2}{21} = -36 \cdot \frac{2}{21}$$

$$x = -\frac{72}{21}$$

Solve the equation correctly.

6   Mr. Springfield goes to the movies. He invites family and friends each time and buys snacks from the concession stand. During two recent trips, he spent the same amount of money. On one trip, Mr. Springfield purchased 3 tickets and spent $12 on snacks. On the second trip, he bought 2 tickets and spent $20 on snacks. Write an equation to determine t, the cost of one movie ticket.

Sketch a model of the equation.

How much does each movie ticket cost?

1 Which equations represent the same value for t?

$$\text{I.} \quad 2t + 5 = 3t - 2$$

$$\text{II.} \quad t - 6 = 8 - t$$

$$\text{III.} \quad 4t + 3.4 = 2t - 11$$

Ⓐ I and III only

Ⓑ I and II only

Ⓒ II and III only

Ⓓ I, II, and III

2 An Internet company chooses to advertise with banners on websites visited by a target customer group. The web advertiser offers two plans with the same final cost. The first plan offers 3,000 banner ads for x dollars each plus a set-up fee of $50. The second plan offers 2,000 banner ads for x dollars each plus a set-up fee of $100. What is the cost per banner for each of these plans?

Ⓕ $0.05

Ⓖ $0.50

Ⓗ $5.00

Ⓙ $50.00

3 Charlene paints portraits at a local art fair. She sells the portraits for $40 each. She spends $160 for paint and brushes. If the canvas for each painting costs $8, which equation and solution can be used to determine p, the number of portraits Charlene sells before making a profit?

Ⓐ $40p - 160 = 8p$; $p = 3$

Ⓑ $40p + 160 = 8p$; $p = 5$

Ⓒ $40p + 8p = 160$; $p = 3$

Ⓓ $40p = 160 + 8p$; $p = 5$

4 Which model represents a solution of $v = 4$?

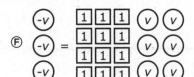

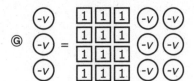

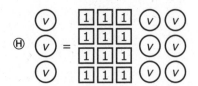

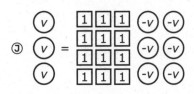

5 Customers have two options when renting video games from a rental store. Plan A requires a $5 monthly fee and $1 per video rental. Plan B requires an $8 monthly fee and $0.75 per video rental. How many video rentals would be required each month for the plans to cost the same amount?

Ⓐ 8 video rentals

Ⓑ 10 video rentals

Ⓒ 12 video rentals

Ⓓ 16 video rentals

 motivation**math**™LEVEL 8 mentoring**minds**.com

1 Look at the equation modeled.

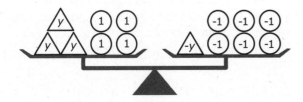

Which value of *y* balances the scale?

Ⓐ $-\frac{1}{5}$

Ⓒ $-\frac{1}{2}$

Ⓑ $-\frac{5}{3}$

Ⓓ $-\frac{5}{2}$

2 Which model does NOT represent a solution of *x* = 4?

Ⓕ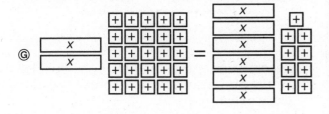

Ⓖ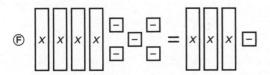

Ⓗ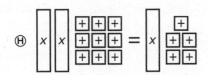

Ⓙ

3 Sally is 1 year older than 3 times the age of Joe. Chris is 5 years younger than 6 times the age of Joe. If Sally and Chris are the same age, how old is Joe?

Ⓐ $\frac{4}{9}$ year old

Ⓑ 2 years old

Ⓒ $2\frac{1}{3}$ years old

Ⓓ 7 years old

4 Two different meal combinations at a chicken restaurant have the same number of total calories. The first meal has 8 chicken nuggets and a large order of fries, while the second meal has 12 nuggets and a small order of fries. The large order of fries contains 288.5 calories and the small order of fries has 193.5 calories. Which equation and solution can be used to determine *n*, the number of calories in each chicken nugget?

Ⓕ $12n - 288.5 = 8n - 193.5$; $n = 24.1$

Ⓖ $8n + 193.5 = 12n + 288.5$; $n = 23.75$

Ⓗ $193.5 + 12n = 288.5 + 8n$; $n = 24.1$

Ⓙ $8n + 288.5 = 12n + 193.5$; $n = 23.75$

5 Which best represents the solution to the equation described?

Two and twenty-five hundredths less the quotient of x and two is equal to the sum of three and six tenths and quadruple x.

Ⓐ $x = -1.3$

Ⓑ $x = -0.3$

Ⓒ $x = -1.6$

Ⓓ $x = -0.8$

Unit 26 Assessment

1 Shawn solves the following equation as shown.

$$\frac{2}{5}x - 4 = 8 - \frac{3}{5}x$$

$$\underline{+ 4 + 4}$$

$$\frac{2}{5}x = 12 - \frac{3}{5}x$$

$$\underline{-\frac{3}{5}x \qquad + \frac{3}{5}x}$$

$$(-5)\text{-}\frac{1}{5}x = 12(-5)$$

$$x = -60$$

Shawn's solution is marked incorrect. Which best explains Shawn's error?

Ⓐ Shawn added 4 to both sides of the equation instead of subtracting 4.

Ⓑ Shawn multiplied by -5 on both sides of the equation instead of multiplying by $-\frac{1}{5}$.

Ⓒ Shawn multiplied by -5 on both sides of the equation instead of dividing by $-\frac{1}{5}$.

Ⓓ Shawn subtracted $\frac{3}{5}x$ on the left side of the equation instead of adding $\frac{3}{5}x$.

2 Which shows all the equations that represent the same solution?

  I. $7x - 5 = 8x$

  II. $5x + 11 = x - 5$

  III. $3x - 3 = 4x + 1$

Ⓕ I and II only

Ⓖ I and III only

Ⓗ II and III only

Ⓙ I, II, and III

3 Lorna has $60 and her sister has $120. Lorna saves $7 per week, and her sister saves $5 per week. Which equation and solution represent the number of weeks, *w*, it will take for the girls to have the same amount of money?

Ⓐ $60w + 7 = 120w + 5$; $w = 30$

Ⓑ $7w + 60 = 5w + 120$; $w = 30$

Ⓒ $7w - 60 = 5w - 120$; $w = 30$

Ⓓ Not here

4 What value of *n* balances the scale?

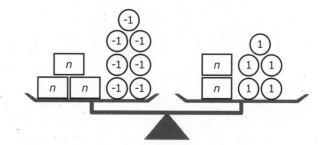

Record your answer and fill in the bubbles on the grid below. Be sure to use the correct place value.

1   Write an equation that contains one or more grouping symbols, the variable on both sides of the equal sign, and a solution of -5. Then, justify your equation is correct by sketching a model of the equation and solving the equation using the model.

2   Write a real-world problem that can be represented by the following equation.

$$30 - 4n = 9n - 9$$

_____

_____

_____

_____

_____

Show a solution for your problem.

Journal

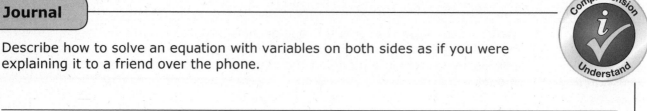

Describe how to solve an equation with variables on both sides as if you were explaining it to a friend over the phone.

_____

_____

_____

_____

Vocabulary Activity

Define and illustrate the following terms.

Coefficient

Definition	Illustration

Constant

Definition	Illustration

Equation

Definition	Illustration

Model

Definition	Illustration

Rational Number

Definition	Illustration

Variable

Definition	Illustration

motivation**math**™LEVEL 8

mentoring**minds**.com

We're at WAR!

Play *We're at WAR!* with a partner. Each pair of players needs a game board and a standard deck of cards with the jacks, queens, kings, and aces removed from the deck. Each player needs a pencil and a sheet of paper. Player 1 shuffles the cards and deals each player 18 cards facedown. Red cards represent negative values, and black cards represent positive values. Both players turn over the top card in their stack. The player with the higher value showing selects the model or equation to begin. Both players solve the selected model or equation on their own sheet of paper. The player whose card is closest to the value of *x* or that makes the equation true wins the round and places his/her initials in the box. If both players' cards satisfy the model or equation or are equally close to the value of *x*, both players place their initials in the appropriate box. The game ends when all models and equations are solved. The player with more initials wins.

Model/Equation	Player 1	Player 2	Model/Equation	Player 1	Player 2
$\boxed{x}\ \boxed{\begin{array}{cc}+&+\\+&+\end{array}} = \boxed{x}\ \boxed{x}\ \boxed{\begin{array}{cc}-&\\-&\end{array}}\boxed{\begin{array}{c}-\\-\end{array}}$			$\frac{5}{4}x + 7 = \frac{3}{4}x + 3$		
-3*x* + 8 = -4*x* + 13			5*x* – 2 = 4*x* – 9		
(balance scale model)			-4*x* + 2 = -3*x* – 4		
4*x* – 24 = -5*x* + 12			8*x* + 40 = 2*x* + 100		
$6x - 3\frac{2}{3} = \frac{2}{3}x + 7$			4*x* – 7 = 5*x* + 1		
10*x* = 6*x* – 20			-9*x* – 9 = *x* + 21		
2*x* – 8 = 6*x* + 8			0.8*x* – 8 = 2*x* + 4		
13*x* + 29 = 5*x* – 51			8*x* – 9 = 7*x* – 15		
3.6*x* – 1.8 = 2.8*x* + 5.4			(algebra tiles model)		

Use the information to answer questions 1 and 2.

$$6w - 2 = 8w - 5$$

1 Create a model to represent the equation.

2 Solve the equation for w.

3 Explain, in words, the mistake in the solution.

$$3x - 5 = 7x + 11$$

$$-3x + 3x - 5 = 7x + 11 - 3x$$

$$-5 + 11 = 4x + 11 - 11$$

$$6 = 4x$$

$$\frac{3}{2} = x$$

What is the correct value for x?

Use the information to answer questions 4 and 5.

Jamal buys a new racing bicycle. Two shops charge the same price for the bicycle but offer different payment plans. Shop 1 requires $260 down and a monthly payment of $20. Shop 2 requires $140 down and a monthly payment of $30.

4 Write an equation to represent the payment plans where m is the number of months payments are made.

5 After how many months will Jamal have paid both shops an equal amount of money?

6 Write and solve an equation to represent the following sentence.

The sum of two-thirds of a number and eight is equal to the difference of seven-thirds of the same number and two.

Connections

Using grocery store ads, write an equation with variables on both sides of the equal sign to represent purchasing different numbers of the same item together with a different additional item. The total for each set of items will be equivalent. Use the ad to create a model to represent the equation, and solve the equation to prove the variable has the same value on each side. Share your example with the class.

                   motivation**math**™LEVEL 8   mentoring**minds**.com

1 Parallel lines *a* and *b* are cut by a transversal *h*.

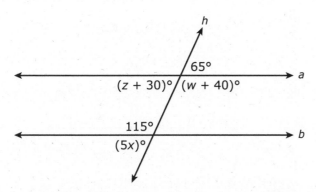

For each of the following equations, write *true* if the equation is true and justify your response. Write *false* if the equation is false, rewrite the equation so that it is true, and explain the new equation.

a. $z + 30 = 65$

b. $w + 40 + 65 = 360$

c. $z + 30 = 115$

d. $w + 40 = 115$

e. $5x = 65$

2 Look at the diagram.

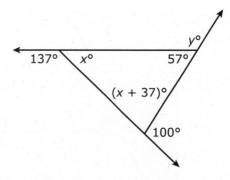

For each of the following, write an equation to show the relationship and justify your answer.

a. An interior angle and its exterior angle

b. The interior angles of a triangle

c. An exterior angle of a triangle and the two non-adjacent interior angles

d. The exterior angles of a triangle

3 Use the angle-angle criterion to explain whether the triangles shown are similar.

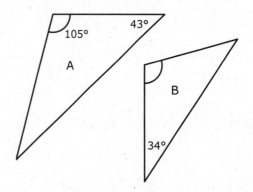

1 Parallel lines l_1 and l_2 are cut by a transversal t.

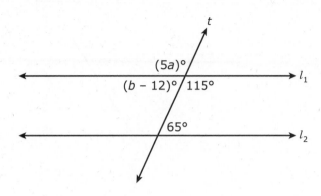

Which of the following statements are true?

I. Vertical angles are congruent, so
   $5a = 115$.

II. Alternate interior angles are congruent,
   so $b - 12 = 65$.

III. Corresponding angles are congruent
   and linear angle pairs sum to 180°,
   so $5a + 65 = 180$.

IV. Alternate interior angles sum to 180°,
   so $(b - 12) + 65 = 180$.

Ⓐ I and II only

Ⓑ II and III only

Ⓒ I, II, and III only

Ⓓ I, II, III, and IV

2 Look at the diagram below.

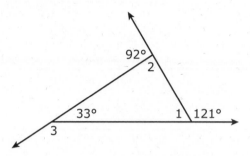

Which of the following is NOT true?

Ⓕ $m\angle 1 + 121 = 180$; the sum of an interior
angle of a triangle and the adjacent
exterior angle is 180°.

Ⓖ $121 + m\angle 2 + 33 = 180$; the sum of the
interior angles of a triangle is 180°.

Ⓗ $33 + m\angle 1 = 92$; the measure of an
exterior angle of a triangle is equal to the
sum of the measures of the non-adjacent
interior angles of a triangle.

Ⓙ $121 + 92 + m\angle 3 = 360$; the sum of the
exterior angles of a triangle is 360°.

3 Look at triangles ACB and HGF.

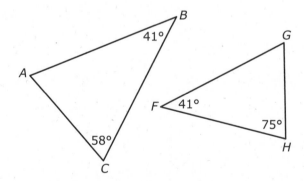

Which equation must be true if and only if the
figures are similar?

Ⓐ $m\angle A + 41 + 58 = 180$

Ⓑ $180 - (41 + 58) = 180 - (41 + 75)$

Ⓒ $41 + m\angle G + 75 = 180$

Ⓓ $180 - (41 + 58) = m\angle H$

1 Look at the diagram.

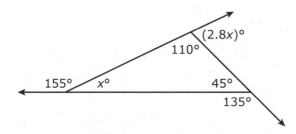

Three students are asked to write and explain an equation to determine the value of x. The answers for each student are shown in the table.

Sebastian	$x + 110 + 45 = 180$, because the sum of the interior angles of a triangle equals 180°.
Lilly	$x + 110 = 2.8x$, because the sum of the measures of non-adjacent interior angles is equal to the measure of the exterior angle.
LaShonda	$155 + 2.8x + 135 = 360$, because the sum of the exterior angles of a triangle equals 360°.

Which student wrote a correct equation and explanation?

Ⓐ Sebastian only

Ⓑ Lilly and Sebastian only

Ⓒ LaShonda and Sebastian only

Ⓓ Lilly, Sebastian, and LaShonda

2 Lines a and b are cut by a transversal t.

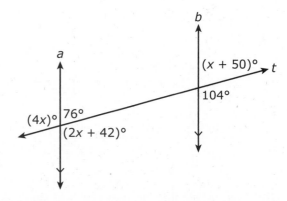

Which of the following could NOT be used to determine the value of x?

Ⓕ Alternate exterior angles are congruent, therefore $4x = 104$.

Ⓖ Corresponding angles are congruent, therefore $2x + 42 = 76$.

Ⓗ Vertical angles are congruent, therefore $4x = 2x + 42$.

Ⓙ Linear angle pairs sum to 180°, therefore $x + 50 + 104 = 180$.

3 Minha says triangle A with angles measuring 34° and 57° is similar to triangle B with angles measuring 57° and 89°. Is Minha correct?

Ⓐ There is not enough information to determine if the triangles are similar.

Ⓑ Yes, because each triangle has an angle measuring 57°

Ⓒ No, because $34 + 57 \neq 57 + 89$ which means there are not two angles in triangle A that are congruent to two angles in triangle B

Ⓓ Yes, because $180 - (34 + 57) = 89$ which means two angles in triangle A are congruent to two angles in triangle B

Use the triangle to answer questions 1 and 2.

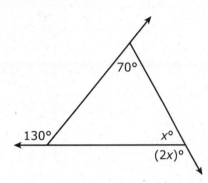

70°

130°

$x°$

$(2x)°$

1 Which equation can be used to find the value of x?

Ⓐ $3x = 90$, because linear angle pairs sum to 90°

Ⓑ $3x = 180$, because linear angle pairs sum to 180°

Ⓒ $130 + 70 + x = 180$, because the sum of the interior angles of a triangle sum to 180°

Ⓓ $130 + 70 + 3x = 360$, because the sum of the exterior angles of a triangle sum to 360°

2 Which equation shows the sum of the exterior angles of the triangle?

Ⓕ $x + 70 + 130 = 360$

Ⓖ $x + 70 + 50 = 180$

Ⓗ $2x + 130 + (180 - 70) = 360$

Ⓙ $3x + 130 + 110 = 180$

3 Third Street and Fourth Street are parallel, and Broadway Avenue cuts across both.

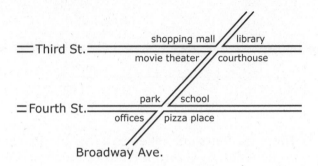

shopping mall   library

═Third St.═══════════════

movie theater   courthouse

park   school

═Fourth St.════════════

offices   pizza place

Broadway Ave.

If the measure of the angle where the library is located equals 42°, and the angle where the school is located measures $x°$, which equation is true?

Ⓐ $x = 42$, because vertical angles are congruent

Ⓑ $x = 42$, because alternate interior angles are congruent

Ⓒ $x = 42$, because alternate exterior angles are congruent

Ⓓ $x = 42$, because corresponding angles are congruent

4 Triangles LMO and PNO are shown.

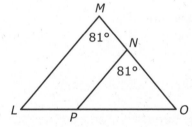

M

81°

N

81°

L P O

Are the triangles similar?

Ⓕ Yes, $\angle LMO$ and $\angle PNO$ are congruent and only one pair of corresponding angles must be congruent in similar triangles.

Ⓖ Yes, $\angle O$ is shared by both triangles and $\angle LMO$ and $\angle PNO$ are congruent so the triangles are similar by angle-angle similarity.

Ⓗ No, $\angle LMO$ and $\angle PNO$ are congruent so the triangles are congruent.

Ⓙ No, $\angle O$ is shared by both triangles so the triangles cannot be similar.

1 Prove that the sum of the angles of the quadrilateral shown is 360°. Label the diagrams as needed, but no measuring tools should be used. Justify your solution.

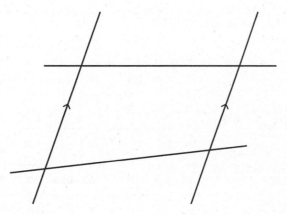

2 Use the Triangle Sum Theorem to prove the exterior angle sum of any triangle is 360°. Use expressions, equations, and models to justify your reasoning.

Journal

Describe two different ways an exterior angle of a triangle is related to the interior angles of the triangle.

_____

_____

_____

_____

Vocabulary Activity

Sketch and label an example of each set of vocabulary terms.

a. exterior angles and non-adjacent interior angles

b. parallel lines and transversal

c. alternate interior angles and alternate exterior angles

d. corresponding angles and vertical angles

motivation**math**™ LEVEL 8

Equation Elation

Play *Equation Elation* with a partner. Each pair of players needs a number cube and a game board. Each player needs a pencil. Player 1 begins by rolling the number cube to determine a figure. He/She writes an equation that can be used to determine the missing value in the figure. Player 1 then records a reason to justify the equation written. If the equation is written correctly, player 1 earns 4 points. If the reason provided is correct, player 1 earns 5 points. Play passes to player 2 who repeats the process. If a number is rolled for a figure already completed, the player loses a turn. The game ends when the equations and reasons for all six figures have been recorded. The player with more points wins.

Figure 1 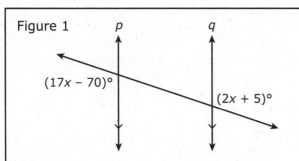	**Figure 4** 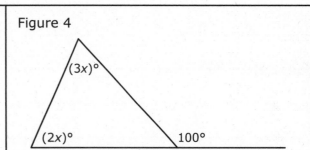
Equation _____	Equation _____
Reason _____	Reason _____
Figure 2 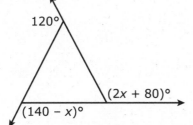	**Figure 5** 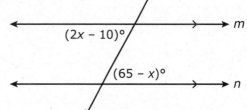
Equation _____	Equation _____
Reason _____	Reason _____
Figure 3 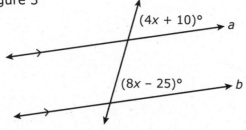	**Figure 6** 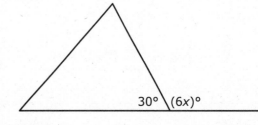
Equation _____	Equation _____
Reason _____	Reason _____

1 Two triangles are shown.

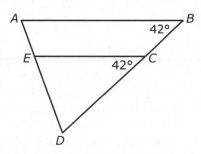

Explain how to prove that triangle *ABD* is similar to triangle *ECD*.

_____

_____

_____

_____

2 Look at the triangle.

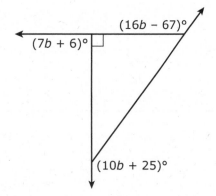

Explain how to find the measure of each exterior angle using the model.

_____

_____

_____

3 Parallel lines *a* and *b* are cut by intersecting transversals *g* and *h*.

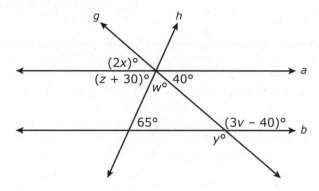

Use the properties of angles created when a transversal intersects two parallel lines to prove that the sum of the angles of the triangle shown is 180°.

Connections

Find an example of parallel lines in a magazine or newspaper. Draw a transversal line across the parallel lines. Measure one interior angle created. Write equations that can be used to find the measures of the remaining angles. Provide a justification with each equation. Share the results with the class.

1 Mrs. Silva needs to hire a math tutor for her son. A+ Tutors charges $20 per hour plus a $25 supply fee. Tutor Time charges $25 per hour plus a $10 supply fee. The graph of the total cost for each option is shown.

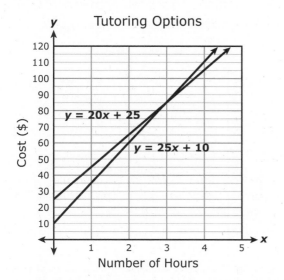

a. Explain the meaning of the point (3, 85) in terms of the situation.

b. Write and evaluate two expressions to verify that the point (3, 85) satisfies both equations.

c. Is there another point that simultaneously satisfies both equations? Explain your answer.

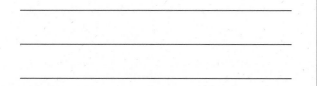

2 The graphs for equations $y = \frac{1}{2}x - 4$ and $y = -\frac{3}{2}x + 4$ are shown.

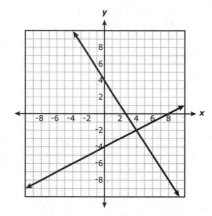

Identify the values of x and y that satisfy both linear equations.

Use the equations of the lines to verify that the values satisfy the equations.

3 Look at the linear function.

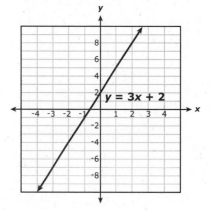

Thomas determines that the point (-2, -4) is true for $y = 3x + 2$ and $y = x - 2$. Graph the function $y = x - 2$ on the coordinate plane. Is Thomas correct? Justify your answer graphically and algebraically.

1 The equations $y = 2x - 5$ and $y = -x + 1$ are shown on the coordinate plane.

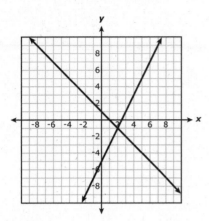

Which ordered pair correctly identifies the values of x and y that satisfy both linear equations?

Ⓐ (1, 1)　　　　Ⓒ (-5, 2.5)

Ⓑ (2, -1)　　　　Ⓓ (-1, 2)

2 Look at the graph.

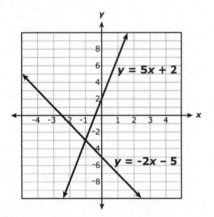

Which of the following is NOT true?

Ⓕ When $x = -1$, $y = -3$ is true for both equations.

Ⓖ The equations $5(-1) + 2 = -3$ and $-2(-1) - 5 = -3$ can be used to justify the solution.

Ⓗ For each equation, -3 can be substituted for x and the resulting value is -1.

Ⓙ There is exactly one point, (-1, -3), where the two equations intersect.

3 Southlake Cable charges $50 per month for basic cable and $5.00 for each premium movie channel. Lakeview Cable charges $41 per month for the same cable package and $6.50 for each premium movie channel. The graph of the equations representing the costs for each company is shown.

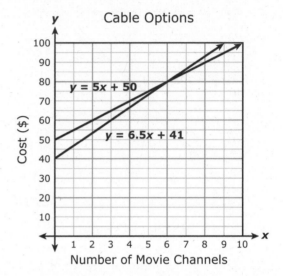

How many movie channels would a customer need to purchase in order for both cable companies to cost the same?

Ⓐ Four movies channels, because $5(4) + 50 = 70$ and $6.5(4) + 41 = 70$

Ⓑ Five movies channels, because it would cost $75 for 5 movies at both cable companies

Ⓒ Six movies channels, because $5(6) + 50 = 6.5(6) + 41$

Ⓓ Seven movies channels, because it would cost $85 for 7 movies at both cable companies

1 Shipping Company A charges $3 per pound to ship a package plus a $2 handling fee. Shipping Company B charges $2 per pound plus a $4 handling fee. The graph shows the equations representing the shipping costs for each company.

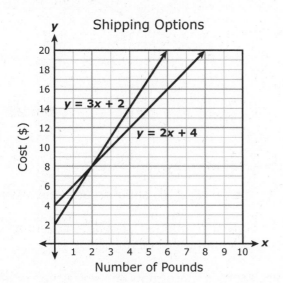

What is the weight of a package, in pounds, that results in an equivalent cost for both companies?

Ⓐ One pound, because the difference between 3(1) + 2 and 2(1) + 4 is 1

Ⓑ Two pounds, because 3(2) + 2 = 8 and 2(2) + 4 = 8

Ⓒ Four pounds, because 3(4) + 2 = 14 and 2(4) + 4 = 12

Ⓓ Eight pounds, because the lines intersect at point (2, 8)

2 Look at the graph containing the lines $y = 2x + 8$ and $y = -\frac{2}{3}x$.

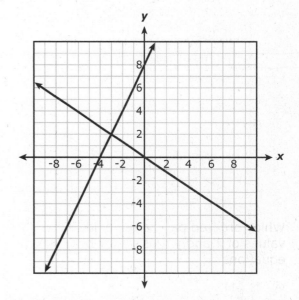

What value of x satisfies both equations?

Record your answer and fill in the bubbles on the grid below. Be sure to use the correct place value.

1 A graph modeling the growth of two plants is shown.

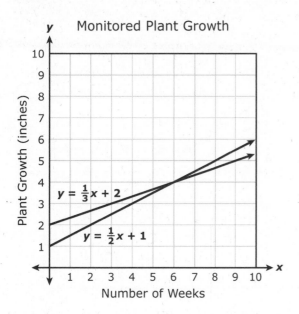

Which of the following is true for this situation?

Ⓐ The plants grow at the same rate because the ordered pair (1, 2) satisfies both equations.

Ⓑ The plants will both reach a height of 6 inches at 4 weeks because the ordered pair (4, 6) satisfies both equations.

Ⓒ One plant grows twice as fast as the other because the y-intercepts are 2 and 1.

Ⓓ The plants will both reach a height of 4 inches at 6 weeks because the ordered pair (6, 4) satisfies both equations.

2 Look at the graph.

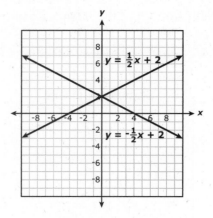

Which of the following is true?

Ⓕ The point (2, 0) satisfies both equations.

Ⓖ For each equation, 2 can be substituted for x and the resulting value is 0.

Ⓗ There is more than one point that satisfies both equations.

Ⓙ The equations $\frac{1}{2}(0) + 2 = 2$ and $-\frac{1}{2}(0) + 2 = 2$ can be used to verify the point that satisfies both equations.

3 Two linear functions are graphed.

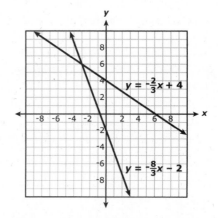

Which ordered pair correctly identifies the values of x and y that are true for both equations?

Ⓐ (6, -3) Ⓒ (-3, 6)

Ⓑ (6, 0) Ⓓ (0, -2)

 motivation**math**™LEVEL 8 mentoring**minds**.com

Name _____

Standard 8.9(A) – Supporting

Unit 28 Critical Thinking

1 The solution to a pair of simultaneous linear equations is (-3, -2). The slope of one line is 3. The slope of the second line is the negative reciprocal of the first. Graph the two lines on the coordinate plane.

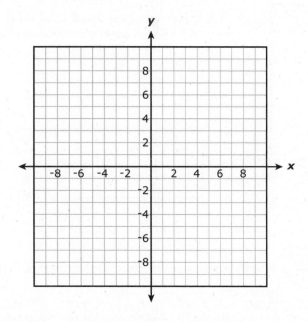

Write and evaluate two expressions that justify (-3, -2) is a solution for both lines.

2 Consider the linear equations $y = -3x - 1$ and $y = 5x + 15$. The tables show the relationship between x and y in each equation.

x	-2	0	2	4
y	5	-1	-7	-13

x	-4	-3	-2	-1
y	-5	0	5	10

What values for x and y simultaneously satisfy both equations? Explain your answer.

What is true about the graph of the two equations? Explain your answer.

mentoring**minds**.com   motivation**math**™ LEVEL 8   ILLEGAL TO COPY   **227**

Journal

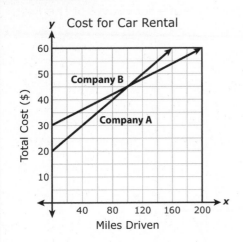

Cost for Car Rental

The graph shows the total cost for renting a car from two different companies based on the number of miles the car is driven.
Explain how the graph can be used to compare costs and find the better deal, including the meaning of the point of intersection shown.

_____

_____

_____

_____

Vocabulary Activity

An acrostic poem uses the letters in a word to begin each line of a poem. Each line of the poem relates to or describes the word used. For this activity, create an acrostic poem using the word *simultaneous*.

S _____

I _____

M _____

U _____

L _____

T _____

A _____

N _____

E _____

O _____

U _____

S _____

motivation**math**™LEVEL 8   mentoring**minds**.com

Interesting Intersections

Play *Interesting Intersections* with a partner. Each pair of players needs a number cube and a paper clip to use with the spinners. Each player needs a pencil and a sheet of paper. Player 1 spins the spinners and rolls the number cube. Using the point associated with the number rolled and the two values for the *y*-intercepts, player 1 draws two lines on the graph. On his/her sheet of paper, player 1 writes the equations for the two lines and then verifies algebraically that the point of intersection satisfies both equations. If the point satisfies the equations, player 1 records the two equations and his/her initials in any space. If the point does not satisfy both equations, player 2 may steal the lines by correctly recording two equations and verifying. The first player to complete three spaces vertically, horizontally, or diagonally wins.

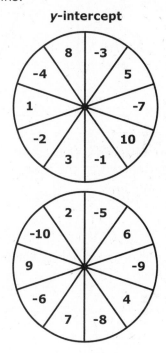

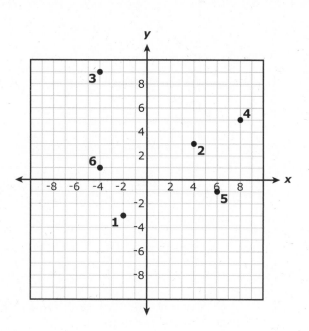

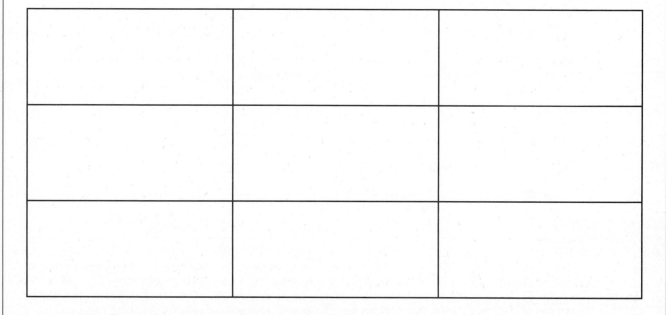

1 Look at the graphs of lines $y = x + 6$ and $y = -2x + 9$.

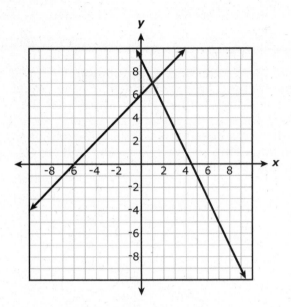

Write the ordered pair that satisfies both equations shown on the graph.

Verify your ordered pair is a solution to both equations.

2 Two families held garage sales last weekend. The graph shows the number of hours each family worked and the amounts earned.

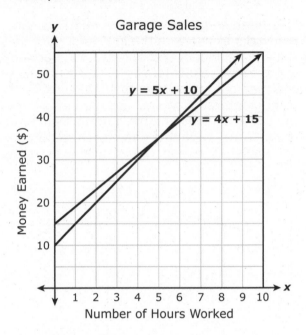

Garage Sales

$y = 5x + 10$

$y = 4x + 15$

At what value for x did the two families work the same number of hours and earn the same amount of money?

How much money did each family earn for that number of hours?

Verify the x and y values satisfy both equations.

Connections

Research the cost of a new car. Create two different payment plans to pay for the car. For each payment plan, select different amounts for the down payments and different monthly payment amounts. Write the equations for both payment plans and graph them on the same graph. Find the ordered pair that satisfies both payment plan equations. Verify and explain your solution. Share your results with the class.

Use the graph to answer questions 1–3.

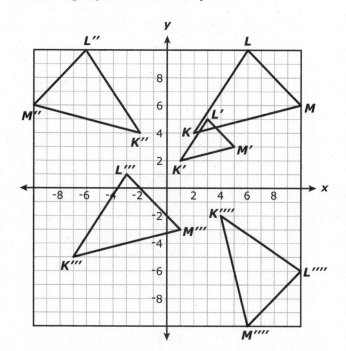

1 Triangle *KLM* is the pre-image for triangles *K'L'M'*, *K"L"M"*, *K'''L'''M'''*, and *K''''L''''M''''*. Which images are congruent to the pre-image? Explain your answer.

2 Which images have the same orientation as the pre-image? Explain your answer.

3 Identify the transformation applied to triangle *KLM* that yields each image.

K'L'M' _____

K"L"M" _____

K'''L'''M''' _____

K''''L''''M'''' _____

4 For each representation, determine whether the transformation results in an image that is congruent to its pre-image. Explain your answers.

	Original Vertices	New Vertices
a.	$X(-3, 6)$	$X'(-1, 2)$
	$Y(-9, -7)$	$Y'(-3, -\frac{7}{3})$
	$Z(1, -6)$	$Z'(\frac{1}{3}, -2)$

b. $(x, y) \rightarrow (x, y - 3)$

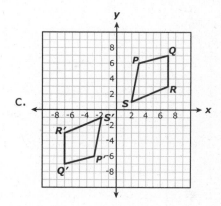

c.

d. A dilation by a scale factor of 3

e. $(x, y) \rightarrow (0.5x, 0.5y)$

	Original Vertices	New Vertices
f.	$D(-5, 3)$	$D'(-5, -3)$
	$E(4, -7)$	$E'(4, 7)$
	$F(-2, -10)$	$F'(-2, 10)$

1 Which of the following transformations results in an image that is congruent to its pre-image?

    I.   270° rotation about the origin

II.

Original Vertices	New Vertices
A(4, 5)	A′(-4, 5)
B(10, 4)	B′(-10, 4)
C(7, -2)	C′(-7, -2)

III. $(x, y) \rightarrow \left(\frac{2}{3}x, \frac{2}{3}y\right)$

IV.

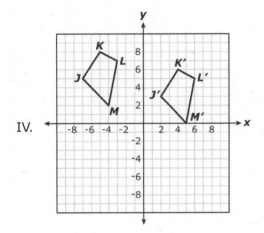

Ⓐ   III and IV only

Ⓑ   I and IV only

Ⓒ   I, II, and IV only

Ⓓ   I, II, III, and IV

2 Triangle *C′D′E′* is a dilation of triangle *CDE* with a scale factor of 1.5. Triangle *C″D″E″* is a translation of triangle *CDE*.

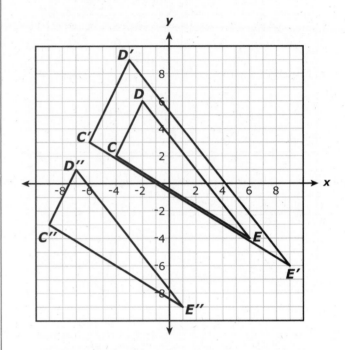

Which of the following is NOT true?

Ⓕ   Triangles *CDE* and *C′D′E′* preserve orientation because the figures are identical in shape and direction.

Ⓖ   Triangles *CDE* and *C″D″E″* do not preserve orientation because the transformation is a dilation with a scale factor greater than 1.

Ⓗ   Triangles *CDE* and *C″D″E″* are congruent because the transformation is a translation.

Ⓙ   Triangles *CDE* and *C′D′E′* are not congruent because the transformation is a dilation with a scale factor greater than 1.

1 Quadrilateral *W'X'Y'Z'* is a reflection of quadrilateral *WXYZ* across the *x*-axis. Quadrilateral *W"X"Y"Z"* is a 180° rotation of quadrilateral *WXYZ* counterclockwise about the origin.

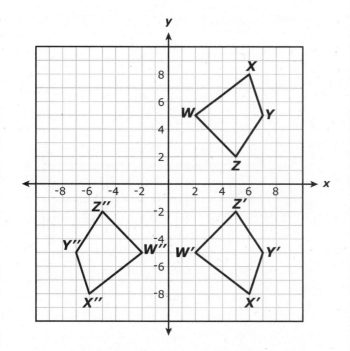

Which of the following statements is true?

Ⓐ Orientation is preserved for quadrilateral *W'X'Y'Z'* therefore only reflections across the *x*-axis preserve orientation.

Ⓑ Orientation is preserved for quadrilateral *W"X"Y"Z"* therefore only 180° rotations counterclockwise about the origin preserve orientation.

Ⓒ Orientation is not preserved for quadrilateral *W"X"Y"Z"* therefore all rotations do not preserve orientation.

Ⓓ Orientation is not preserved for quadrilateral *W'X'Y'Z'* therefore all reflections do not preserve orientation.

2 Which of the following transformations results in an image that is NOT congruent to its pre-image?

I. Dilation with a scale factor of 1

II. $(x, y) \rightarrow (-x, -y)$

III.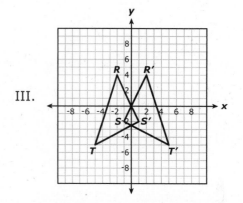

IV.

Original Vertices	New Vertices
$F(-2, 3)$	$F'(-4, 6)$
$G(-7, -6)$	$G'(-14, -12)$
$H(5, -\frac{1}{2})$	$H'(10, -1)$
$J(3, 10)$	$J'(6, 20)$

Ⓕ IV only

Ⓖ I and IV only

Ⓗ I, II, and III only

Ⓙ I, II, and IV only

1 Look at triangle *XYZ* on the coordinate plane.

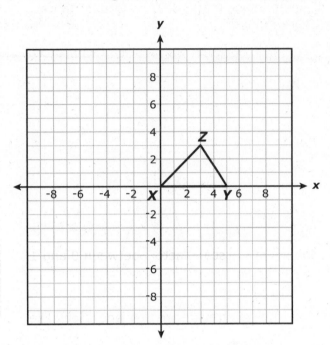

If triangle *XYZ* is rotated counterclockwise 90° about the origin to form triangle *X'Y'Z'*, which of the following is true?

Ⓐ Triangle *X'Y'Z'* is congruent to triangle *XYZ* but does not have the same orientation as triangle *XYZ*.

Ⓑ Triangle *X'Y'Z'* is not congruent to triangle *XYZ* but does have the same orientation as triangle *XYZ*.

Ⓒ Triangle *X'Y'Z'* is not congruent to triangle *XYZ* and does not have the same orientation as triangle *XYZ*.

Ⓓ Triangle *X'Y'Z'* is congruent to triangle *XYZ* and does have the same orientation as triangle *XYZ*.

2 Which of the following transformations does NOT preserve orientation?

Ⓕ translations

Ⓖ reflections

Ⓗ dilations

Ⓙ rotations

3 Which of the following preserves congruence?

Ⓐ
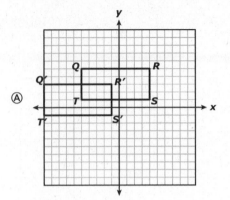

Ⓑ

Original Vertices	(-8, -6)	(-7, 3)	(3, -1)
New Vertices	(-12, -9)	(-10.5, 4.5)	(4.5, -1.5)

Ⓒ A dilation by a scale factor of $\frac{2}{5}$

Ⓓ $(x, y) \rightarrow (0.7x, 0.7y)$

4 Pentagon *ABCDE* is reflected across the *y*-axis to form pentagon *A'B'C'D'E'*.

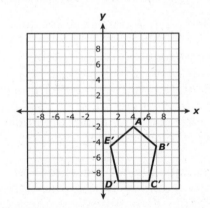

Which statement is NOT true?

Ⓕ Pentagon *A'B'C'D'E'* does not have the same orientation as pentagon *ABCDE*.

Ⓖ Pentagon *A'B'C'D'E'* has the same orientation as pentagon *ABCDE*.

Ⓗ Pentagon *A'B'C'D'E'* is congruent to pentagon *ABCDE*.

Ⓙ Pentagon *A'B'C'D'E'* is a transformation of pentagon *ABCDE*.

Analysis
Analyze

1 As students enter Mr. Nin's math class, each receives a card with a set of dilated figures drawn on a coordinate plane. Two examples of cards are shown.

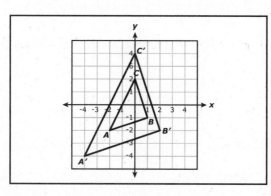 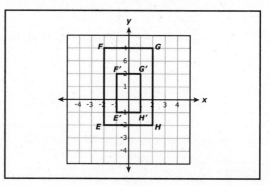

Label each example with one of the following descriptions of the scale factor: between 0 and 1, equal to 1, greater than 1. Explain your choices.

For the description of a scale factor not used, describe what the transformation would look like on the coordinate plane.

Analysis
Analyze

2 Tim and Kate study the properties of transformations in math class. As part of an assignment, the students are asked to create a graphic organizer showing the properties of congruence and orientation for different transformations. Tim and Kate's organizer is shown.

	Yes	No
Preserves Congruence	Rotation Reflection Translation	Dilation
Preserves Orientation	Reflection Translation	Dilation Rotation

Provide feedback on Tim and Kate's organizer. Make suggestions for changes as needed and give justification for your remarks.

_____

_____

_____

Journal

Explain why the image of a figure after a translation, a rotation, or a reflection is congruent to its pre-image, but the image of a figure after a dilation by a scale factor other than 1 is not.

_____

_____

_____

Vocabulary Activity

For this activity, work with a partner. Each pair of players needs an activity page and a paper clip to use with the spinner. Each player needs a sheet of paper and a pencil. Player 1 secretly writes a vocabulary term from the list on the paper, and then spins the spinner and follows the directions for the secret term. Player 2 tries to guess the vocabulary term. If the term is guessed correctly, it is marked off the list. Players switch roles and continue until all vocabulary terms have been marked off the list.

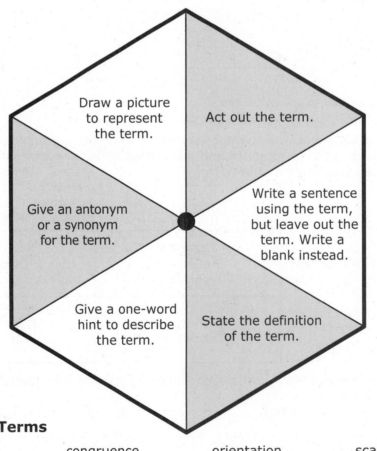

Vocabulary Terms

transformation	congruence	orientation	scale factor
reflection	translation	dilation	pre-image
rotation	image	clockwise	counterclockwise

Transform Me

Play *Transform Me* with a partner. Each pair of players needs a game board and a paper clip to use with the spinner. Each player needs a different color pencil. Player 1 spins the spinner and calls out a transformation that fits the description. If correct, player 1 shades one space containing the transformation identified. If incorrect, player 1 loses a turn and player 2 repeats the process. The game ends when all the spaces have been shaded. The winner is the player with more spaces shaded in his/her color.

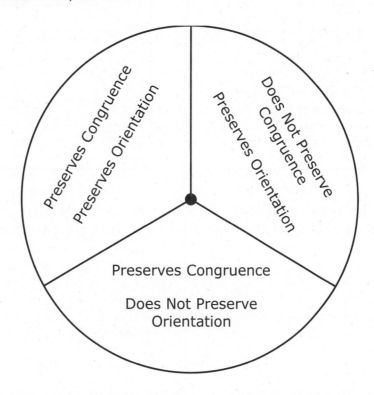

Reflection (across *x*-axis)	Translation	Dilation (scale factor = 1)	Rotation (clockwise 90°)
Translation	Dilation (scale factor > 1)	Rotation (clockwise 270°)	Reflection (across *y*-axis)
Rotation (clockwise 180°)	Rotation (clockwise 360°)	Translation	Dilation (scale factor < 1)
Reflection (across *y*-axis)	Reflection (across *x*-axis)	Dilation (scale factor > 1)	Translation

1   Look at the graph.

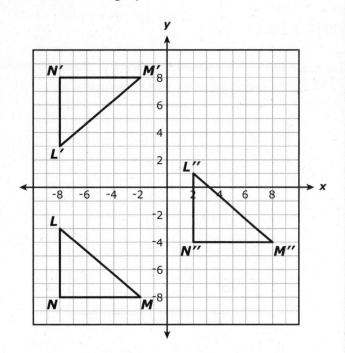

How do the orientation and congruence of triangle *L'M'N'* compare to triangle *LMN*?

What conclusion can be made about all reflections?

How do the orientation and congruence of triangle *L"M"N"* compare to triangle *LMN*?

What conclusion can be made about all translations?

2   Look at the graph.

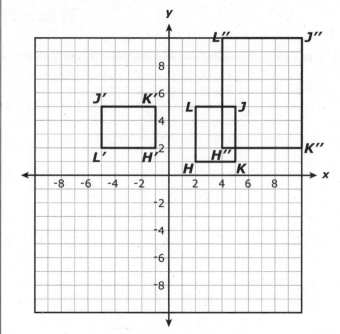

How do the orientation and congruence of rectangle *H'L'J'K'* compare to rectangle *HLJK*?

What conclusion can be made about all rotations?

How do the orientation and congruence of rectangle *H"L"J"K"* compare to rectangle *HLJK*?

What conclusion can be made about all dilations?

Connections

Research various amusement park rides. Identify rides that rotate, reflect, or translate. For each ride, create a display with a picture of the ride and a description of the type of transformation seen in the ride. Include in your description information about whether the ride preserves orientation and/or congruence. Share your displays with the class.

1 Look at the translation shown.

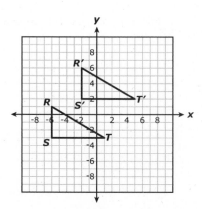

Complete the table to show the relationship between the coordinates of the vertices of triangles *RST* and *R'S'T'*.

△*RST*	Relationship	△*R'S'T'*
R(-6, 1)	(-6 + 4, 1 + 5)	R'(-2, 6)
S(-6, -3)	(-6 + 4, -3 + 5)	S'(-2, 2)
T(1, -3)	(1 + 4, -3 + 5)	T'(5, 2)

Write an algebraic representation to describe the translation of each *x*- and *y*-value of the vertices of triangle *RST* to form triangle *R'S'T'*.

2 Look at the reflection.

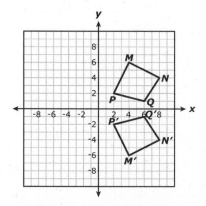

Write an algebraic representation to describe the reflection of each *x*- and *y*-value of the vertices of figure *MNQP* to form figure *M'N'Q'P'*.

Across which axis did the reflection occur?

3 Parallelogram *ABCD* is rotated 90° counterclockwise about the origin to form parallelogram *A'B'C'D'*.

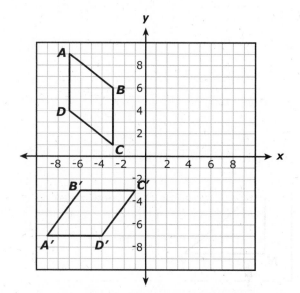

Complete the table to show the relationship between the coordinates of the vertices of figures *ABCD* and *A'B'C'D'*.

Vertices of Figure *ABCD*	Corresponding Vertices of Figure *A'B'C'D'*

Write a general algebraic representation to describe the rotation of each *x*- and *y*-value of the vertices from figure *ABCD* to form figure *A'B'C'D'*.

1 Look at triangles *TUV* and *T'U'V'*.

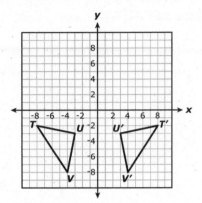

Which best explains the transformation of triangle *TUV* to form triangle *T'U'V'*?

Ⓐ Translation to the right 6 units
$(x, y) \rightarrow (x + 6, y)$

Ⓑ Reflection across the *x*-axis
$(x, y) \rightarrow (x, -y)$

Ⓒ 180° rotation
$(x, y) \rightarrow (-x, -y)$

Ⓓ Reflection across the *y*-axis
$(x, y) \rightarrow (-x, y)$

2 Look at the transformation.

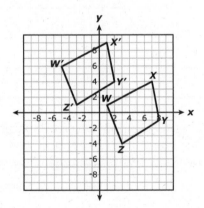

Which rule maps quadrilateral *WXYZ* to quadrilateral *W'X'Y'Z'*?

Ⓕ $(x, y) \rightarrow (x + 5, y - 6)$

Ⓖ $(x, y) \rightarrow (x - 6, y + 5)$

Ⓗ $(x, y) \rightarrow (x + 6, y - 5)$

Ⓙ $(x, y) \rightarrow (x - 5, y + 6)$

3 Tremont uses the rule $(x, y) \rightarrow (-x, -y)$ to show a transformation of rectangle *JKLM* to form rectangle *J'K'L'M'*. Which best shows this transformation?

Ⓐ 180° rotation counterclockwise

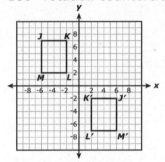

Ⓑ 90° rotation counterclockwise

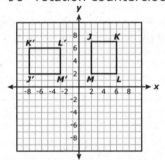

Ⓒ 180° rotation counterclockwise

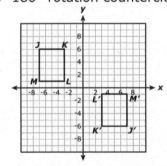

Ⓓ 90° rotation counterclockwise

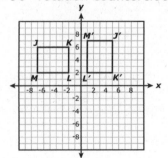

1 Look at the graph of triangle *DEF*.

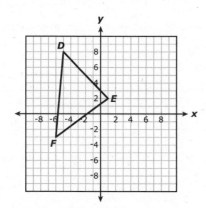

If Drew applies the transformation
$(x, y) \rightarrow (x - 4, y + 3)$ to triangle *DEF*,
what is true about triangle *D'E'F'*?

Ⓐ Triangle *D'E'F'* is a translation 4 units
down and 3 units to the right.

Ⓑ Triangle *D'E'F'* is a dilation by a scale
factor of $-\frac{4}{3}$.

Ⓒ Triangle *D'E'F'* is a translation 4 units to
the left and 3 units up.

Ⓓ Triangle *D'E'F'* is a dilation by a scale
factor of $\frac{3}{4}$.

2 Which of the following would result in a
rotation 360° counterclockwise about the
origin?

Ⓕ $(x, y) \rightarrow (-y, -x)$

Ⓖ $(x, y) \rightarrow (-y, x)$

Ⓗ $(x, y) \rightarrow (-x, -y)$

Ⓙ $(x, y) \rightarrow (x, y)$

3 The graph shows the resulting figure after
parallelogram *ABCD* is reflected across the
y-axis.

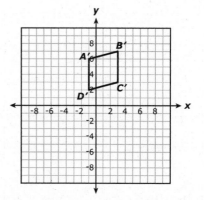

Which best explains the transformation that
occurred?

Ⓐ $(x, y) \rightarrow (x, y)$ Ⓒ $(x, y) \rightarrow (-x, -y)$

Ⓑ $(x, y) \rightarrow (-x, y)$ Ⓓ $(x, y) \rightarrow (x, -y)$

4 Look at the figures shown.

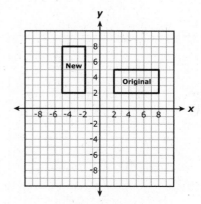

Which transformation best describes the
figures?

Ⓕ 270° rotation counterclockwise about the
origin using the rule $(x, y) \rightarrow (-y, x)$

Ⓖ 90° rotation counterclockwise about the
origin using the rule $(x, y) \rightarrow (x, -y)$

Ⓗ 270° rotation counterclockwise about the
origin using the rule $(x, y) \rightarrow (-x, y)$

Ⓙ 90° rotation counterclockwise about the
origin using the rule $(x, y) \rightarrow (-y, x)$

Unit 30 Assessment

1 Ryan reflects rectangle *LMNO* across the x-axis.

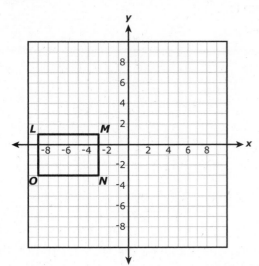

Which best shows the rule for the reflection?

Ⓐ $(x, y) \rightarrow (x, y)$ Ⓒ $(x, y) \rightarrow (-x, -y)$

Ⓑ $(x, y) \rightarrow (-x, y)$ Ⓓ $(x, y) \rightarrow (x, -y)$

2 Look at the graph.

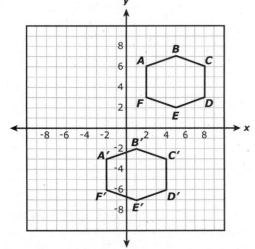

Which best explains the transformation?

Ⓕ A translation following the rule $(x + 4, y + 9)$

Ⓖ A translation following the rule $(x - 4, y - 9)$

Ⓗ A translation following the rule $(x + 9, y + 4)$

Ⓙ A translation following the rule $(x - 9, y - 4)$

3 Which graph shows the use of the rule $(x, y) \rightarrow (y, -x)$ to transform triangle *VWX*?

Ⓐ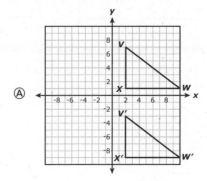

Ⓑ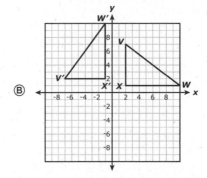

Ⓒ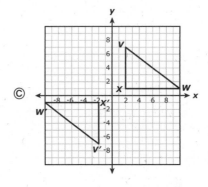

Ⓓ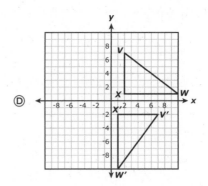

Application

Apply

1   The following composition of transformations is performed on quadrilateral *ABCD*.

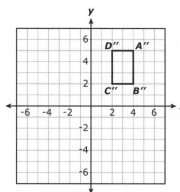

$(x, y) \rightarrow (x + 5, y + 7)$ followed by $(x, y) \rightarrow (-x, y)$

The resulting quadrilateral, *A"B"C"D"*, is shown.

What are the coordinates for quadrilateral *ABCD*?

Analysis

Analyze

2   Consider the transformation of triangle *ABC* to triangle *A'B'C'* shown on the coordinate plane.

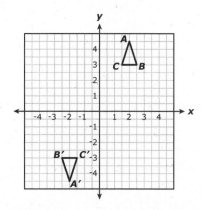

Explain three different transformations or compositions of transformations that could have resulted in triangle *ABC* being transformed to triangle *A'B'C'*. Use algebraic representations to justify your work.

a.

b.

c.

Journal

Verbally describe one transformation that yields the same results as a composition of two transformations. Explain how you know the results are the same.

_____

_____

_____

Vocabulary Activity

Label each of the examples with the name of the transformation shown. Then record the general algebraic representation used to create the transformation.

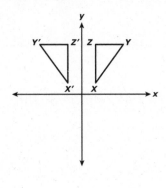   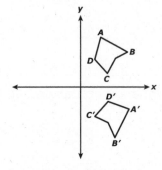   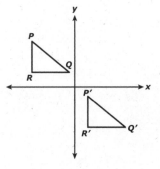

_____   _____   _____

_____   _____   _____

Use the following terms to label the diagram: *transformation, origin, x-axis, y-axis, image, pre-image.*

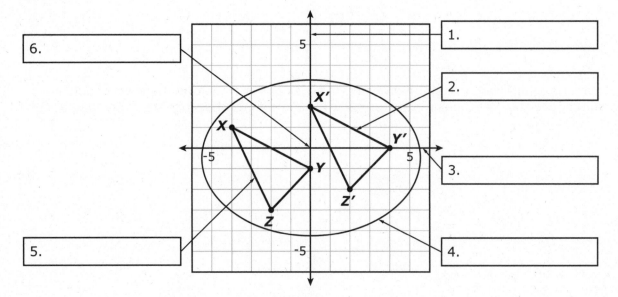

Transformatch

A triangle is graphed on the coordinate plane. For each transformation provided, record the letter of the graph that matches the transformation. Then record the algebraic representation of the transformation. Finally, record the coordinates for each vertex on the graph. All rotations are counterclockwise about the origin.

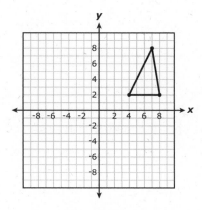

1. Translation _____

   $(x, y) \rightarrow ($_____, _____$)$

2. 90° Rotation _____

   $(x, y) \rightarrow ($_____, _____$)$

3. Reflection over y-axis _____

   $(x, y) \rightarrow ($_____, _____$)$

4. 270° Rotation _____

   $(x, y) \rightarrow ($_____, _____$)$

5. Reflection over x-axis _____

   $(x, y) \rightarrow ($_____, _____$)$

6. 360° Rotation _____

   $(x, y) \rightarrow ($_____, _____$)$

7. 180° Rotation _____

   $(x, y) \rightarrow ($_____, _____$)$

A.
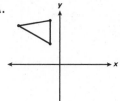

B.
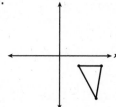

C.
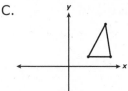

D.
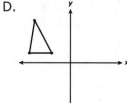

E.
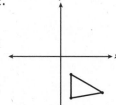

F.
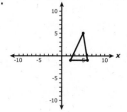

G.
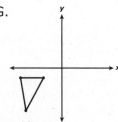

Unit 30 Homework

1 Look at the pentagons on the graph.

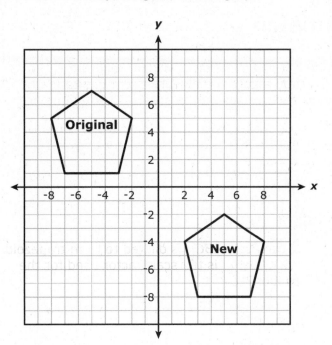

Write the rule for the transformation shown.

2 Ingrid rotates a triangle 90° counterclockwise about the origin. She explains the rotation using the rule $(x, y) \rightarrow (-x, -y)$. Is Ingrid's rule correct? Explain your answer.

3 Look at the parallelogram *EFGH* on the graph.

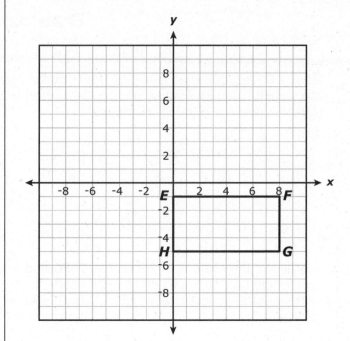

Use the rule $(x, y) \rightarrow (-x, y)$ to transform rectangle *EFGH* and create rectangle *E′F′G′H′*.

What transformation created rectangle *E′F′G′H′*?

Use the rule $(x, y) \rightarrow (x, -y)$ to transform rectangle *EFGH* and create rectangle *E″F″G″H″*.

What transformation created rectangle *E″F″G″H″*?

Connections

Create a set of cards to play Memory with family members or friends. On one card, write the name of a transformation, on a second card sketch a picture of the transformation, and on a third card record the algebraic representation for the transformation. Place the cards facedown in an array and play a game of Memory, with each player attempting to match all three representations of the transformation.

Use the information to answer questions 1–3.

Rectangle *D'E'F'G'* is a dilation of rectangle *DEFG* by a scale factor of $\frac{1}{2}$.

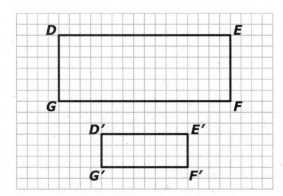

1   Label the dimensions of rectangle *DEFG* and rectangle *D'E'F'G'*. How do the corresponding side lengths of rectangles *D'E'F'G'* and *DEFG* compare?

_____

_____

2   What is the perimeter of rectangle *DEFG*?

What is the perimeter of rectangle *D'E'F'G'*?

How do the perimeters of rectangles *D'E'F'G'* and *DEFG* compare?

_____

_____

3   What is the area of rectangle *DEFG*?

What is the area of rectangle *D'E'F'G'*?

How do the areas of rectangles *D'E'F'G'* and *DEFG* compare?

_____

_____

4   Trapezoid *ABCD* is similar to trapezoid *WXYZ*.

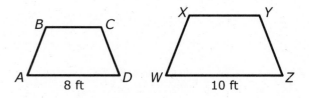

If trapezoid *WXYZ* is dilated to form trapezoid *ABCD*, what is the scale factor used for the dilation?

If trapezoid *ABCD* is dilated to form trapezoid *WXYZ*, what is the scale factor used for the dilation?

If the perimeter of trapezoid *ABCD* is 24 feet, write and evaluate an expression to determine the perimeter of trapezoid *WXYZ*.

If the area of trapezoid *WXYZ* is 50 square feet, write and evaluate an expression to determine the area of trapezoid *ABCD*.

5   The radius of a circle is tripled. Write a statement about the change in the circumference of the circle.

_____

_____

Write a statement about the change in the area of the circle.

_____

_____

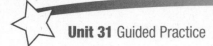

Unit 31 Guided Practice

1 Heather draws a triangle with an area of 192 square centimeters.

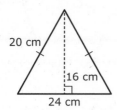

20 cm

16 cm

24 cm

If Heather's triangle is dilated by a scale factor of $\frac{3}{4}$, what is the area of the new triangle?

Ⓐ 108 cm²   Ⓒ 48 cm²

Ⓑ 144 cm²   Ⓓ 216 cm²

2 Parallelogram *WXYZ* is dilated by a scale factor of 2.5 to form parallelogram *W′X′Y′Z′*.

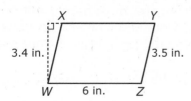

X   Y

3.4 in.   3.5 in.

W   6 in.   Z

Which expression CANNOT be used to calculate the perimeter of parallelogram *W′X′Y′Z′*?

Ⓕ (6 + 3.5 + 6 + 3.5)(2.5)

Ⓖ 2(6 + 2.5) + 2(3.5 + 2.5)

Ⓗ 2(6 · 2.5) + 2(3.5 · 2.5)

Ⓙ 2.5 · 2(6 + 3.5)

3 What effect does a dilation by scale factor *x* have on the area of a rectangle?

Ⓐ The area remains the same.

Ⓑ The area changes by a factor of *x*.

Ⓒ The area changes by a factor of 2*x*.

Ⓓ The area changes by a factor of *x*².

4 Charley paints the circumference of a large circle on a poster.

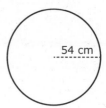

54 cm

If Charley paints a smaller circle with a radius $\frac{1}{3}$ the measure of the larger circle, which best represents the circumference of the smaller circle?

Ⓕ 18π cm   Ⓗ 36π cm

Ⓖ 108π cm   Ⓙ 54π cm

5 A figure is dilated by a scale factor of 4. Which of the following is true about the figure and its dilation?

Ⓐ The perimeter of the image is 4 times as large as the perimeter of the pre-image.

Ⓑ The perimeter of the image is 8 times as large as the perimeter of the pre-image.

Ⓒ The perimeter of the image is 16 times as large as the perimeter of the pre-image.

Ⓓ The perimeter of the image is the same as the perimeter of the pre-image.

6 The ratio formed by the corresponding sides of two similar triangles is 3 : 5. The area of the smaller triangle is 180 square feet. Which expression can be used to determine the area of the larger triangle?

Ⓕ $180\left(\frac{3}{5}\right)$ Ⓗ $180\left(\frac{3}{5}\right)^2$

Ⓖ $180\left(\frac{5}{3}\right)$ Ⓙ $180\left(\frac{5}{3}\right)^2$

 motivation**math**™LEVEL 8   mentoring**minds**.com

1 Two rectangles are similar. The length of the larger rectangle is 20 inches and the corresponding length of the smaller rectangle is 15 inches. If the perimeter of the larger rectangle is 52 inches, which expression can be used to determine the perimeter of the smaller rectangle?

Ⓐ $52\left(\frac{4}{3}\right)$

Ⓑ $52\left(\frac{4}{3}\right)^2$

Ⓒ $52\left(\frac{3}{4}\right)$

Ⓓ $52\left(\frac{3}{4}\right)^2$

2 The ratio of the area of triangle *ABC* to triangle *A'B'C'* is $\frac{49}{4}$. What is the scale factor used to dilate triangle *ABC* to form triangle *A'B'C'*?

Ⓕ $\frac{49}{4}$

Ⓖ $\left(\frac{49}{4}\right)^2$

Ⓗ 12.25

Ⓙ $\frac{2}{7}$

3 What effect does a dilation by scale factor *z* have on the perimeter of a parallelogram?

Ⓐ The perimeter remains the same.

Ⓑ The perimeter changes by a factor of *z*.

Ⓒ The perimeter changes by a factor of 2*z*.

Ⓓ The perimeter changes by a factor of z^2.

4 A park has a circular splash pool and a smaller wading pool.

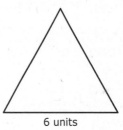

Splash Pool   Wading Pool

The radius of the splash pool is 3 times the radius of the wading pool. Which best represents the area of the splash pool?

Ⓕ πr^2 　　　　　　Ⓗ $6\pi r^2$

Ⓖ $3\pi r^2$ 　　　　　Ⓙ $\pi(3r)^2$

5 The side length of an equilateral triangle is 6 units.

6 units

If the triangle is dilated by a scale factor of $\frac{2}{3}$, what is the perimeter of the dilated figure?

Ⓐ 6 units 　　　　　Ⓒ 12 units

Ⓑ 9 units 　　　　　Ⓓ Not here

6 Marta has a photograph with an area of 80 square inches. She prints a similar photograph that is half the length and width of the original photograph. Which expression can be used to determine the area of Marta's second photograph?

Ⓕ $80\left(\frac{1}{4}\right)$ 　　　　Ⓗ $80\left(\frac{1}{2}\right)$

Ⓖ $80(2)$ 　　　　　Ⓙ $80(1)$

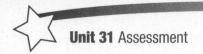
Use the diagram to answer questions 1 and 2.

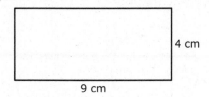

4 cm

9 cm

1 If the dimensions of the rectangle are tripled, which expression can be used to find the perimeter of the dilated figure?

Ⓐ 4(3) + 9(3)

Ⓑ 4(3) • 9(3)

Ⓒ 2 • 4(3) + 2 • 9(3)

Ⓓ 2 • 4(3) • 2 • 9(3)

2 If the dimensions of the rectangle are dilated by a scale factor of $\frac{1}{2}$, which expression shows a correct method to find the area of the dilated rectangle?

Ⓕ 36 • 2

Ⓖ 36 • $\frac{1}{2}$

Ⓗ 36 • $\left(\frac{1}{2}\right)^2$

Ⓙ 36 • 2^2

3 The radius of a circle is 18 meters. A second circle has a radius of 12 meters. If the area of the original circle is 324π square meters, what is the area of the second circle?

Ⓐ 324π • $\frac{2}{3}$

Ⓑ 324π • $\left(\frac{2}{3}\right)^2$

Ⓒ 324π • $\frac{3}{2}$

Ⓓ 324π • $\left(\frac{3}{2}\right)^2$

Use the diagram to answer questions 4 and 5.

Josie and Jake are discussing options for changing the dimensions of their backyard vegetable garden.

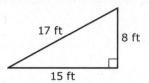

17 ft

8 ft

15 ft

4 Josie wants to increase the dimensions by a factor of 1.5. How many feet of fencing would be needed to surround the new vegetable garden?

Ⓕ 51.5 ft   Ⓗ 56 ft

Ⓖ 52.5 ft   Ⓙ 60 ft

5 Jake's plan is to change the dimensions by a factor of $\frac{4}{5}$. Which of the following statements is true?

Ⓐ The area of the new garden would be $\frac{4}{5}$ the area of the original garden.

Ⓑ The area of the new garden would be $\frac{2}{5}$ the area of the original garden.

Ⓒ The area of the new garden would be $\frac{16}{25}$ the area of the original garden.

Ⓓ The area of the new garden would be $\frac{4}{25}$ the area of the original garden.

6 The ratio of the areas of two figures is 1 to 25. Which expression can be used to determine the scale factor used to dilate the original figure?

Ⓕ $\frac{5^2}{1^2}$ Ⓗ $\frac{\sqrt{25}}{\sqrt{1}}$

Ⓖ $\frac{25}{1}$ Ⓙ $\frac{25^2}{1^2}$

Application

Apply

1 Isosceles trapezoid *A′B′C′D′* is shown.

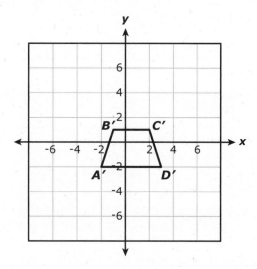

If trapezoid *ABCD* was dilated by a scale factor of $\frac{2}{3}$ to form trapezoid *A′B′C′D′*, what is the area of trapezoid *ABCD*?

Application

Apply

2 A designer replicates a Texas star as part of a lighting design. The original star has a perimeter of 4 feet. The lit star uses 30 feet of rope lighting to surround it. The original star has an area of *x* square feet. What is the difference, in square feet, of the areas of the two stars?

Journal

Explain how to determine the ratio of the perimeters of a shape and its dilation if the ratio of the areas of the two shapes is $\frac{9}{16}$.

_____

_____

_____

Vocabulary Activity

Create math "graffiti" using vocabulary terms from the unit. For each term listed, write the word in a way that gives a clue to the meaning. An example for *perimeter* is provided.

area, circumference, diameter, dilation, dimensions, perimeter, radius, scale factor

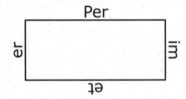

Effective Dilations

Play *Effective Dilations* with a partner. Each pair of players needs a game board, a paper clip to use with the spinner, a number cube, and two game tokens. Each player needs a pencil and a sheet of paper. Player 1 rolls the number cube and moves his/her token the number of spaces indicated. Player 1 then spins the spinner to determine a scale factor (outer ring) and whether he/she will calculate the area or perimeter of the figure in the space (inner ring). Player 1 determines the area or perimeter/circumference for the dilation of the shape shown using the scale factor. If correct, player 1 earns 4 points for the area or 2 points for perimeter/circumference. Play passes to player 2, who repeats the process. The first player to earn at least 40 points wins.

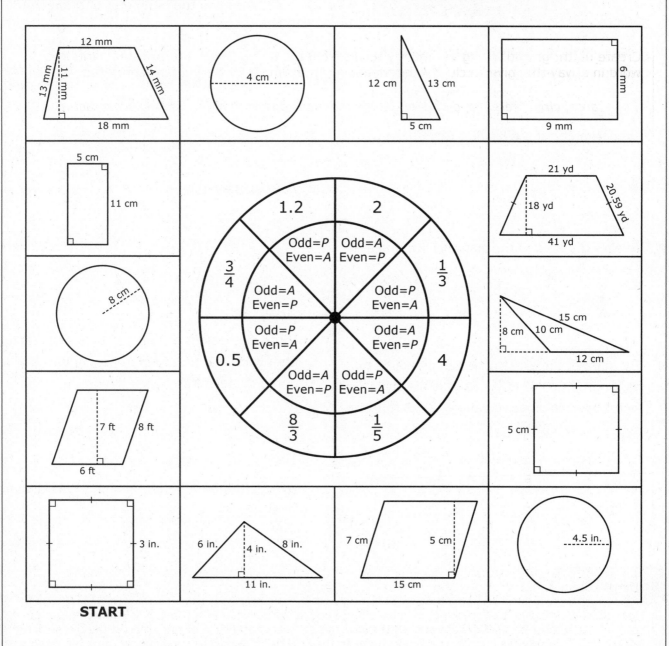

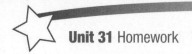
Use the picture to answer questions 1 and 2.

60 in.

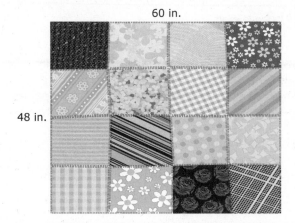

48 in.

1 Eliza is making a blanket using the fabric shown in the picture. She cuts the fabric so the dimensions are reduced by a factor of $\frac{2}{3}$. Write an expression that can be used to find the perimeter of the blanket Eliza makes.

2 What is the area of the blanket Eliza makes?

3 The ratio of the areas of rectangle *WXYZ* to rectangle *W'X'Y'Z'* is $\frac{4}{25}$. What is the scale factor used to dilate rectangle *WXYZ* to form rectangle *W'X'Y'Z'*?

4 Look at the isosceles triangles.

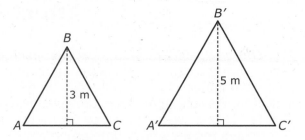

a. If the perimeter of triangle *A'B'C'* is 30 meters, write an expression to determine the perimeter of triangle *ABC*.

b. If the area of triangle *ABC* is 12 square meters, write an expression to determine the area of triangle *A'B'C'*.

5 Look at the circle.

If the dimensions are dilated by a scale factor of $\frac{9}{4}$, what is the circumference, in terms of π, of the dilated circle?

What is the area, in terms of π, of the dilated circle?

Connections

Measure the dimensions of an object in your home, such as a television or a window. Draw a diagram of your object with its original dimensions. Determine the perimeter and area of the object if the dimensions are tripled. Compare the change in the perimeter to the change in the area. Explain how the scale factor is used to find the perimeter and area of the dilated figure.

Use the scatterplot to answer questions 1 and 2.

Thermophiles are microorganisms that thrive in extreme temperatures ranging from 60°C to 75°C. A growth rate graph is shown for one species of thermophile.

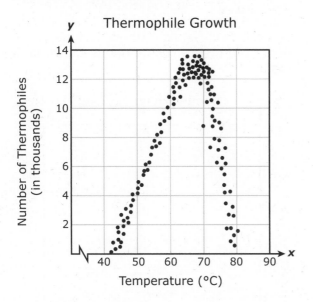

1 What type of association exists between the number of thermophiles and temperature?

_____

2 Explain what the association given in problem 1 means in terms of the number of thermophiles and temperature.

_____

_____

_____

_____

_____

_____

Use the information to answer questions 3–5.

The following bivariate data is given.

(10, -2), (1, 5), (-4, 8),
(2, 3), (-6, 10), (6, 2)

3 Construct a scatterplot using the data.

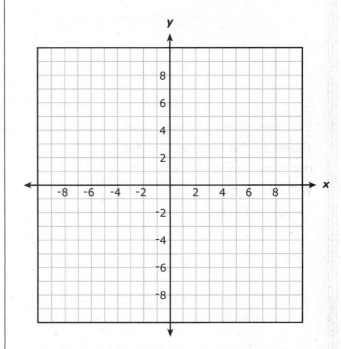

4 Based on the scatterplot, describe the association shown in the data.

5 Describe the relationship between x- and y-values based on your response to problem 4.

6 If a scatterplot shows a positive, linear association, describe the relationship between the x- and y-values.

Unit 32 Guided Practice

Use the scatterplot to answer questions 1 and 2.

Weather conditions are recorded daily. The following scatterplot shows the dew point versus the maximum humidity for a given time period.

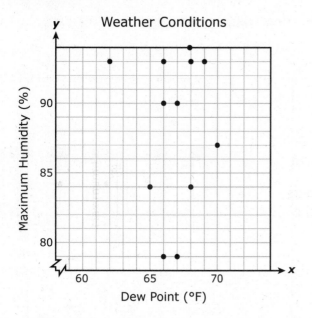

1 Which best describes the association shown in the scatterplot?

Ⓐ Linear

Ⓒ Non-linear

Ⓑ Increasing

Ⓓ Decreasing

2 Based on the scatterplot, which statement is a valid conclusion?

Ⓕ As the dew point increases, the maximum humidity increases.

Ⓖ As the dew point decreases, the maximum humidity increases.

Ⓗ As the dew point decreases, the maximum humidity decreases.

Ⓙ There appears to be no association between dew point and maximum humidity.

Use the scatterplot to answer questions 3 and 4.

Ms. Ellis' nine math classes investigated the link between regular handwashing and the incidence of flu. During the school year, 3 classes agreed to wash their hands 2 times each day, 3 classes agreed to wash their hands 4 times each day, and 3 classes agreed to wash their hands 6 times each day. The data from their investigation is shown in the graph.

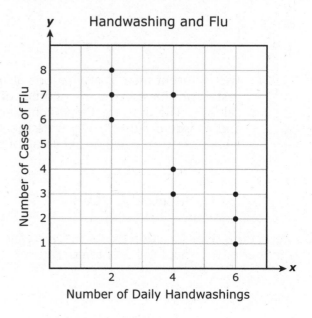

3 Which best describes the trend shown in the scatterplot?

Ⓐ Positive trend

Ⓒ No trend

Ⓑ Negative trend

Ⓓ Average trend

4 Which statement best describes the association in the scatterplot?

Ⓕ The association of the data is non-linear.

Ⓖ The association of the data is linear.

Ⓗ The association of the data is absolute.

Ⓙ The data is not associated.

1 The noble gases from the periodic table are colorless, tasteless, and odorless gases that are virtually non-reactive. The relationship between atomic mass and density of the gases is shown in the scatterplot.

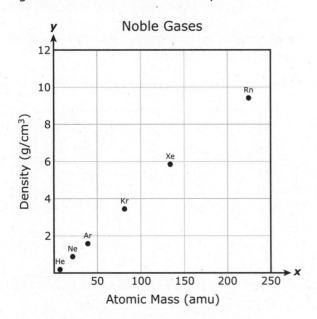

Which statement best describes the association that exists between the atomic mass and density of the noble gases?

Ⓐ There is no association between the atomic mass and density of the noble gases.

Ⓑ A positive, linear association exists between the atomic mass and density of the noble gases. As the atomic mass decreases, the density increases.

Ⓒ A negative, non-linear association exists between the atomic mass and density of the noble gases. As the atomic mass increases, the density decreases.

Ⓓ A positive, linear association exists between the atomic mass and density of the noble gases. As the atomic mass increases, the density increases.

Use the scatterplot to answer questions 2 and 3.

Mr. Chen created a scatterplot to model the relationship between the number of questions on a test and student scores on the test.

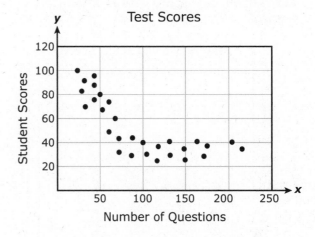

2 Which best describes the trend that exists between the number of questions on a test and the student scores?

Ⓕ Positive trend

Ⓖ Negative trend

Ⓗ No trend

Ⓙ Average trend

3 Based on Mr. Chen's scatterplot, which type of association exists?

Ⓐ There is no association that exists between the number of questions on a test and student scores.

Ⓑ A linear association exists between the number of questions on a test and student scores.

Ⓒ A non-linear association exists between the number of questions on a test and student scores.

Ⓓ An average association exists between the number of questions on a test and student scores.

Use the scatterplot to answer questions 1 and 2.

Standardized assessment creators determine a final scale score for exams by determining the difficulty of each question. A mathematics assessment raw score versus scale score is shown.

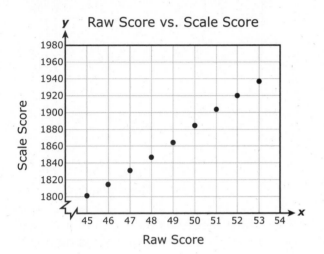

1 Which best describes the trend shown in the scatterplot?

Ⓐ No trend

Ⓑ Positive trend

Ⓒ Negative trend

Ⓓ Not here

2 Which best describes the relationship between the raw scores and scale scores for this mathematics assessment?

Ⓕ There is no association. As the raw scores decrease, the scale scores increase.

Ⓖ There is a linear association. As the raw scores increase, the scale scores decrease.

Ⓗ There is a linear association. As the raw scores increase, the scale scores increase.

Ⓙ There is a non-linear association. As the raw scores increase, the scale scores decrease.

Use the scatterplot to answer questions 3 and 4.

The Old Faithful Geyser in Yellowstone National Park was discovered in 1870. Old Faithful erupts every 35 to 120 minutes and the eruptions last between 1.5 and 5 minutes. The scatterplot shows several consecutive eruptions.

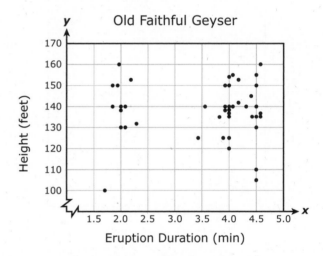

3 Which statement best describes the relationship between the duration and height of the Old Faithful Geyser eruptions?

Ⓐ The data suggests an average association.

Ⓑ The data suggests a positive, linear association.

Ⓒ The data suggests a negative, linear association.

Ⓓ The data suggests no association.

4 Which best describes the trend shown in the data?

Ⓕ Average trend   Ⓗ No trend

Ⓖ Negative trend   Ⓙ Positive trend

The table shows the numbers of black-and-white televisions in American households versus color televisions from 1955 to 1995.

Year	Black-and-White TVs	Color TVs
1955	7,638,000	20,000
1960	5,709,000	122,000
1965	8,743,000	2,694,000
1970	4,704,000	5,320,000
1975	4,975,000	6,486,000
1980	6,684,000	10,997,000
1985	3,683,000	16,995,000
1990	1,411,000	20,584,000
1995	484,000	25,600,000

Create a scatterplot of the two data sets. Use a different color pencil for each set.

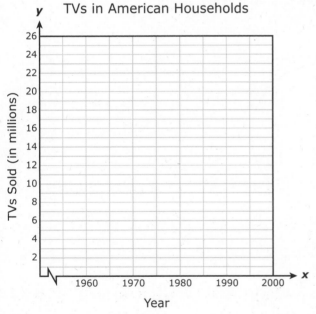

Describe the trends seen in each set of data.

Black-and-white television _____

Color television _____

Based on the information in the plot, what would the trend be between the number of black-and-white televisions in American homes versus the number of color televisions? Explain your answer.

_____

_____

After 20+ years, what do you predict about the number of black-and-white televisions in American homes? Explain your answer.

_____

_____

Journal

Describe three different situations. One situation should represent a positive data trend, one should represent a negative data trend, and one should represent no trend in the data.

_____

_____

_____

_____

Vocabulary Activity

Complete the graphic organizer by creating graphs that show *no association*, a *positive association*, and a *negative association*. If the relationship is *linear*, color the circle red. If the relationship is *non-linear*, color the circle green.

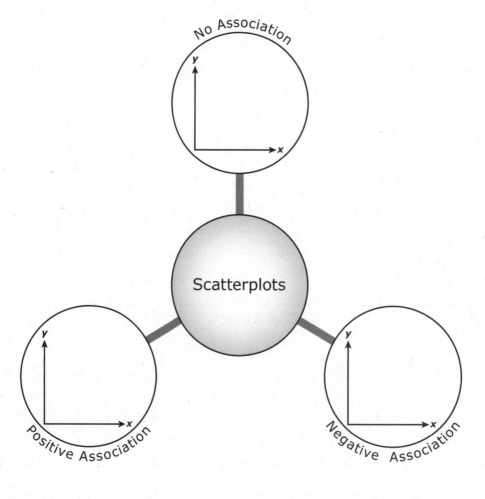

What's Trending

Play *What's Trending* with a partner. Each pair of players needs a game board and a number cube. Each player needs a sheet of paper and a pencil. Player 1 rolls the number cube and uses the chart to determine the trend of a data set. Player 1 then selects a data set that matches the trend and plots the data to verify that the set is correct. If correct, player 1 initials the plot and the data set used, and play passes to player 2. If incorrect, player 1 erases his/her work and play passes to player 2. If a player rolls a number and there are no more data sets available to match the trend, the player loses a turn. Play continues until all the data sets have been plotted. The player with more plots and data sets initialed is the winner.

Prime Number	Positive Trend
Composite Number	Negative Trend
One	No Trend

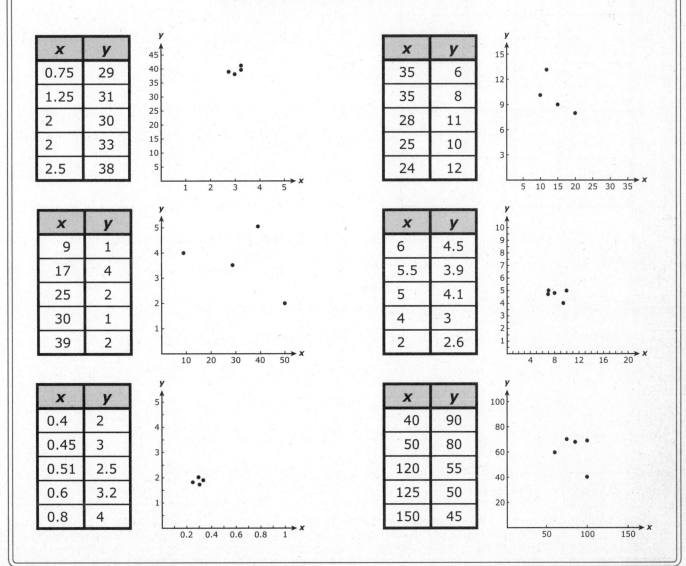

x	y
0.75	29
1.25	31
2	30
2	33
2.5	38

x	y
35	6
35	8
28	11
25	10
24	12

x	y
9	1
17	4
25	2
30	1
39	2

x	y
6	4.5
5.5	3.9
5	4.1
4	3
2	2.6

x	y
0.4	2
0.45	3
0.51	2.5
0.6	3.2
0.8	4

x	y
40	90
50	80
120	55
125	50
150	45

Use the information to answer questions 1–3.

The Centers for Disease Control collects data every year to determine death rates among the population due to a variety of causes. The table shows data collected for the influenza and pneumonia death rates for children under the age of 1 between the years 1999 and 2010.

Influenza and Pneumonia Death Rates
Children < 1 year

Year	Death Rate per 100,000
1999	8.4
2000	7.6
2001	7.5
2002	6.7
2003	8.1
2004	6.8
2005	6.6
2006	6.5
2007	5.4
2008	5.5
2009	6.3
2010	4.9

1 Construct a scatterplot using the data from the table.

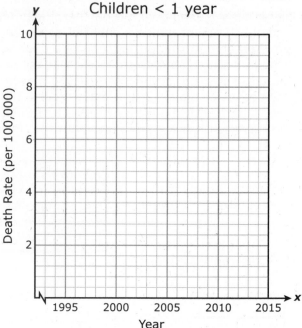

Influenza and Pneumonia Death Rates
Children < 1 year

2 What type of trend describes the data in the scatterplot?

3 Explain the association shown in the scatterplot.

1 A popular movie series has made a total of 6 movies. The length of each movie is shown.

Movie Length (minutes)

139	161	153	142	157	130

(a) What is the mean of the data?

(b) What is the absolute value of the difference between 139 and the mean?

What is the absolute value of the difference between 161 and the mean?

What is the absolute value of the difference between 153 and the mean?

What is the absolute value of the difference between 142 and the mean?

What is the absolute value of the difference between 157 and the mean?

What is the absolute value of the difference between 130 and the mean?

(c) What is the average of the differences found in part (b)?

(d) What does the value found in part (c) tell about the data?

2 Mrs. Wright gave a 10-question pretest to her students. The dot plots show the top 8 scores from her first-period class and her seventh-period class.

First-Period Class

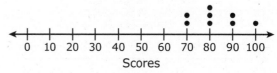

Seventh-Period Class

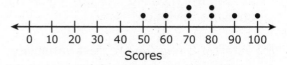

What is the mean absolute deviation of the scores from Mrs. Wright's first-period class?

What is the mean absolute deviation of the scores from Mrs. Wright's seventh-period class?

3 Complete each statement by filling in the blanks.

The smaller a mean absolute deviation is, the _____ variability there is in the data around the _____.

The larger a mean absolute deviation is, the _____ variability there is in the data around the _____.

Unit 33 Guided Practice

1 Two data sets collected during an investigation are shown.

Data Set A

| 75.8, 79.2, 78.6, 82.1, 76.7, 77.3 |

Data Set B

| 89.1, 85.4, 87.2, 88.9, 86.7, 90.9 |

Which of the following is true?

Ⓐ Data set A has the greatest variability around the mean due to the higher mean absolute deviation.

Ⓑ Data set B has the greatest variability around the mean due to the higher mean absolute deviation.

Ⓒ Data sets A and B have the same variability around the mean due to the same mean absolute deviation.

Ⓓ There is not enough information to determine the variability difference between data sets A and B.

2 The last six days of August 2011 set all-time records for high temperatures in Austin, Texas.

Date	Temperature (°F)
26	103
27	110
28	112
29	109
30	105
31	103

Which of the following values best identifies the mean absolute deviation for these temperatures?

Ⓕ 4

Ⓖ 107

Ⓗ 103

Ⓙ 3.3

3 Look at each set of data.

Data Sets

W	11, 7, 28, 46, 36
X	5.7, 7.5, 9.4, 6.4, 8.9
Y	10.75, 11.5, 11.9, 10.25, 10.1
Z	80, 77, 79, 78, 76

Which data set has a mean absolute deviation of 0.64?

Ⓐ Data set W

Ⓑ Data set X

Ⓒ Data set Y

Ⓓ Data set Z

4 The yearly salaries for each of four employees at Mattress City are shown in the table.

Salary

| $50,000 |
| $45,000 |
| $32,000 |
| $30,000 |

Which statement is NOT supported by the data?

Ⓕ The average distance between each salary and the mean salary is $8,250.

Ⓖ The salary of the employee that has been with the company the longest is the largest.

Ⓗ The mean salary for an employee of Mattress City is $39,250.

Ⓙ The salaries for employees at Mattress City show a variation from the mean that is greater than $6,000.

1 What information does the mean absolute deviation provide about a data set?

ⓐ The mean absolute deviation describes the average distance each value in the data set is from the median.

ⓑ The mean absolute deviation describes the average distance each value in the data set is from the mean.

ⓒ The mean absolute deviation describes the average distance each value in the data set is from zero.

ⓓ The mean absolute deviation describes the average distance each value in the data set is from the range.

2 Four groups measure how long it takes a toy car to travel one meter down a ramp. Each group's data is presented in the table.

Group	Data Set
1	10.5, 9.8, 10.9, 10.0, 10.3
2	9.7, 9.9, 10.5, 10.6, 10.8
3	9.6, 9.8, 10.2, 10.8, 11.1
4	10.7, 10.6, 9.5, 9.7, 11.0

Which group's data shows the least amount of variability around the mean?

ⓕ Group 1

ⓖ Group 2

ⓗ Group 3

ⓙ Group 4

3 Final scores for seven high school baseball games played are shown in the table.

Team	Final Score	Final Score	Team
Wildcats	8	6	Eagles
Bulldogs	3	4	Mustangs
Rams	10	1	Huskies
Hornets	2	3	Comets
Cougars	9	6	Patriots
Roadrunners	8	2	Bears
Owls	1	7	Bobcats

Which of the following is true?

ⓐ The winning teams' scores and the losing teams' scores show the same variability because they have the same mean absolute deviation.

ⓑ The losing teams' scores show the greatest variability.

ⓒ The winning teams' scores show the greatest variability.

ⓓ There is not enough information to determine the difference in variability between the winning teams' scores and the losing teams' scores.

4 Ten customers enter a convenience store during their lunch hour on Monday. The age of each customer is identified on the dot plot.

Customer Ages

Age (years)

What is the mean absolute deviation of the ages?

ⓕ 30 years   ⓗ 3.8 years

ⓖ 5.6 years   ⓙ 4.2 years

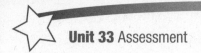
1 Two researchers in the marketing department of a grocery company look at the numbers of times consumers purchase a frozen food item in one month. They plan to use this information to predict how many containers of the item to keep in stock for consumers to purchase in future months. The results of the research are shown.

> **Researcher 1 Results**
>
> | |
> |---|
> | Mean: 15 |
> | Mean Absolute Deviation: 1.8 |

> **Researcher 2 Results**
>
> | |
> |---|
> | Mean: 22 |
> | Mean Absolute Deviation: 7.5 |

Which of the following statements is true?

Ⓐ The results from researcher 2 show a greater variability because the mean is larger than the mean in the results from researcher 1.

Ⓑ The results from researcher 1 show a greater variability because the mean is smaller than the mean in the results from researcher 2.

Ⓒ The results from researcher 2 show less variability because the mean absolute deviation is larger.

Ⓓ The results from researcher 1 show less variability because the mean absolute deviation is smaller.

2 A survey found the following numbers of pets in different households.

4	1	0	2	1	3	1

What is the mean absolute deviation for the number of pets?

Ⓕ 2

Ⓖ 1.7

Ⓗ 1.1

Ⓙ 0.7

3 Miles and Mazie find the mean absolute deviation for the set of numbers shown.

8	2	3	4	13	18

Their steps are shown.

Step 1: $\dfrac{8 + 2 + 3 + 4 + 13 + 18}{6} = 8$

Step 2: $\dfrac{0 + \text{-}6 + \text{-}5 + \text{-}4 + 5 + 10}{6} = 0$

Which of the following is true?

Ⓐ There are no mistakes, and the mean absolute deviation for the data is 0.

Ⓑ Step 1 shows how to calculate the mean absolute deviation, while step 2 shows how to justify the mean absolute deviation.

Ⓒ Step 1 is incorrect because the mean of the data set is calculated using only the highest and lowest values in the data set.

Ⓓ Step 2 is incorrect because mean absolute deviation uses the absolute value of the differences.

4 Look at each set of data.

Data Sets

A	28, 36, 30, 44, 46
B	13, 15, 9, 35, 25
C	7.6, 4.1, 2.7, 3.4, 16.2
D	108, 101.5, 125, 100.2, 100.3

Which set of data shows the greatest amount of variability around the mean?

Ⓕ Set A

Ⓖ Set B

Ⓗ Set C

Ⓙ Set D

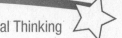

1 The seventh- and eighth-grade students have a competition to see which group can raise the most money for new computers for the school. The amount of money raised by each group over six months is shown in the graph.

	October	November	December	January	February	March
7th Grade	$880	$1,160	$940	$1,080	$1,120	$1,240
8th Grade	$1,440	$910	$970	$1,220	$1,280	$1,320

Explain the differences between the two data sets in terms of the mean absolute deviations.

2 Create two different data sets, each with five values, that meet the following criteria.

The mean absolute deviation of Set A is greater than the mean absolute deviation of Set B.

The mean of Set B is greater than the mean of Set A.

Analysis
i
Analyze

Journal

Mr. Timms writes the following statement on the board.

The mean absolute deviation for a set of data is 2.89.

Explain what the statement means in terms of the data points.

_____

_____

_____

Vocabulary Activity

Complete the graphic organizer using each vocabulary term. Write a term from the list in the first column and a definition of the term in the second column. In the third column, draw an illustration representing the vocabulary term.

mean   *absolute value*   *deviation*

Vocabulary Term	Definition	Illustration

Based on the information in the table, develop a definition for mean absolute deviation in your own words.

_____

_____

     motivation**math**™LEVEL 8   mentoring**minds**.com

M.A.D. for Data

Play *M.A.D. for Data* with a partner. Each pair of players needs a game board, a number cube, a calculator, and two different colors of pencils. Each player needs a pencil and a sheet of paper. Player 1 rolls the number cube and calculates the mean absolute deviation (MAD) for the data set matching the number rolled. If calculated correctly, player 1 shades the matching MAD and data bubbles using his/her colored pencil. If incorrect, play passes to player 2 who repeats the process. If a player rolls the number of a data set already shaded, he/she loses a turn. The game ends when all matching data sets and MAD values have been shaded. The winner is the player with more bubbles shaded.

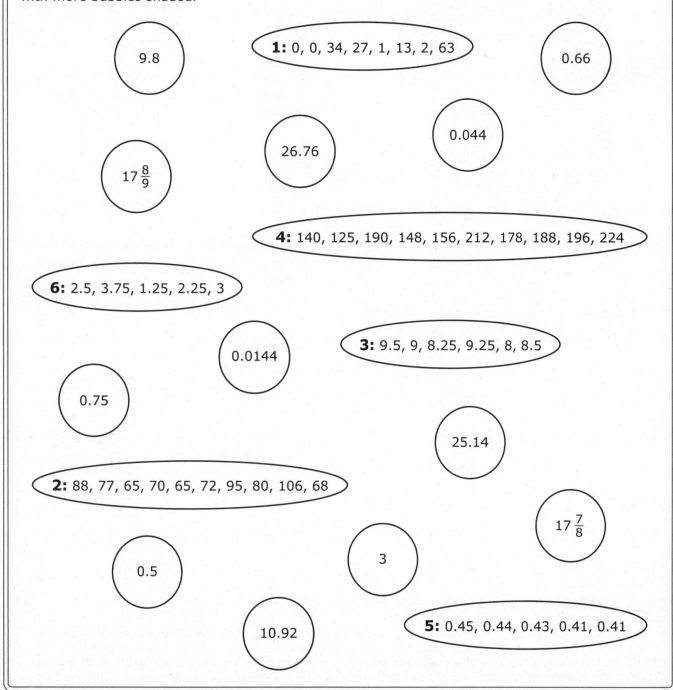

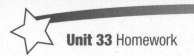
1 Kathryn and Cole looked at previous T-shirt sales to determine how many T-shirts to order for the next basketball season. The data each found are shown.

Kathryn

85	40	77	86	80	82

Cole

90	86	88	84	87	81

(a) Find the mean absolute deviation for Kathryn's data and for Cole's data.

(b) What information does the mean absolute deviation found in part (a) give about the two data sets?

2 The mean absolute deviation for the heights of several students is 2 inches. Explain the meaning of the value.

3 Sam and Fred are both bowlers. A comparison of their recent bowling scores is shown in the table.

Sam	250	255	275	230	250	270
Fred	300	250	225	200	275	250

Determine the mean score for each bowler.

What is the mean absolute deviation for the bowlers' scores?

Which bowler is the more consistent? Use the mean absolute deviation to justify your answer.

_____

_____

_____

Connections

When planning a budget, it is important to know what expenses will occur each month. Some expenses, such as electricity, vary from month to month. Use the amounts of your home's electricity bills for the past ten months to determine the mean and the absolute mean deviation for the electricity bills. Write a paragraph explaining how the values were calculated.

1 Suzie conducts a survey to determine the favorite athletic shoe brand among the students at her school. She gets an attendance roster for all eighth-grade math classes and numbers each group of students separately. She then uses a random number generator on her calculator to select one student from each math class roster. She finds each of the selected students and asks them the survey question.

(a) Identify the population.

(b) Identify the sample.

(c) Describe the method used to sample the population. Include the process used to gain a random sample and the identification of the students the sample is selected from.

(d) Is the sample representative of the population? Explain your answer.

(e) Is the sample random? Explain your answer.

(f) If either of your responses to part (d) or (e) were no, what would you change about the sampling method?

2 A local hospital is interested in determining the number of people in the town that received a flu shot this year. To conduct the study, they ask all the local doctors to poll their patients when they come for an appointment to determine if they have had a flu shot.

(a) Identify the population.

(b) Identify the sample.

(c) Will the results of the hospital's study yield valid information about the number of people in the town that received a flu shot last year? Explain your answer.

(d) Describe a different method of collecting a random sample of the population to use for the study.

3 Serena plans to open a business selling cookies and cupcakes to the students in her school. She needs to determine a fair price for the cupcakes. She wants to poll a random sample of the students at her school to determine a fair price for a cupcake. Describe a simulation Serena could use to obtain her sample without bias.

1 During after-school practice, Diego surveys all the members of the football team about their favorite sport. The results are shown in the table.

Favorite Sport

Sport	Number of Students
Football	30
Basketball	9
Soccer	5
Baseball	11

From these results, Diego concludes that football is the favorite sport among all the students at his school. Which is the best explanation for why his conclusion might NOT be valid?

Ⓐ The survey is biased because only randomly selected members of the football team should have been included in the survey.

Ⓑ The survey is biased because it was not administered in two parts.

Ⓒ The survey is biased because football players do not represent the interests of the entire population.

Ⓓ The survey is biased because the sample did not include coaches.

2 The principal of a junior high school wants to know how many students like the current cafeteria food. Which method might the principal use to ensure a good representation of the population in his survey?

Ⓕ On a day chosen at random, the principal asks the counselor to provide a list of student ID numbers and selects every tenth person on the list. He finds each student between classes to ask if they like the cafeteria food.

Ⓖ On a day chosen at random, the principal goes to the cafeteria and asks the first 50 students who enter the cafeteria if they like the cafeteria food.

Ⓗ On a day chosen at random, the principal walks through the cafeteria and asks students who brought their own lunch if they like the cafeteria food.

Ⓙ On a day chosen at random, the principal walks through the cafeteria and asks students eating the cafeteria meal if they like the cafeteria food.

3 Billy wants to determine how many of the students in his eighth-grade class like to play video games. He stands in front of the school and watches as the students enter the school. When he sees an eighth grader whose name he knows, he asks if he/she likes to play video games. Is Billy's sample a good representation of the population?

Ⓐ No, because Billy does not determine the grade of the students

Ⓑ Yes, because Billy surveys everyone in the eighth grade

Ⓒ No, because Billy only surveys students he knows by name

Ⓓ Yes, because he asks his survey question to eighth-grade students

1 The coaches of a school football team want to know how many families from the school plan to attend this week's game. Each coach takes a different approach to obtain this information. Which sampling method would provide a good representation of the population?

Ⓐ Call all the parents of the football players to ask if their families will attend the game.

Ⓑ Stop every fifth car that enters the school parking lot one morning to ask if their families will attend the game.

Ⓒ Ask all the students in the last period PE class if their families will attend the game.

Ⓓ Choose every fourth student from an alphabetical list of the entire student body and ask if their families will attend the game.

2 Last week Carlos surveyed customers leaving Mega Food. Of the 500 people surveyed, 447 said that Mega Food was their favorite grocery store. From these survey results, Carlos concluded that Mega Food was the favorite grocery store among all the people in his town. Which is the best explanation for why his conclusion might not be valid?

Ⓕ The sample may not have been representative of all the people in Carlos' town.

Ⓖ Carlos asked every customer coming out of the store rather than asking every fifth customer who left the store.

Ⓗ The survey Carlos used did not ask how old the customers were.

Ⓙ The sample size was too small due to the population of the town being small.

3 The administration of AT&T Stadium would like to determine which snack food is most preferred at football games held in the stadium. For a select game, a computer program is used to generate a list of 200 seat numbers. The purchasers of the tickets for those seats are contacted and asked about their favorite snack food. Is the sample a good representation of the population?

Ⓐ Yes, because the sample contains 200 people

Ⓑ Yes, because the sample is random and representative of the people who attend football games at AT&T Stadium

Ⓒ No, because the sample is not randomly selected

Ⓓ No, because the sample is not representative of all people who attend football games at AT&T Stadium

4 The city council plans to conduct a survey and use the results to improve city services. The council wants to select citizens at random to participate in the survey. Which sampling method will NOT produce results representative of the population?

Ⓕ Obtain a list of customer names from the water department and survey each member of every tenth household over the age of 18.

Ⓖ Survey every person who attends a city council meeting each month for six months.

Ⓗ Survey each member of households with even house numbers.

Ⓙ Use a computer program to generate a list of addresses.

1 The student council event committee is planning an international food event for the school and would like to feature foods from other countries that might interest students. The committee decides to conduct a survey of students to determine which countries to feature. They interview several students in the cafeteria during lunch and all the students from the Spanish club. Which of the following statements is true?

Ⓐ The survey results are unbiased because the committee surveyed students in the cafeteria and from the Spanish club.

Ⓑ The survey results are unbiased because the Spanish club is the largest foreign language club in the school.

Ⓒ The survey results are biased because they did not interview the teachers of the students.

Ⓓ The survey results are biased because the sample did not represent all students in the school.

2 A survey is conducted to find the most popular sport among eighth-grade students at Ellis Junior High. Which of the following methods would provide a sample that would best represent the population?

Ⓕ Select every fourth student from an alphabetical list of all eighth-grade students.

Ⓖ Select every teacher and parent of an eighth-grade student.

Ⓗ Select every fourth student from an alphabetical list of all eighth-grade girls.

Ⓙ Select every eighth-grade student that has been on an athletic team at Ellis Junior High.

3 The headmaster at a private school wants to update the student dress code. He wishes to survey a select group of parents of the students enrolled at the school to determine their opinion on the addition of a blazer to the school uniform. Which method can be used to ensure an unbiased sample is obtained for the survey?

Ⓐ All parents attending the next PTO meeting are surveyed.

Ⓑ Every fifth person on a list of parent volunteers is surveyed.

Ⓒ All parents waiting in the pick-up line after school are surveyed.

Ⓓ All parents of students whose birthday is an even numbered day are surveyed.

4 The dean of the math department at a local university plans the fall schedule. She needs to know how many 8 A.M. classes to schedule for the fall semester. She obtains a list of students living on campus from the housing department. The list is numbered and a random number generator is used to generate 200 student names to survey about their preference for early morning classes. Are the survey results representative of the population?

Ⓕ No, more than 200 students will have an 8 A.M. class during the fall semester.

Ⓖ Yes, a random number generator is used to determine the students surveyed.

Ⓗ No, only students living on campus are included in the survey.

Ⓙ Yes, all students living on campus are included in the population.

1   A researcher for a cell phone manufacturer's product development division conducts a survey to determine interest in a new cell phone that will be marketed for teens. One idea the division is considering is to make the phone available with different features, one that appeals to teenage girls and another that appeals to teenage boys. The researcher begins by surveying 500 students, 250 girls and 250 boys, from each of 10 high schools located in the test market area. Some of the results of the survey are shown in the table.

	Own a Cell Phone		Gender-based Cell Phone	
	Yes	No	Yes	No
Boys	2,026	474	1,872	628
Girls	1,982	518	1,913	587

Based on the data in the table, did the researcher use an unbiased method to select students to participate in the survey? Justify your response.

_____

_____

_____

2   Describe a simulation that can be used to generate a random sample of 300 middle school students to be surveyed about a new after-school activity. Explain how you know the simulation will guarantee an unbiased sample that is representative of the whole student body.

_____

_____

_____

_____

_____

Journal

Analysis

Analyze

Wildlife biologists in Texas estimate the number of white-tailed deer each year in order to maintain an appropriate buck-to-doe ratio. Wildlife biologists capture a set number of deer, tag one ear of each deer with a unique number, and then release the deer. The following year, the biologists capture the same number of deer and use the ratio of tagged deer to the total number captured to estimate the number of deer in the area. Explain why this method does or does not result in a sample that is both random and representative of the population in the area.

_____

_____

_____

Vocabulary Activity

Describe each vocabulary term and provide an example.

Population

Random Sample

Sample Results

Biased	Unbiased

Does It or Does It Not?

Complete *Does It or Does It Not?* individually. For each of the following, a population being studied is described as well as a method of sampling the population to obtain a random sample to be surveyed. Sort each into the categories *Representative* if the sample is a good representation of the entire population or *Not Representative* if the sample is not a good representation of the entire population. Record the letter for each response in the appropriate box.

a. Population: Residents of a town
    Sampling Method: 500 people are chosen from all shoppers at a mall over a three-day
    period

b. Population: Students at a middle school
    Sampling Method: 200 students are chosen from a numbered list of student ID numbers
    using a random number generator

c. Population: Largemouth bass in one Texas lake
    Sampling Method: The lake is divided into four zones and 50 fish are caught in each zone

d. Population: Adults over the age of 50 with high blood pressure
    Sampling Method: All adults using a blood pressure machine at a supermarket in one week

e. Population: All athletes attending a local university
    Sampling Method: All students working out in the school's weight room and gym

f. Population: A box containing three different colors of marbles
    Sampling Method: A marble is selected from the box without looking

g. Population: Credit card holders from five upscale department stores
    Sampling Method: A computer program generates a list of 700 cardholder names

h. Population: People that own at least one cat and one dog
    Sampling Method: 350 customers purchasing cat food at a local pet store

Representative	Not Representative

Unit 34 Homework

1 An airport considers installing more phone and computer charging stations around waiting areas and restaurant areas. A survey is conducted of 500 travelers who are all under the age of 12 inside the airport. Would the results of the survey be useful for making a decision about installing additional charging stations? Explain your answer.

2 Genna plans to survey students in the eighth grade to determine how many hours of sleep they get each night. Describe a method Genna could use to generate a random sample that would represent the population.

3 Before Craig and Jennifer open their bakery, they decide to conduct a survey in the town they are considering as the location for the bakery. They select every twentieth resident of the town from the phone book to participate in the survey. Will this method of selecting a sample be representative of the population? Explain your answer.

4 The school newspaper wants to print an article about the favorite pastime of students at the school. Reporters survey thirty students at a skateboard park. Will the survey yield unbiased results that are representative of the population? Explain your answer.

5 Student DJs for a school radio station want to determine which type of music the eighth-grade students prefer in order to plan their programming. Describe two different methods the DJs could use to conduct a survey that would give a representative sample of the population without bias.

Connections

Create and design a survey to conduct at your school. Describe a method for selecting a random sample of students at the school that will provide valid results. Conduct the survey using at least 50 students and organize the results. Present your findings on a poster or in a multimedia presentation to the class.

motivation**math**™
Financial Literacy

Unit 35:   Standards 8.12(A) – Supporting, 8.12(B), 8.12(E)

Unit 36:   Standards 8.12(C) – Supporting, 8.12(D) – Readiness

Unit 37:   Standard 8.12(F)

Unit 38:   Standard 8.12(G) – Supporting

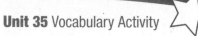

The following terms and phrases will be used throughout this unit.

annual percentage rate (APR)	interest rate	principal
balance	lender	refinance
credit card	loan	repayment
credit limit	loan term	service charge (fee)
debit card	minimum payment	stored-value card
debt	payoff	withdrawal
easy access loan (payday or title loan)		

Four-in-a-Row

Play *Four-in-a-Row* with a partner. Player 1 begins by choosing a term and giving the definition. Player 2 verifies the definition using the glossary. If correct, player 1 initials the space containing the term. The players then switch roles and continue with the next term chosen by player 2. The first player to initial four spaces in a row horizontally, vertically, or diagonally is the winner.

lender	stored-value card	loan term	debt
repayment	credit limit	easy access loan (payday or title loan)	minimum payment
refinance	withdrawal	annual percentage rate (APR)	loan
interest rate	principal	credit card	debit card

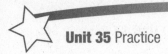

Mr. and Mrs. Barnes decide to apply for a home improvement loan to renovate the kitchen and main bathroom of their home. The amount required to complete the remodeling work of the home is $25,000. Mr. and Mrs. Barnes receive offers from four lenders. The loan options are detailed in the table.

Lender	Loan Details	Minimum Payment	Total Cost of Loan	Total Interest Paid
Best Loans Today	Loan Term: 10 years Interest Rate: 6.9%			
EZ Loans	Loan Term: 10 years Interest Rate: 5.9%			
Low Rate Loans	Loan Term: 15 years Interest Rate: 6.9%			
Time-4-Loan	Loan Term: 15 years Interest Rate: 5.9%			

1 For each option, use the free loan calculator at www.bankrate.com/calculators/managing-debt/loan-calculator.aspx to determine the minimum payment. Also, calculate the total cost of the loan and total interest paid over the loan term. Complete the table using the calculated values.

2 What is the difference between the cost of the loan from Best Loans Today and the cost of the loan from EZ Loans? What accounts for this difference?

3 What is the difference between the cost of the loan from Best Loans Today and the cost of the loan from Low Rate Loans? What accounts for this difference?

4 Which loan offer should Mr. and Mrs. Barnes choose? Explain your answer.

_____

_____

_____

Austin needs to buy tires for his truck but has not budgeted money for the purchase. He needs $650 to cover all costs associated with purchasing a new set of tires. Different methods of paying for the tires are shown in the table.

Debit Card	Stored-value Card
Account Balance: $655.00 Service Charge: • $5.00 per month unless minimum balance of $250.00 maintained Advantages of a debit card: Disadvantages of a debit card:	Stored-value Card Balance: $660.00 Service Charges: • Monthly Activation Fee: $4.95 • Transaction Fee: $2.00 per purchase Advantages of a stored-value card: Disadvantages of a stored-value card:
Credit Card	**Easy Access Loan**
Beginning Credit Card Balance: $0.00 Credit Limit: $750.00 APR: 19.9% Advantages of a credit card: Disadvantages of a credit card:	<u>Loan Details</u> Loan Amount: $750.00 Loan Term: 2 weeks Loan Fees: $131.25 Advantages of an easy access loan: Disadvantages of an easy access loan:

1 For each method of payment, record the advantages and disadvantages of using the method to pay for a large purchase, such as tires, in the spaces provided.

2 Use the online calculator at
www.bankrate.com/calculators/credit-cards/credit-card-minimum-payment.aspx
to calculate the amount of Austin's monthly credit card payment if he pays 5% of his balance each month.

How many months will Austin need to pay off his credit card making only the minimum payment calculated?

How much total interest will he pay on the tire purchase?

3 What is the total amount Austin will repay if he chooses an easy access loan and pays the loan in full at the end of the loan term?

What is the APR for the easy access loan? (loan fees ÷ loan amount • 365 ÷ loan term (in days) • 100)

4 Based on all of the information, which payment method should Austin use to purchase his truck tires? Justify your answer.

Use the information to answer questions 1–3.

Darius wants to buy a new car. The car he chooses has a total purchase price of $18,500. Darius uses a multi-offer website to apply for a car loan. He receives three offers with minimum payments he can afford. The terms for each loan are shown in the table.

Option	APR	Loan Term (months)	Minimum Payment
A	2.99%	60	$332.34
B	3.99%	36	$546.11
C	1.99%	48	$401.28

1 How much interest will Darius pay over the entire loan term if he chooses loan option B?

Ⓐ $1,440.40

Ⓑ $678.96

Ⓒ $761.44

Ⓓ $1,159.96

2 What is the total cost difference between loan options A and C?

Ⓕ $3,309.12

Ⓖ $678.96

Ⓗ $4,136.40

Ⓙ $2,481.84

3 Which loan option allows Darius to purchase his new car at the lowest overall cost?

Ⓐ Option A

Ⓑ Option B

Ⓒ Option C

Ⓓ Both options A and C are the same cost.

Use the information to answer questions 4–7.

Linda has an accident and accumulates $1,200 in medical bills. She reviews her options for paying off the bills.

Credit Card	APR: 18.99% Minimum payment: $40
Car Title Loan	Loan term: 30 days Loan fees: $389.97

4 Using the website www.bankrate.com/ calculators/credit-cards/credit-card-payoff-calculator.aspx, how many months will it take Linda to pay off the debt using her credit card and making minimum monthly payments?

Ⓕ 30 months   Ⓗ 41 months

Ⓖ 36 months   Ⓙ 48 months

5 Making the minimum monthly payments, what is the total amount Linda will repay using her credit card?

Ⓐ $1,200   Ⓒ $1,440

Ⓑ $1,640   Ⓓ $1,920

6 What is the APR charged on the car title loan? (fees ÷ loan amount • 365 ÷ term • 100)

Ⓕ 0.0395%   Ⓗ 6.63%

Ⓖ 529.99%   Ⓙ 395.39%

7 If Linda plans to repay her medical debt in one year, which method should she use?

Ⓐ A car title loan because she will pay less overall for the loan

Ⓑ A credit card because the car title loan charges loan fees every 30 days

Ⓒ A car title loan because she can still drive her car while she repays the loan

Ⓓ A credit card because she earns points when she uses the card

Wheel of Choices

Play *Wheel of Choices* with a partner. Each pair of players needs a game board, a paper clip to use with the spinner, and a computer with internet access. Each player needs a sheet of paper and a pencil. Player 1 spins the spinner. Using the online calculator found at www.bankrate.com/calculators/managing-debt/loan-calculator.aspx, player 1 works the problem on his/her paper. Player 1 announces his/her answer. If correct, player 1 writes the answer inside the space, and initials the space along the outside edge. If incorrect, player 1 loses a turn. Player 2 spins the spinner and repeats the process. If the spinner lands on a space that is already initialed, the player moves clockwise to the next open space and solves the problem. The game ends when all spaces have initials. The player with more initialed spaces is the winner.

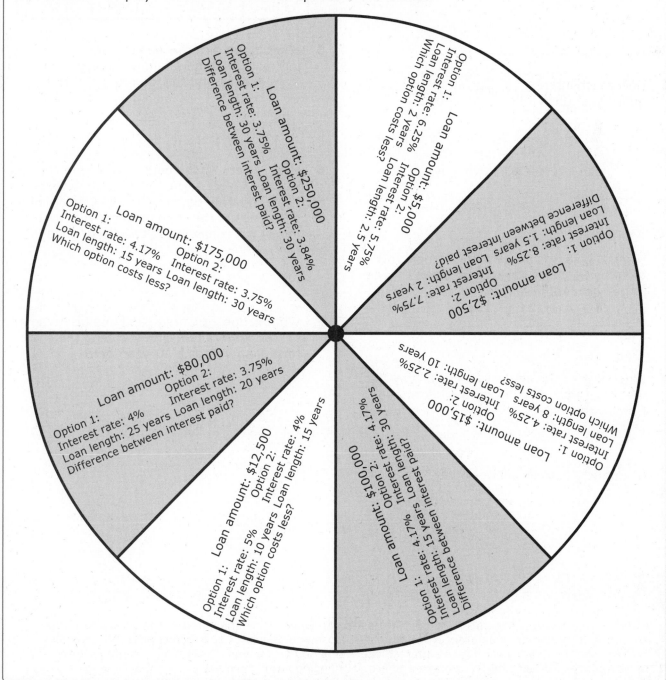

Use the information to answer questions 1–4.

Kevin uses his credit card regularly and has accumulated a balance of $2,500. He pays an APR of 23.9% on the balance.

1 Using the credit card payoff calculator, calculate the number of months Kevin will need to pay off his debt if he does not make any additional charges on the card and only pays the minimum monthly payment of $50. www.bankrate.com/calculators/credit-cards/credit-card-payoff-calculator.aspx

2 What is the total amount Kevin will pay the credit card company using the information from problem 1?

How much interest will Kevin pay?

3 Using the same calculator, determine the monthly payment Kevin must make in order to pay his debt in full in 3 years.

4 What is the total amount Kevin will pay the credit card company using the information from problem 3?

How much interest will Kevin pay?

Use the information to answer questions 5–7.

The Rogers family purchases a new vacation home for $175,000. Before making the purchase, Mr. Rogers researches various loan options.

Bank	Loan Length	Interest Rate	Monthly Payment
Harring	30 years	3.75%	$648
eLoans	30 years	3.99%	$668
Tebonic	30 years	4.125%	$689

5 What is the difference in the amount of interest the Rogers family will pay on the loan from eLoans and the loan from Tebonic?

6 Mrs. Rogers finds another loan from Harring with a 15-year term and 3.75% interest rate. If the monthly payment is $993, what is the difference in the total amounts the Rogers family will repay in the two Harring loans?

7 What is one advantage and one disadvantage for the Rogers family in choosing the shorter term loan versus a 30-year loan?

Connections

Visit the website www.bankrate.com/calculators.aspx and investigate the different calculators available to calculate repayment of different types of debt. Choose one calculator and record different scenarios for repaying the debt by varying the interest rate and period of the loan. Determine advantages and disadvantages for using this type of loan. Share your findings with the class.

The following terms and phrases will be used throughout this unit.

accrue	interest rate	principal
certificate of deposit (CD)	maturity	savings account
compound interest	money market account	simple interest
interest		

Use the graphics to complete the steps 1–6.

Advantage Bank and Trust

Savings Account #967218   Cindy Linn

Account Activity

Balance 01/02/13 . . . . $1,500.00

Interest earned $67.50

Withdrawals $0.00

Balance 01/02/15 . . . . $1,567.50

Interest Overview

Simple

Annual percentage rate. 2.25%

Interest deposit $67.50

Advantage Bank and Trust

Money Market Account #3081948   Cindy Linn

Account Activity

Balance 01/02/13 . . . . $5,000.00

Interest earned $356.13

Withdrawals $0.00

Balance 01/02/15 . . . . $5,356.13

Interest Overview

Compounded Annually

Annual percentage rate. 3.5%

Interest deposit $356.13

1   Draw an oval around the *principal* for each account.

2   Draw a star next to the account that earns *compound interest*.

3   Draw a lightning bolt next to the account that earns *simple interest*.

4   Draw a heart around the *interest rate* for each account.

5   Draw a rectangle around the *interest* earned.

6   Underline the type of account in each statement.

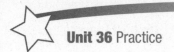
Steven is 25 years old when he starts saving money for retirement. Steven opens an account with an initial deposit of $5,000. The bank offers several retirement savings options.

Retirement Savings Options

Account Type	Basic Savings Account	Premium Savings Account	CD	Money Market Savings Account
Minimum Account Balance	$0	$500	$1,000	$5,000
Interest Rate	0.85%	2.00%	2.00%	1.50%
Interest Type	Simple	Compounded annually	Simple	Compounded annually

1 How much interest would Steven earn at the end of 5 years with each savings account?

Basic Savings Account:

Premium Savings Account:

CD:

Money Market Savings Account:

2 Which savings account should Steven choose to earn the greatest amount of interest over the next 5 years? Justify your response.

3 Steven earns a $2,500 bonus at work. He invests the money in a CD that earns 1.25% annually. Assuming the interest is compounded each year and Steven reinvests the interest rather than withdrawing it, complete the chart to show the amount Steven earns for the first 4 years the money is invested.

	Principal	Interest Earned	Account Balance
Year 1	$2,500		
Year 2			
Year 3			
Year 4			

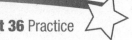
4 If Steven begins adding an additional $500 each year to the CD at the beginning of the fifth year, how much will the investment be worth after an additional four years? Assume the interest is calculated at the end of each year.

	Principal	Contribution	Interest Earned	Account Balance
Year 5				
Year 6				
Year 7				
Year 8				

5 Steven wants to teach his younger brother, who is 8 years old, about the importance of saving for things he wants in the future such as a car or going to college. Answer the following questions Steven's brother asks about saving money.

I only have $20 right now. Shouldn't I wait until I have a lot more money to start saving?

Doesn't my money just sit in an account until I take it out? How does that help me pay for college or buy a car when I get older?

What type of account should I put my money in? Which type of account earns the most money over time?

6 Steven's brother decides to invest his $20 in either a money market savings account or a CD. The savings account earns interest at a rate of 1.8% compounded annually. The CD has a maturity date of 10 years, meaning the money cannot be removed from the account without a penalty for 10 years. The CD earns 2.9% simple interest. What is the difference in the amount of the interest earnings between the two accounts after 10 years?

7 If Steven decides to add money to his account from his allowance each month, what effect will the additional savings have on his long-term savings goals?

1 LaTonya opens two savings accounts with an initial deposit of $100 in each. The graph shows the anticipated growth of each savings account over a 20-year period.

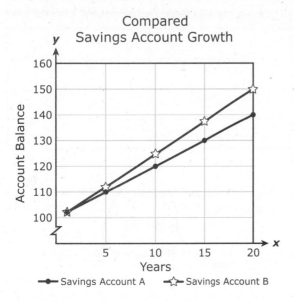

Compared Savings Account Growth

Assuming both accounts earn interest at the same rate, which statement best explains the difference in the account balances?

Ⓐ Savings account A earns interest that is compounded annually, while savings account B accrues simple interest.

Ⓑ Savings account A accrues simple interest, while savings account B earns interest that is compounded annually.

Ⓒ Both savings account A and savings account B earn simple interest, but savings account B has more money added to the account.

Ⓓ Not enough information is provided about the interest being earned on the two accounts to determine the difference.

2 Demitri's parents begin saving for his college fund when Demitri is 10 years old. They invest $5,000 in a CD that earns 1.2% interest compounded annually. When Demitri turns 18, he decides to attend a local community college for two years. One year of courses at the community college costs approximately $2,700. Is there enough money available from the CD to pay for the first two years of Demitri's college education?

Ⓕ Yes, the CD earns compound interest so the investment is more than double after 5 years.

Ⓖ No, the CD earns compound interest so the investment is charged a monthly fee and loses money over 8 years.

Ⓗ Yes, the CD earns over $500 in interest over 8 years.

Ⓙ No, the CD earns $480 in interest over 8 years.

3 Allen opens a retirement savings account with an initial deposit of $5,000. He makes annual contributions to the account, and at the end of 5 years the account has grown to $8,650.

Beginning Balance	Contributions	Interest Earned	Ending Balance
$0	$5,000		
	$500		
	$500		
	$500		
	$500		$8,650

Which best describes Allen's investment?

Ⓐ Allen invests in a retirement savings account that earns 5.5% interest compounded annually.

Ⓑ Allen invests in a retirement savings account that earns 3% simple interest.

Ⓒ Allen invests in a retirement savings account that earns 2.75% interest compounded annually.

Ⓓ Allen invests in a retirement savings account that earns 5.5% simple interest.

Grab Bag

Play *Grab Bag* with a partner. Each pair of players needs a game board and two six-sided number cubes of different colors. Each player needs a different colored pencil, a sheet of paper, and a pencil. The players designate one color number cube for the simple interest problems and the second color number cube for the compound interest problems. Player 1 rolls both number cubes and solves the problems corresponding to the numbers rolled. Player 1 finds the difference in the amount of interest earned in both problems. If correct, player 1 shades the money bag with the difference in his/her color. If incorrect, player 1 loses a turn, and play passes to player 2. If a player rolls a number associated with *Player's Choice*, he/she may select any problem in the same column to solve. The game ends when all of the money bags are colored. The player with more money bags colored in his/her color is the winner.

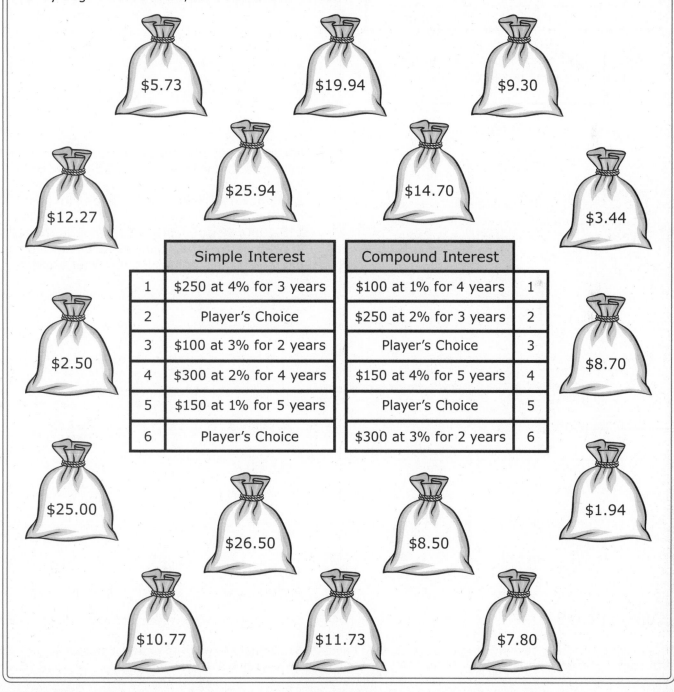

	Simple Interest	Compound Interest	
1	$250 at 4% for 3 years	$100 at 1% for 4 years	1
2	Player's Choice	$250 at 2% for 3 years	2
3	$100 at 3% for 2 years	Player's Choice	3
4	$300 at 2% for 4 years	$150 at 4% for 5 years	4
5	$150 at 1% for 5 years	Player's Choice	5
6	Player's Choice	$300 at 3% for 2 years	6

Money bags: $5.73, $19.94, $9.30, $12.27, $25.94, $14.70, $3.44, $2.50, $8.70, $25.00, $26.50, $8.50, $1.94, $10.77, $11.73, $7.80

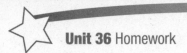

Use the information to answer questions 1–4.

Lochlan works nights and weekends at a local grocery store. Over the past several years, he has saved $3,000. Lochlan would like to invest the money so he can buy a house in 20 years. The table shows two different investment options at Lochlan's bank.

CD	Money Market Account
1.75% annual simple interest	1.85% annual compound interest
$1,500 minimum	$3,500 minimum

1 Which type of account can Lochlan open with the money he has saved? Explain your answer.

2 The CD has a maturity date of 2 years. How much will Lochlan's investment be worth after 2 years?

3 After 10 years, Lochlan transfers his investment into a money market account. The account now earns compounded interest of 1.95% annually with a maturity date of 5 years. How much will Lochlan's investment be worth after 5 years in the new account?

4 Lochlan keeps his money in the money market account for a total of 10 years. He is now ready to purchase a home. He needs a 3% down payment for the house he has chosen. The purchase price of the house is $162,000. Does Lochlan have enough money in his investment account to cover the down payment on his home? Explain your answer.

Connections

Research historical data about interest rates, today and 1985. Compare the growth of a $1,000 savings account at these interests over a 5- and 10-year period. Share your findings with the class.

       motivation**math**™LEVEL 8   mentoring**minds**.com

The following terms and phrases will be used throughout this unit.

benefit	expense	income
budget	financial irresponsibility	need
cost	financial responsibility	want
credit card		

Use the clues to complete the crossword puzzle.

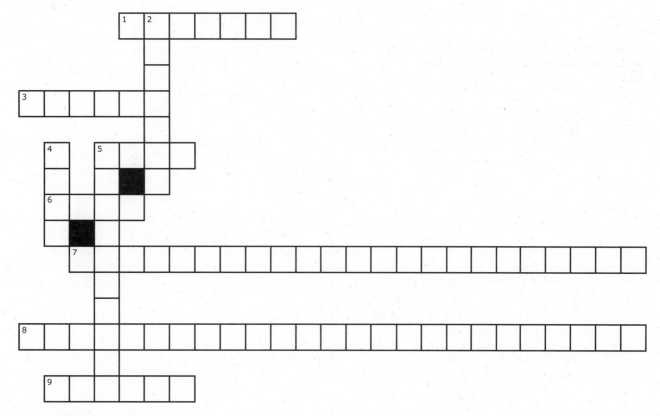

Across
1. an advantage
3. the amount of money received in a particular time (weekly, monthly, yearly) in exchange for work
5. the price or amount paid for something
6. an item that is necessary for life, including food, clothing, water, and shelter
7. the act of managing money in a way that is considered in the best interests of the individual or family
8. the failure to meet one's financial responsibilities
9. a plan for how much money is spent and saved based on income and goals

Down
2. an amount of money used to buy goods or services
4. an item that a person would like to have but is not necessary for survival
5. a card, issued by a bank, store, or other business, that is used to borrow money or buy goods and services on credit

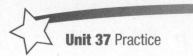
For each scenario described, identify the decisions that are financially responsible and those that are not. Then discuss the benefits or costs associated with each decision.

Scenario	Responsible/Not Responsible Benefits/Costs
1. Cecilia is offered two concert tickets to see her favorite band. The tickets cost $85 each. Cecilia has budgeted $50 for entertainment. She has a credit card with a balance close to her credit limit. Cecilia really wants to see the band, so she pays for the balance of the tickets with her credit card.	
2. Rebekah is paid weekly from her job at a retail clothing store. She has scheduled her bank to automatically transfer $20 each week from her checking account to her savings account.	
3. The Dyson family wants to purchase a larger home. They have enough money in savings for a down payment on a home costing no more than $225,000. After searching for several weeks, the family finds their dream home, costing $250,000. The family waits to purchase the home and begins saving additional money for the down payment.	
4. Andrew sees an ad online for a new cell phone. The phone has several features his current phone does not have and costs $450. Andrew has not had any issues with his current cell phone and does not have any money in his budget for a new cell phone. He takes out a payday loan for $500 to purchase the new phone.	

Use the information to answer questions 1 and 2.

The Shirley family is a one-income family with two children that both attend elementary school. The family budget is shown for the month of May.

Family Budget: May

Income	
Monthly Net Income	$4,520.00
Monthly Expenses	
Savings	$200.00
Mortgage, including insurance	$1,175.00
Utilities: electric, water, internet, cable	$450.00
Car 1	$217.93
Car 2	$378.15
Car insurance	$115.60
Health insurance	$545.00
Other Insurance: dental and life insurance	$89.25
Car expenses: gas, oil, tires, maintenance	$250.00
Cellular service	$160.00
Food	$325.00
Credit card	$275.00
Clothing	$120.00
Miscellaneous expenses	$150.00
Total Monthly Expenses	$4,450.93

1 List at least two items in the Shirley family budget that reflect financially responsible decision making.

2 Identify each of the following actions taken by the Shirley family as being financially responsible or financially irresponsible.

Mr. Shirley calls the cell phone company and negotiates a lower family plan rate for their service.

Mrs. Shirley purchases the entire family new clothes for an upcoming family outing using the credit card.

Mrs. Shirley transfers an extra $25 left over at the end of the month from the money budgeted for food into the family's savings account.

Mr. Shirley gets a raise at his job. He divides the extra income between savings and paying down the credit card debt.

1 Which of the following represents financially responsible actions?

    I. Spending within your means

   II. Paying minimum credit card payments each month

  III. Paying yourself first

  IV. Spending money according to budget

Ⓐ I and IV only

Ⓑ I, III, and IV only

Ⓒ II and III only

Ⓓ IV only

2 Dakota asks Taylor to go to a professional tennis match. The trip costs approximately $2,000. Taylor has $1,500 in the bank, but Dakota wants him to use a credit card for the remaining $500. Taylor agrees to use a credit card to pay. Which is a possible cost for his financial irresponsibility?

Ⓕ Taylor depletes his emergency fund for unexpected expenses.

Ⓖ Taylor pays finance charges each month the credit card balance is not paid in full.

Ⓗ Taylor is unable to pay one of his bills after the trip.

Ⓙ All of the above

3 Jeff has $8,000 in his savings account. He is purchasing a car for $15,000. He plans to use the money in the savings account as a down payment and finance the remaining $7,000. Jeff can only afford a monthly payment of $175. The car dealership has two payment options to meet this amount. Option A has a monthly payment of $156.96 for 60 months. Option B has a monthly payment of $166.00 for 48 months. Which payment option should Jeff choose?

Ⓐ Option A because Jeff saves $18.04 per month

Ⓑ Option A because Jeff makes smaller payments over 60 months

Ⓒ Option B because Jeff pays only $968.00 in interest

Ⓓ Either option because there is no difference in the total amount

4 Lindsey is denied a home loan to buy her first house. The mortgage company says that her credit score is too low. Which decision is financially responsible and will increase her credit score over time?

Ⓕ Apply for another credit card to consolidate all of her debt onto one credit card.

Ⓖ Make a budget to reduce spending and apply savings to payments on debt each month.

Ⓗ Find a new mortgage company and reapply for the home loan.

Ⓙ Take out another loan to reduce payments on current debt.

Money Choices

Play *Money Choices* with a partner. Each pair of players needs a game board, a number cube, and two different game tokens. Each player needs a sheet of paper and a pencil. Each player has a $200 bank account balance to begin the game. Player 1 begins by rolling the number cube and moving his/her game token the indicated number of spaces. Player 1 reads the situation and decides whether it represents a responsible financial decision or not. If it does, player 1 adds the indicated money amount to his/her balance. If not, the money is deducted from the balance. Play passes to player 2. Each player moves around the game board to the finish space. The player with more money in his/her bank account at the finish wins the game.

Stop using credit card. $5	Use coupons to buy groceries. $10	Apply for another credit card. $50		FINISH	START
Consolidate debt to pay off faster. $20		Use debit card to buy shoes. $5		Eat dinner at home. $30	Use credit card to buy lunch. $10
Forget to pay water bill. $25		Skip utility payment. $75		Stay home and watch movie on TV. $10	Use coupon for 25% off. $25
Earn a degree and increase salary. Move forward.			Use savings to buy a TV. $100	Take out a payday loan. Move back.	Fail to make minimum payment. Lose a turn.
Pay self first each month. $25					Save $50 each month. $50
					Make a late house payment. $25
Spend more than budgeted. $75					Pay off car loan early. $50
Buy game with a gift card. $10	Save $100 by using old cell phone. Move forward.	Buy groceries in sale ad. $5	Buy clothes at full price. $20	Share rent with a friend. $25	Overdrawn bank account. $40

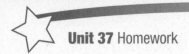

For each scenario described, identify the decisions that are financially responsible and those that are not. Then discuss the benefits or costs associated with each decision.

Scenario	Responsible/Not Responsible Benefits/Costs
1. Shea has a budget of $40 to buy groceries and a list of things to purchase. Shea has everything on the list in her basket but sees a magazine that has her favorite actress on the cover. She does not have enough money to purchase the magazine and the groceries on her list. She considers removing an item from her basket but puts the magazine back instead.	
2. Carter uses his credit card frequently to make everyday purchases. He has accumulated debt of $785 on his card. Carter does not use his card again for six months while he makes regular payments on the balance.	
3. Patrick is looking for his first apartment to rent. He has a budget of $475 per month for rent. Patrick finds a one-bedroom apartment in a neighborhood he really likes for $525 per month. He also finds a two-bedroom apartment in the same neighborhood for $800. His best friend is also looking for a place to rent. Patrick decides to rent the one-bedroom apartment.	
4. Karla loves to wear the latest fashion trends. She budgets $75 each month for clothing and accessories. She also budgets $50 each month for savings. During the last six months, Karla has spent $125 each month shopping. She has not saved any money during the six months.	

Connections

Create a spending plan for an item that you are interested in purchasing. Display the purchase price of the item, describe how money for the purchase will be earned, and demonstrate ways the purchase can show financial responsibility. Share your spending plan with the class.

The following terms and phrases will be used throughout this unit.

associate's degree	Federal Application for Student Aid (FAFSA)	salary
bachelor's degree	financial aid	scholarship
certification	grant	semester
cost	income	tuition
doctoral degree	master's degree	work-study
estimate	occupation	

Complete the activity with a partner. Each pair needs one six-sided number cube. Each student needs a sheet of paper and a pencil. Take turns rolling the number cube, choose a vocabulary term, and follow the directions that match the number rolled.

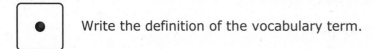

Write the definition of the vocabulary term.

Give one real-world example and one non-example for the vocabulary term.

Give a synonym and antonym for the vocabulary term.

Sketch the vocabulary term and have your partner guess the term.

Act out the vocabulary term and have your partner guess the term.

Choose two vocabulary terms and describe how the terms are related.

Unit 38 Practice

Use the information to answer questions 1–6.

Trevor wants to attend college and pursue a degree in information systems. He answers an online survey to help determine college costs at his preferred colleges. Use the information provided to complete the online survey for Trevor at www.collegeforalltexans.com/apps/CollegeMoney/.

- Preferred Colleges:
    - 1 – University of North Texas (4-year college)
    - 2 – Eastfield College (2-year college, in-district tuition)
    - 3 – The University of Texas at Dallas (4-year college)
- Trevor will live at home while attending all of these colleges.
- Trevor is 17 years old, single, and has no dependents.
- Trevor is a U.S. citizen and resident of Texas.
- Trevor lives in a single-parent household.
- Trevor's parent had an income of $35,000 in the previous year and paid $4,500 in income tax.
- Trevor did not have a job during the previous year.
- Trevor lives at home with his 2 younger sisters.

Use the survey results to complete the table.

College	University of North Texas	Eastfield College	The University of Texas at Dallas
Where will Trevor live?			
Tuition and Fees			
Books			
Room and Board*			
Other Expenses			

* Room and Board is calculated for both on-campus and off-campus living situations.

1 Based on the estimates provided in the survey, what is the total cost for each university?

University of North Texas:

Eastfield College:

The University of Texas at Dallas:

2 How much money will Trevor save by attending Eastfield College for 2 years and then transferring to the University of North Texas compared to attending the University of North Texas for all 4 years?

Trevor talks with his family about his choices for college. They discuss the advantages and disadvantages of living at home while attending college and attending a two-year school to complete basic courses then transferring to a four-year university to complete his major. Also, they discuss how Trevor will pay for college.

3 Trevor begins a part-time job working 25 hours per week and earns $7.50 per hour. His total expenses, taxes, and transportation to and from work are $75 per week. He will work for 67 weeks before starting college. Assuming he does not spend any additional money, how much will Trevor have saved towards college expenses during this time period?

4 What is the difference in the cost of the first year for each school and the amount Trevor will have saved in his college fund?

List at least 2 ways Trevor could make up the shortfall, if necessary, to pay for the first year of college.

Trevor files a FAFSA (Free Application for Federal Student Aid) application. The application determines he qualifies for federal student aid. Trevor qualifies for $5,845 of federal student aid that does not require repayment. The aid includes $4,380 in a Federal Pell Grant and $1,465 in work-study assistance.

5 How does the federal student aid change the amount of money required for Trevor's first year of college at each school?

University of North Texas:

Eastfield College:

The University of Texas at Dallas:

6 What is the total cost, after financial aid and family contribution, for Trevor to attend school in each of the following situations?

University of North Texas (4 years):

Eastfield College (2 years) + University of North Texas (2 years):

The University of Texas at Dallas (4 years):

Eastfield College (2 years) + The University of Texas at Dallas (2 years):

Use the information to answer questions 1–5.

Denisha compares the tuition costs for a two-year community college and a public four-year university. The community college allows students to stay at home or live off campus, while the four-year university requires students to live on campus for the first two years.

	Two-year Community College		Four-year Public University	
	At home	Off campus	On campus	Off campus
Tuition and fees	In-district: $83 per semester hour Out-of-district: $262 per semester hour		$4,832 per semester	
Books and other expenses	$4,462 per year	$5,789 per year	$9,521 per year	$10,848 per year

1 Denisha wants to attend the public four-year university. She wants to live on campus for two years and then move off campus. If Denisha completes her bachelor's degree in 4 years plus 1 semester, how much will the degree cost?

Ⓐ $86,332.50

Ⓑ $89,650

Ⓒ $135,812

Ⓓ $67,906

2 Denisha's family convinces her that attending the community college will save money her first 2 years. If she takes 15 hours each semester and pays the out-of-district tuition rate, will Denisha save money on tuition and fees compared to attending the public university for all four years?

Ⓕ No, it costs $902 more per semester.

Ⓖ Yes, it costs $902 less per semester.

Ⓗ No, it costs $3,587 more per semester.

Ⓙ Yes, it costs $3,587 less per semester.

3 Denisha's parents deposited $2,500 into a college savings account when she was born. The account has accrued interest at a rate of 5% compounded annually. If the investment matures when Denisha turns 18, how much money will she have in her college savings account?

Ⓐ $2,725.00

Ⓑ $2,734.82

Ⓒ $4,750.00

Ⓓ $6,016.55

4 Denisha's parents begin making additional contributions to a savings account at the beginning of her ninth-grade year. Her family's income after taxes is $68,560 annually, and they save 3% each year in the account. How much money will Denisha's family contribute over the next 4 years?

Ⓕ $2,056.80

Ⓖ $82,272

Ⓗ $8,227.20

Ⓙ $20,568

5 Which best describes ways Denisha can raise additional funds needed to pay for her college education?

    I. Work at a summer camp earning $1,900 each summer for 4 summers.

    II. Receive a scholarship for $1,500 per semester for good grades in high school.

    III. Work weekends at the Burger Barn throughout high school, and deposit $50 each week into a savings account.

Ⓐ I only

Ⓑ II only

Ⓒ III only

Ⓓ I, II, and III

The Cost of an Occupation for One Year

Visit the *CareerOneStop* website, www.careerinfonet.org. Use the instructions to complete the table.

- Click on the link *Occupation Information*.
- Click on the first bullet point, *Occupation Profile*.
- In the *Keyword Search* box, enter three occupations, one at a time, and search.
- Highlight the occupation entered and click *Continue*.
- Scroll to find *Texas* and click *Continue*.
- Use the information on the page to complete the table.
- Click the link *Occupation Profile* on the left-hand side of the page to return to the search box.

Career Interests

Occupation			
Texas Median Yearly Salary			
Education/ Training			

1 Select your top two choices from the table. Assume the following regarding paying for college.

- The average time needed for each certification or degree type is: certification–1 year, associate's degree–2 years, bachelor's degree–4 years, master's degree–2 additional years with bachelor's, doctoral degree–2–4 additional years with master's.

- The average number of hours required for college enrollment is 12 per semester.

- The average cost per semester hour for tuition and fees is $82 at a two-year community college, $276 at a four-year public university, or $891 at a four-year independent university. A certification costs an average of $1,000.

Calculate the cost for tuition and fees to earn the degree needed at each type of school for each of your top occupation choices. If the occupation chosen requires any type of certification, add that into the cost of obtaining a degree.

2 Describe a plan for saving the money needed to earn the degree(s) chosen in problem 1. Include anticipated family contribution, possible financial aid resources, and your own contribution in the plan. Use the website www.collegeforalltexans.com to assist in your planning.

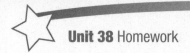
Use the information to answer questions 1–3.

Rosemary is 18 years old and lives near Austin. She loves traveling, staying in hotels, and eating at restaurants. She wants a career managing an upscale hotel. Rosemary's mother died at a young age and her father works to take care of his four children. His salary is about $35,000 a year, and he paid $1,793 in income tax last year. Rosemary earns money babysitting for her neighbors. Last year she earned $1,500 and paid no taxes. As the oldest, Rosemary wants to set an example for her siblings by being the first member of her family to attend college.

1 Visit the website www.actstudent.org and select *Career Planning* from the top menu. Use the *World-of-Work Map* to locate the area Rosemary's chosen career falls in. Click on the area and scroll through the list of career areas to find Rosemary's choice. Use the information that pops up to answer the following questions.

What should Rosemary plan to major in?

What degree option should Rosemary pursue to prepare for her career?

In her college search, Rosemary researches three public universities that offer her degree program. She ranks them according to her preference.

1. Texas Tech University
2. University of Houston
3. Sam Houston State University

2 Visit the website www.collegeforalltexans. com/apps/CollegeMoney/ and use Rosemary's information to complete the online survey. Complete the table showing the costs per year for each school.

	TTU	U of H	SHSU
Tuition and Fees			
Books			
Room and Board			
Other			
Total Cost per Year			

3 Rosemary chooses to attend Texas Tech University to earn her degree. Rosemary qualifies for $7,195 of federal student aid that does not require repayment. The aid includes $5,730 in a Federal Pell Grant and $1,465 in the work-study program per year. What is the estimated contribution needed from other sources to pay for Rosemary's first year?

4 Describe a savings plan for Rosemary to follow in order to save the needed funds for at least her first year of college.

Connections

Research how an advanced degree, such as a master's (6 years) or doctoral (8–10 years), would increase annual earning potential in an entry-level position. You can find this information using job ads online. Determine education cost if the median tuition and fees for a master's or doctoral degree is $10,500 per year and $1,200 per year for books. Discuss the advantages and disadvantages of obtaining an advanced degree and future earnings potential.

Performance Assessment A: Growing Pains

Performance Assessment B: Move-a-Thon Mathematics

motivation**math**™LEVEL 8

mentoring**minds**.com

Problem Stimulus

The town of Mentorville has become a thriving, prosperous community. As the town grows, new schools are needed, new shopping centers are developed, and new neighborhoods are built. Numerous families have decided to move to Mentorville due to the growing number of jobs and new homes available. Mentorville has always been known for its tree-lined streets and beautiful parks. Improvements to the town's largest park have become necessary in order to accommodate the growth being experienced by the town.

The town council holds a meeting to discuss possible park improvements. The meeting includes an open forum for residents to voice their opinions. Everyone is in agreement that improvements should be started during the spring of the current year. The town council selects members of the council, local builders, business people, and private citizens to form a park improvement committee. The committee begins collecting data and making plans for the new and improved town park.

Task Overview

The committee collects data and makes interpretations to use in the decision making process.

mentoring**minds**.com
motivation**math**™LEVEL 8
ILLEGAL TO COPY
307

Performance Task

Part A

One of the most important factors the park improvement committee must take into consideration when planning improvements is the population growth of Mentorville. A graph showing the changes in the population of Mentorville over the last several years is shown.

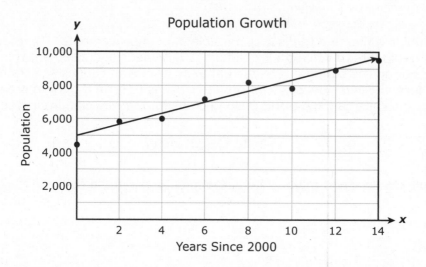

1 Write an equation in the form $y = mx + b$ to represent the trend line shown in the graph.

2 Using the equation written in problem 1, predict the approximate number of residents that will live in Mentorville in 2024 and 2034.

The park improvement committee decides to survey a random sample of Mentorville residents to get a better idea of how the population feels about the planned improvements for the town's park.

3 Describe a method the town council could use to obtain a random sample of residents that would give an accurate representation of the population.

4 Part of the improvements to the park will include additional features for children. Use the data collected during the survey to create a scatterplot showing the number of children per family compared to the number of park visits the family makes each week. Include a title and labels on the axes.

Number of Children per Family	Number of Park Visits per Week
1	2
3	3
6	5
4	5
2	2
1	1
5	6
3	5
2	4
6	7
2	3
4	4

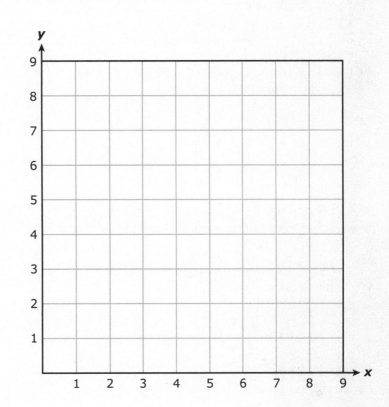

5 Based on the data in the scatterplot, what type of association exists between the number of children in a family and the number of times the family visits the park per week? Explain your answer.

Performance Assessment A

Part B

The town council plans the specific improvements to be made to the park. The largest improvement made will be the addition of a wading pool to the current pool facility to accommodate more families with small children. The diagram for the wading pool is shown.

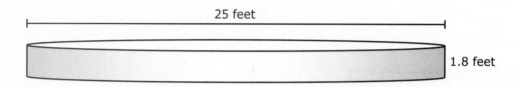

25 feet

1.8 feet

1   The volume of the pool can be found using the formula $V = Bh$. Write an expression that can be used to determine the value of B.

2   The pool will be filled to $\frac{7}{8}$ of its maximum capacity. Determine the number of cubic feet of water the wading pool will contain when filled. Use $\pi \approx \frac{22}{7}$.

3   The sides and bottom of the pool will be painted with an ocean life theme. How many square feet of pool surface will be painted? Explain your answer. Use $\pi \approx \frac{22}{7}$.

         motivation**math**™LEVEL 8   mentoring**minds**.com

Part C

The entrance to the park will be remodeled as part of the improvement. A design of the new entrance is shown.

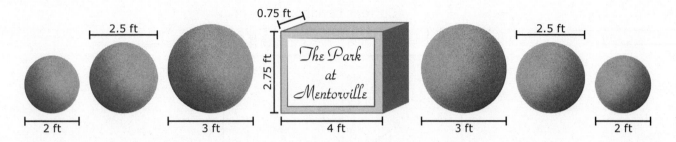

1   The spheres shown will be formed using a colored concrete mix. What is the volume of concrete mix, in cubic feet, needed to create one of each size of the spheres used at the park entrance? Use π ≈ 3.14. Round your answers to the nearest hundredth.

2-foot sphere _____

2.5-foot sphere _____

3-foot sphere _____

2   How many total cubic feet of concrete mix will be used to create the park entrance spheres?

3   The sign displaying the name of the park will be a rectangular prism centered between the concrete spheres. The sign will rest on the ground so visitors to the park may pose for pictures. The total visible surface area of the sign will be painted purple. How many square feet of the sign will be painted?

Performance Assessment A

Part D

The final improvement to the park will be to enlarge the sandbox in the children's play area. The current sandbox is shown, with one unit on the graph equal to a length of one foot.

Current Sandbox

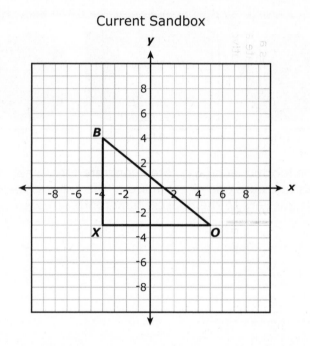

1 Find the perimeter of the current sandbox, in feet. Round your answer to the nearest tenth.

2 The new sandbox will be an enlargement of the current sandbox by a scale factor of 1.5. Use an algebraic representation to describe the effect of the scale factor on the current sandbox.

Use the algebraic representation to determine the coordinates of the new sandbox. Then, sketch the new sandbox, *B'O'X'*, on the grid.

B' _____   O' _____   X' _____

3 What scale factor is applied to the perimeter of the current sandbox to determine the perimeter of the new sandbox? Explain your answer.

What scale factor is applied to the area of the current sandbox to determine the area of the new sandbox? Explain your answer.

motivation**math**™LEVEL 8
mentoring**minds**.com

Name: _____

Performance Assessment A: Growing Pains

Task	Score Point: 1 Undeveloped	Score Point: 2 Developing	Score Point: 3 Developed	Student's Score (Circle)		
A.1 Write an equation in the form $y = mx + b$ to model a linear relationship.	Student is unable to write the equation of the line.	Student correctly writes the slope of the line but not the y-intercept or vice versa.	Student correctly writes the equation of the line.	Score: 1	2	3
A.2 Use a trend line to make predictions.	Student is unable to correctly use the equation of the trend line to make predictions.	Student correctly substitutes values into the equation of the trend line but records incorrect predictions.	Student correctly uses the equation of the trend line to make predictions.	Score: 1	2	3
A.3 Simulate generating a random sample that is representative of the population.	Student does not show an understanding of simulations or how to generate a random sample.	Student shows some understanding of simulations but does not correctly describe a method to generate a random sample.	Student correctly describes a simulation that will generate a random sample representative of the population.	Score: 1	2	3
A.4 Construct a scatterplot.	Student incorrectly plots 6 or more points on the graph.	Student incorrectly plots 1–5 points on the graph.	Student correctly plots all 12 points on the graph.	Score: 1	2	3
A.5 Describe the association between bivariate data in a scatterplot.	Student incorrectly describes the association shown in the data.	Student correctly describes the association shown in the data but is unable to explain what the association means.	Student correctly describes the association shown in the data and correctly explains what the association means.	Score: 1	2	3
B.1 Describe the volume formula of a cylinder in terms of its base area and height.	Student incorrectly records an expression that can be used to determine B.	Student records an expression that can be used to determine the volume of the cylinder instead of B.	Student correctly records an expression that can be used to determine B.	Score: 1	2	3
B.2 Solve a problem involving the volume of a cylinder.	Student incorrectly calculates the volume of the cylinder.	Student correctly calculates the volume of the cylinder but does not solve the problem stated.	Student correctly calculates the volume of the cylinder and solves the problem stated.	Score: 1	2	3
B.3 Solve a problem involving the surface area of a cylinder.	Student incorrectly calculates the surface area of the cylinder.	Student correctly calculates the surface area of the cylinder but does not solve the problem stated.	Student correctly calculates the surface area of the cylinder and solves the problem stated.	Score: 1	2	3

Task	Score Point: 1 Undeveloped	Score Point: 2 Developing	Score Point: 3 Developed	Student's Score (Circle)
C.1 Solve a problem involving the volume of a sphere.	Student incorrectly calculates the volume of all three spheres.	Student incorrectly calculates the volume of 1 or 2 spheres.	Student correctly calculates the volume of all three spheres.	Score: 1 2 3
C.2 Solve a problem involving the volume of a sphere.	Student incorrectly calculates the total volume of the spheres.	Student calculates the total volume for only one of each size sphere.	Student correctly calculates the total volume of all six spheres.	Score: 1 2 3
C.3 Solve a problem involving the surface area of a rectangular prism.	Student incorrectly calculates the surface area of the prism.	Student calculates the total surface area of the prism, including the bottom.	Student correctly calculates the surface area of the prism and solves the problem stated.	Score: 1 2 3
D.1 Use the Pythagorean Theorem to solve problems.	Student is unable to use the Pythagorean Theorem to determine the length of the hypotenuse.	Student correctly uses the Pythagorean Theorem to determine the length of the hypotenuse but does not find the perimeter of the triangle.	Student correctly uses the Pythagorean Theorem to determine the length of the hypotenuse and finds the perimeter of the triangle.	Score: 1 2 3
D.2 Use an algebraic representation to describe the effect of a dilation using a positive rational scale factor.	Student incorrectly records the algebraic representation of the dilation.	Student correctly records the algebraic representation of the dilation but does not correctly determine the coordinates of the new triangle.	Student correctly records the algebraic representation of the dilation and correctly determines the coordinates of the new triangle.	Score: 1 2 3
D.3 Model the effect on linear and area measurements of dilated two-dimensional shapes.	Student is unable to determine the scale factors used to find the perimeter and area of the new triangle.	Student correctly determines the scale factor used to find the perimeter of the new triangle but is unable to correctly determine the scale factor to find the area of the new triangle.	Student correctly determines the scale factors used to find the perimeter and area of the new triangle.	Score: 1 2 3

Student's Total Score

38–42 points = Proficient   31–37 points = Satisfactory   25–30 points = Below Standard   0–24 points = Unsatisfactory

motivation**math**™ LEVEL 8

Problem Stimulus

It was an unusual Monday morning in the halls of North Middle School. Mr. South was having a difficult time calming his first-period mathematics class and getting them started on the day's lesson.

"What's all the excitement and commotion about this morning?" asked Mr. South.

"Mr. South, most of our classmates and their families participated in the physical education department's move-a-thon on Saturday," said Molly. "I think everyone had a great time, and people are excited to share their stories from the event."

"You wouldn't believe how far I biked!" exclaimed Raul. "I've never gone as far as I did on Saturday."

"He's right! I was there with him, Mr. South," added Miranda. "You should have seen how many people where there and how many activities were taking place — it was one of the coolest things ever!"

"Wow," said Mr. South. "I know most of you enjoy physical education, but this sure seems exciting. Because everyone is so enthusiastic, I want to skip today's lesson and talk more about this move-a-thon. Although, I think you'll find we're still going to do some mathematics."

"Huh?" asked Martin. "How was the move-a-thon mathematics? It was a day of fitness and physical activity. I want to see the mathematics."

Task Overview

Mr. South's class will analyze what the students did at the move-a-thon in order to see the mathematics involved in the activities.

Performance Assessment B

Performance Task

Part A

Over the weekend, the school held the first annual move-a-thon to raise money for the school's physical education department, as well as to increase awareness of the importance of fitness. Students and families were encouraged to come to the school and "move" during the course of a day. Most participants moved on teams, with at least one teammate moving at a time. Participants walked or rode bicycles on a course set up around the school. Teams kept records of the total distance and length of time they moved.

1   Molly's team decided to walk. The graph shows the miles her team walked each hour.

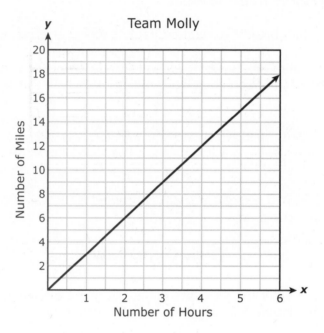

Use similar right triangles to determine the slope of the line. Show your work and explain your answer.

2   The number of miles walked by Team Molly varies directly with the number of hours the team walks. Write an equation to represent the relationship shown in the graph.

How many hours will it take the team to walk 20 miles?

3 What type of relationship, proportional or non-proportional, is shown between the number of miles and the number of hours Molly's team walked? Justify your response.

4 Martin's team also walked in the move-a-thon, but they did not start at the beginning of the course. The team's distances traveled are shown in the table.

Team Martin

Time (hours)	Distance (miles)
1	6.5
3	11.5
5	16.5
6	19.0

Determine the slope and the *y*-intercept for the data.

5 Write an equation to represent the relationship shown in the table.

6 What type of relationship, proportional or non-proportional, is shown between the number of miles and the number of hours Martin's team walked? Justify your response.

Performance Assessment B

7 Raul's team rode bicycles during the move-a-thon. From the starting line, they rode a total of 30 miles in 5 hours. Assuming their speed was constant, create a table, graph, and equation to represent the team's ride. Give titles for the graph and table and label the axes of the graph.

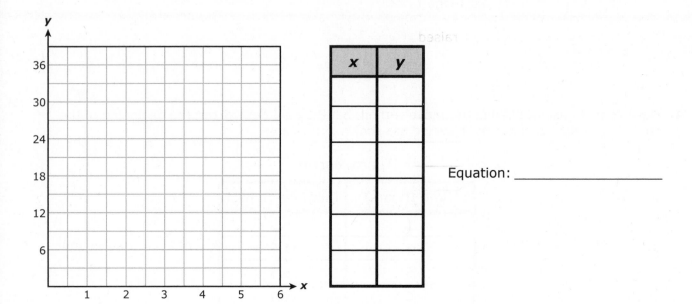

Equation: _____

8 Miranda's team could not make it to the beginning of the move-a-thon. However, they met up with Raul's team after Raul's team had ridden for 1.5 hours. Both teams continue to ride at the same rate for the remainder of the ride. Create a table, graph, and equation to represent team Miranda's ride. Give titles for the graph and table and label the axes of the graph.

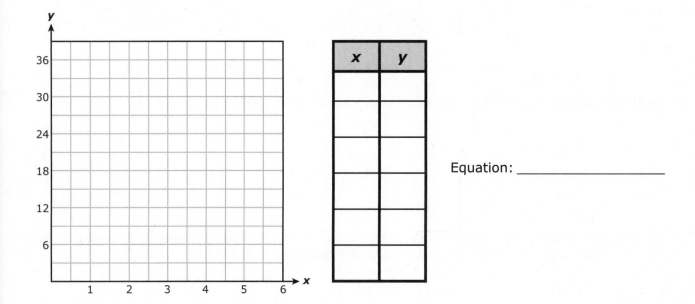

Equation: _____

Part B

The purpose of the move-a-thon was to raise money for the physical education department. The department encouraged participants to collect pledges based on the hours they would walk or the number of miles they would ride. One-time donations were also accepted.

1 The amount of money Miranda raised is shown in the table.

Miranda's Fundraising

Miles Ridden	Dollars Raised
5	$35
10	$40
15	$45
20	$50

Does the data in the table show a proportional or non-proportional relationship? Explain your answer.

2 Raul had different friends and family members sponsor him for each interval of 5 miles. The graph shows the amounts of money Raul collected from different numbers of people.

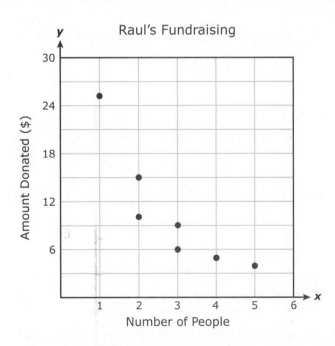

Does the relationship shown in the graph represent a function? Explain your answer.

Performance Assessment B

3 Molly receives a $10 donation from her grandfather. Her mother pledges another $2.25 for each mile Molly walks. Martin's father pledges twice as much per mile as Molly's mother. If Molly and Martin raise the same amount of money, write an equation that can be used to determine m, the number of miles each walked.

How many miles, m, will Molly and Martin each have to walk in order to raise the same amount of money?

4 Samuel's team participated in the move-a-thon by jumping rope. The team's donations were based on the number of minutes participants jumped rope.

Team Samuel

Number of Minutes	Donation ($)
2	9.00
3	13.50
5	22.50
7	31.50

Graph the data from the table. Label the axes and give the graph a title.

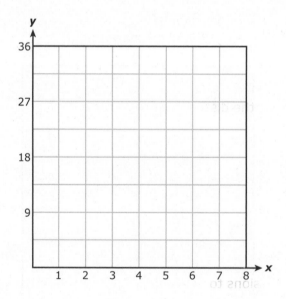

What is the slope of the line graphed? What is the meaning of the slope in terms of the situation?

Part C

Shelly and John's teams participated in the move-a-thon by rollerblading. Shelly's team began at the beginning of the course and skated at a constant rate of 8 miles per hour. John's team began the course at the 15-mile marker and skated at a constant rate of 5 miles per hour. The graph for the distances traveled by each team is shown.

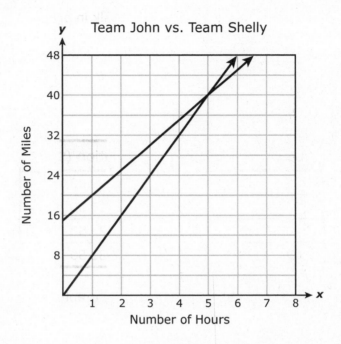

1 Write an equation to represent the distance traveled by John's team.

Write an equation to represent the distance traveled by Shelly's team.

2 Explain the meaning of the point (5, 40) in terms of the situation.

Write and evaluate two expressions to verify that the point (5, 40) satisfies both equations in problem 1.

motivation**math**™LEVEL 8

mentoring**minds**.com

Performance Assessment B: Move-a-Thon Mathematics

Task	Score Point: 1 Undeveloped	Score Point: 2 Developing	Score Point: 3 Developed	Student's Score (Circle)
A.1 Use similar right triangles to determine slope.	Student is unable to create similar triangles using the graphed line.	Student correctly creates similar triangles but is unable to determine the slope of the line.	Student correctly creates similar triangles and determines the slope of the line.	Score: 1 2 3
A.2 Solve problems involving direct variation.	Student is unable to correctly write an equation or answer the question.	Student correctly writes an equation but does not answer the question correctly. OR Student correctly answers the question but does not write a correct equation.	Student correctly writes an equation to represent the graphed line and correctly answers the question.	Score: 1 2 3
A.3 Identify a proportional function arising from a real-world problem.	Student incorrectly identifies the relationship.	Student correctly identifies the relationship but does not justify the response.	Student correctly identifies the relationship and justifies the response.	Score: 1 2 3
A.4 Use data from a table to determine slope and y-intercept.	Student incorrectly determines the slope and y-intercept.	Student correctly determines either the slope or the y-intercept but not both.	Student correctly determines both the slope and y-intercept.	Score: 1 2 3
A.5 Write an equation in the form $y = mx + b$ to model a linear relationship.	Student is unable to write an equation to model the relationship.	Student writes an equation to model the relationship but uses either a slope or y-intercept value that is incorrect.	Student correctly writes an equation to model the relationship.	Score: 1 2 3
A.6 Identify non-proportional function arising from a real-world problem.	Student incorrectly identifies the relationship.	Student correctly identifies the relationship but does not justify the response.	Student correctly identifies the relationship and justifies the response.	Score: 1 2 3
A.7 Represent a linear proportional relationship using a graph, a table, and an equation.	Student is unable to correctly create any representation of the linear proportional relationship.	Student creates 1 or 2 correct representations of the linear proportional relationship.	Student creates 3 correct representations of the linear proportional relationship.	Score: 1 2 3
A.8 Represent a linear non-proportional relationship using a graph, a table, and an equation.	Student is unable to correctly create any representation of the linear non-proportional relationship.	Student creates 1 or 2 correct representations of the linear non-proportional relationship.	Student creates 3 correct representations of the linear non-proportional relationship.	Score: 1 2 3

Task	Score Point: 1 Undeveloped	Score Point: 2 Developing	Score Point: 3 Developed	Student's Score (Circle)
B.1 Identify a proportional function arising from a real-world problem.	Student incorrectly identifies the relationship.	Student correctly identifies the relationship but does not justify the response.	Student correctly identifies the relationship and justifies the response.	Score: 1 2 3
B.2 Identify a function using a graph.	Student incorrectly identifies the relationship.	Student correctly identifies the relationship but does not explain the answer.	Student correctly identifies the relationship and explains the answer.	Score: 1 2 3
B.3 Write and solve a one-variable equation with a variable on both sides to represent a problem.	Student is unable to correctly write or solve an equation.	Student correctly writes an equation but does not solve the equation correctly.	Student correctly writes and solves an equation.	Score: 1 2 3
B.4 Graph a proportional relationship and interpret the unit rate as the slope of the line.	Student is unable to correctly graph the proportional relationship.	Student correctly graphs the proportional relationship but is unable to determine and/or interpret the slope.	Student correctly graphs the proportional relationship and determines and interprets the slope.	Score: 1 2 3
C.1 Write an equation in the form $y = mx + b$ to model a linear relationship.	Student incorrectly writes both equations modeling the linear relationships.	Student correctly writes one, but not both, of the equations modeling the linear relationships.	Student correctly writes both equations modeling the linear relationships.	Score: 1 2 3
C.2 Identify and verify the values of x and y that simultaneously satisfy two equations from the intersection of the graphed equations.	Student is unable to explain the meaning of the point or verify the point satisfies both equations.	Student is able to explain the meaning of the point but is unable to verify the point satisfies both equations. OR Student is able to verify the point satisfies both equations but is unable to explain the meaning of the point.	Student is able to explain the meaning of the point and verify the point satisfies both equations.	Score: 1 2 3

Student's Total Score

38–42 points = Proficient   32–37 points = Satisfactory   25–31 points = Below Standard   0–24 points = Unsatisfactory

motivation**math**™LEVEL 8

mentoring**minds**.com

Chart Your Success

Place a check (✓) in the box if your answer is correct.

Unit 1 Page **10**	Describe relationships between sets of real numbers 8.2(A)–S		1	2	3	4	5				Total Correct	Total Possible **5**
Unit 2 Page **18**	Approximate the value of an irrational number and locate the value on a number line 8.2(B)–S		1	2	3	4	5				Total Correct	Total Possible **5**
Unit 3 Page **26**	Convert between standard decimal and scientific notations 8.2(C)–S		1	2	3	4	5				Total Correct	Total Possible **5**
Unit 4 Page **34**	Order sets of real numbers 8.2(D)–R		1	2	3	4	5				Total Correct	Total Possible **5**
Unit 5 Page **42**	Generalize that ratios of corresponding sides of similar shapes are proportional 8.3(A)–S		1	2	3	4					Total Correct	Total Possible **4**
Unit 6 Page **50**	Compare and contrast attributes of a shape and its dilation 8.3(B)–S		1	2	3						Total Correct	Total Possible **3**
Unit 7 Page **58**	Use an algebraic representation to explain the effect of a scale factor applied to two-dimensional figures 8.3(C)–R		1	2	3	4					Total Correct	Total Possible **4**
Unit 8 Page **66**	Use similar right triangles to develop an understanding of slope 8.4(A)–S		1	2	3						Total Correct	Total Possible **3**
Unit 9 Page **74**	Graph proportional relationships 8.4(B)–R		1	2	3						Total Correct	Total Possible **3**
Unit 10 Page **82**	Use data from a table or graph to determine the rate of change or slope and y-intercept 8.4(C)–R		1	2	3	4					Total Correct	Total Possible **4**
Unit 11 Page **90**	Represent linear proportional and non-proportional situations with tables, graphs, and equations 8.5(A)–S, 8.5(B)–S		1	2	3	4					Total Correct	Total Possible **4**
Unit 12 Page **98**	Contrast bivariate sets of data that suggest a linear relationship with sets that do not 8.5(C)–S		1	2	3						Total Correct	Total Possible **3**

Chart Your Success

Place a check (✓) in the box if your answer is correct.

Unit 13 Page **106**	Use a trend line to make predictions 8.5(D)–R	1	2	3					Total Correct	Total Possible **3**
Unit 14 Page **114**	Solve problems involving direct variation 8.5(E)–S	1	2	3	4	5			Total Correct	Total Possible **5**
Unit 15 Page **122**	Distinguish between and identify examples of proportional and non-proportional situations 8.5(F)–S, 8.5(H)–S	1	2	3	4				Total Correct	Total Possible **4**
Unit 16 Page **130**	Identify functions 8.5(G)–R	1	2	3					Total Correct	Total Possible **3**
Unit 17 Page **138**	Write an equation in the form y=mx+b to model a linear relationship between two quantities 8.5(I)–R	1	2	3	4	5			Total Correct	Total Possible **5**
Unit 18 Page **146**	Describe the volume formula of a cylinder in terms of its base area and height 8.6(A)–S	1	2	3	4				Total Correct	Total Possible **4**
Unit 19 Page **154**	Model the relationship between the volume of a cylinder and a cone 8.6(B)	1	2	3	4				Total Correct	Total Possible **4**
Unit 20 Page **162**	Use models and diagrams to explain the Pythagorean Theorem 8.6(C)–S	1	2	3	4				Total Correct	Total Possible **4**
Unit 21 Page **170**	Solve problems involving the volume of cylinders, cones, and spheres 8.7(A)–R	1	2	3	4				Total Correct	Total Possible **4**
Unit 22 Page **178**	Determine solutions for lateral and total surface area problems involving rectangular prisms, triangular prisms, and cylinders 8.7(B)–R	1	2	3	4	5			Total Correct	Total Possible **5**
Unit 23 Page **186**	Use the Pythagorean Theorem and its converse to solve problems 8.7(C)–R	1	2	3	4				Total Correct	Total Possible **4**
Unit 24 Page **194**	Determine the distance between two points on a coordinate plane using the Pythagorean Theorem 8.7(D)–S	1	2	3	4				Total Correct	Total Possible **4**

   motivation**math**™ LEVEL 8 mentoring**minds**.com

Chart Your Success

Place a check (✓) in the box if your answer is correct.

										Total Correct	Total Possible
Unit 25 Page **202**	Write one-variable equations or inequalities that represent problems and write real-world problems given one-variable equations or inequalities 8.8(A)–S, 8.8(B)–S	1	2	3	4	5					**5**
Unit 26 Page **210**	Model and solve one-variable equations with variables on both sides of the equal sign 8.8(C)–R	1	2	3	4						**4**
Unit 27 Page **218**	Use informal arguments to establish facts about angle relationships 8.8(D)–S	1	2	3	4						**4**
Unit 28 Page **226**	Identify and verify values of x and y that simultaneously satisfy two linear equations 8.9(A)–S	1	2	3							**3**
Unit 29 Page **234**	Generalize properties of orientation and congruence of transformations and differentiate between transformations that preserve congruence and those that do not 8.10(A)–S, 8.10(B)–S	1	2	3	4						**4**
Unit 30 Page **242**	Explain the effect of transformations on a coordinate plane using an algebraic representation 8.10(C)–R	1	2	3							**3**
Unit 31 Page **250**	Model the effect of dilations on linear and area measurements 8.10(D)–S	1	2	3	4	5	6				**6**
Unit 32 Page **258**	Construct a scatterplot and describe the association between bivariate data 8.11(A)–S	1	2	3	4						**4**
Unit 33 Page **266**	Determine the mean absolute deviation using a data set of no more than 10 data points 8.11(B)–S	1	2	3	4						**4**
Unit 34 Page **274**	Simulate generating random samples to develop the notion of a random sample being representative of the population 8.11(C)	1	2	3	4						**4**

Chart Your Success

Place a check (✓) in the box if your answer is correct.

										Total Correct	Total Possible
Unit 35 **Page** 284	Solve problems comparing how interest rate and loan length affect cost of credit; calculate total cost of repaying a loan using online calculators; identify and explain advantages and disadvantages of different payment methods **8.12(A)–S, 8.12(B), 8.12(E)**	1	2	3	4	5	6	7			**7**
Unit 36 **Page** 290	Explain how regular investments grow over time; calculate and compare simple and compound interest **8.12(C)–S, 8.12(D)–R**	1	2	3							**3**
Unit 37 **Page** 296	Analyze and determine if a situation is financially responsible and identify the benefits of financial responsibility and the costs of financial irresponsibility **8.12(F)**	1	2	3	4						**4**
Unit 38 **Page** 302	Estimate the cost of college education and devise a periodic savings plan **8.12(G)–S**	1	2	3	4	5					**5**

ILLEGAL TO COPY   motivation**math**™LEVEL 8   mentoring**minds**.com

Math Glossary

A

absolute value – the distance of a number from zero on a number line

accrue – money or value that is gained over time, either increasing or decreasing

acute angle – an angle measuring less than 90°

acute triangle – a triangle with three acute angles

addends – numbers that are added

addition property of equality – a property that states that if a value is added to both sides of an equality statement (equation), the sides remain equal

additive relationship – a relationship among a set of ordered pairs in which the same value is added to each x-value to find the corresponding y-value

The table shows an additive relationship because 4 is added to each x-value to find each y-value.

x	0	1	2	3
y	4	5	6	7

adjacent – side-by-side; adjoining

adjacent angles – two or more angles with a common ray and a common vertex

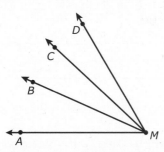

In the drawing, angles *AMB* and *BMC* are adjacent because they share ray *MB* and vertex *M*.

algebraic equation – a number sentence that contains at least one variable and uses the equal sign to show that two expressions are equivalent; for example, $2a = 7$

algebraic expression – an expression that contains at least one variable; for example, $a + b$ or $5n$

algebraic representation (transformation) – the process of recording the effect of a given scale factor applied to a two-dimensional figure on the coordinate plane; for example, a scale factor of 3 is represented by $(x, y) \rightarrow (3x, 3y)$

algorithm – a step-by-step process for solving a problem

alternate exterior angles – a pair of angles on the outer sides of two parallel lines cut by a transversal, but on opposite sides of the transversal

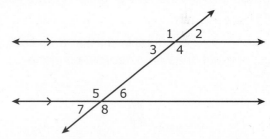

Angles 1 and 8 are alternate exterior angles.

alternate interior angles – a pair of angles on the inner sides of two parallel lines cut by a transversal, but on opposite sides of the transversal

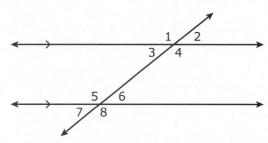

Angles 3 and 6 are alternate interior angles.

altitude – the perpendicular distance from the base of a shape to the highest point of the shape

angle – a figure formed by 2 rays that share a common endpoint

annual percentage rate (APR) – the yearly cost of a financed amount, including interest and fees, expressed as a percentage rate

approximate – *verb*: to estimate; to come close to; *adjective*: almost exact or correct

area – the number of square units needed to cover a surface

area of base (*B*) – in a three-dimensional figure, the area, in square units, of the base of the figure

associate's degree – a degree typically earned after two years of study from a community or career college

associative property – a property of addition or multiplication in which the grouping of the addends or factors does not change the outcome of the operation

$$(a + b) + c = a + (b + c)$$
$$(1 + 2) + 3 = 1 + (2 + 3)$$
or
$$(a \cdot b) \cdot c = a \cdot (b \cdot c)$$
$$(1 \cdot 2) \cdot 3 = 1 \cdot (2 \cdot 3)$$

attribute – a characteristic or property of a shape or thing

axis/axes – the horizontal (*x*-axis) and vertical (*y*-axis) number lines on a coordinate plane

B

bachelor's degree – a degree typically earned after four years of study from a college or university

balance (of a bank account) – the total amount of money in a bank account at any given time

base (2-D figure) – the side of a polygon from which an altitude is drawn

base (3-D figure) – the face or faces of a geometric figure from which an altitude is drawn

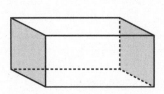

base (of an exponent) – factor appearing the number of times shown by an exponent; for example, 9 is the base in the expression 9^3

biased – having a preference for one over another

bivariate data set – a set of data with two variables; often represented using a scatterplot

borrow – to obtain or use money from a bank or other person in order to purchase goods or services

borrower – a person who borrows money

box plot – a graph that uses a box to represent the middle 50% of a data set and line segments at each end to represent the remainder of the data

braces – symbols used to indicate a set or subset of data; { }

brackets – symbols used to group part of a mathematical expression or equation; [ ]

budget – a plan for how much money is spent and saved based on income and goals

C

capacity – a measure of the amount of liquid a container will hold

center (of a circle) – a point that is equal distance from every point on the circumference of a circle

center of dilation – a fixed point on the coordinate plane about which a figure is enlarged or reduced

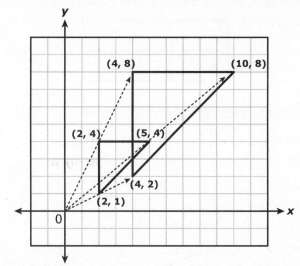

For the dilation shown, the origin is the center of dilation.

central tendency – any of the three measures (mean, median, mode) that represent the center of a set of data

certification – official approval to do a task professionally

certificate of deposit (CD) – a savings certificate that earns interest; a CD typically has a maturity date of 1 month to 5 years from the date it is issued

change in x (Δx) – the change in x quantities often referred to as the run

$$\Delta x = x_2 - x_1$$

change in y (Δy) – the change in y quantities often referred to as the rise

$$\Delta y = y_2 - y_1$$

checking account – an account at a financial institution that allows a person to deposit or withdraw money and write checks to pay for goods and services

circle – a closed curve in which every point is the same distance from a fixed point (the center)

circle graph – a graph that uses a circle to show how a whole is broken into parts; the parts of a circle graph are represented by percents, and the size of each piece is determined by multiplying the part's percent by 360°

circumference – the linear length of the perimeter of a circle

clockwise – in the direction of the moving hands around a clock face

coefficient – a number multiplied by a variable in an algebraic expression; for example, in the expression 6x, 6 is a coefficient

college fund – money saved for a child to help pay for a post-secondary education

combine like terms – the act of combining terms in an algebraic expression that contains the same variable in the same form; for example, in the expression 5x – 4y + 3y – 2x, 5x and -2x are like terms and combine to yield 3x, while -4y and 3y are like terms and combine to yield -y

common denominator – a denominator that is the same in two or more fractions

commutative property – a property of addition or multiplication in which the sum or product stays the same when the order of the addends or factors is changed

$$a + b = b + a$$
$$7 + 8 = 8 + 7$$
$$\text{or}$$
$$a \cdot b = b \cdot a$$
$$3 \cdot 4 = 4 \cdot 3$$

compare – to determine whether two or more numbers or quantities are greater than, less than, or equal to one another

complementary angles – two angles whose measures sum to 90°

composite figure – a figure made up of two or more shapes

composite number – a whole number that has more than two whole-number factors; the number 10 is a composite number because it has more than two factors: 1, 2, 5, and 10

composition (of transformations) – the combination of two or more transformations

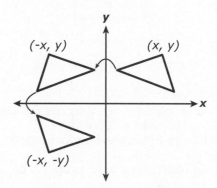

compound interest – interest paid or earned on both the original principal of an investment or a loan and on any accumulated interest during previous periods; the formula $A = P(1 + r)^t$ is used to calculate compound interest, where A is the amount of interest plus the principal, P is the principal invested or borrowed, r is the interest rate written as a decimal, and t is the length of time the money is invested or borrowed, as a year

computation – a calculation of numbers

cone – a three-dimensional shape with a circular base, a curved surface, and one vertex

congruent – having the same size and shape

constant – a number that does not vary; for example, in the expression x + 5, 5 is a constant

constant of proportionality (variation) – the constant ratio of x- and y-values in a proportional relationship; represented by the equation $k = \frac{y}{x}$, where k is the constant of proportionality (variation)

constant rate of change – the ratio of the change in y-values to the change in x-values, represented by the variable m in the equation $y = mx + b$; the constant rate of change can be calculated from a table or graph

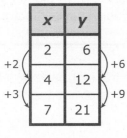

x	y
2	6
4	12
7	21

$+2$ → $+6$
$+3$ → $+9$

$m = \frac{6}{2} = 3$ or $m = \frac{9}{3} = 3$

Therefore, the constant rate of change is 3.

continuous data – any data that has infinite values with connected data points, such as measurements

converse of the Pythagorean Theorem – if the sum of the squares of two sides of a triangle is equal to the square of the third side, then the triangle is a right triangle

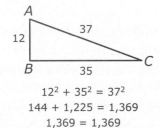

$12^2 + 35^2 = 37^2$
$144 + 1{,}225 = 1{,}369$
$1{,}369 = 1{,}369$

Triangle ABC is a right triangle.

coordinate plane – a plane formed by two perpendicular number lines intersecting at 0

coordinates – an ordered pair of numbers (x, y) used to locate a point on a coordinate plane

correlation – the relationship between the paired data of two variables

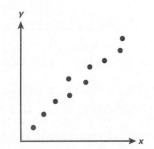

The graph shows a positive correlation between x- and y-values.

corresponding angles – a pair of angles located in the same position in two different congruent or similar shapes

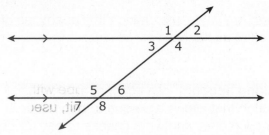

Angles 1 and 5 are corresponding angles.

corresponding angles (similar figures) – a pair of angles located in the same position in two different congruent or similar shapes

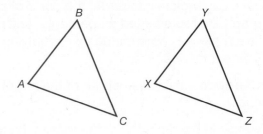

corresponding sides – a pair of sides located in the same position in two different congruent or similar shapes

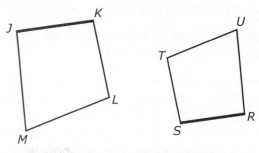

In quadrilaterals $JKLM$ and $RSTU$, segments JK and RS are corresponding sides.

counterclockwise – in the opposite direction of the moving hands around a clock face

counting numbers – the set of numbers used to count objects; does not include 0

credit – an amount of money that a lender or business allows a person to use to purchase goods and services with a promise to repay the money, usually with interest

credit card – a card, issued by a bank, store, or other business, that is used to borrow money or buy goods and services on credit; borrowers make regular payments to repay the amount of money borrowed with interest and fees

motivation**math**™LEVEL 8
mentoring**minds**.com

credit limit – the maximum amount a credit card will allow someone to borrow on a single card

cube – a three-dimensional figure with six congruent square faces

cubed – raised to a power of 3; for example, 4 cubed = 4^3

cubic unit – a unit, shaped like a cube with dimensions of 1 unit $\times$ 1 unit $\times$ 1 unit, used to measure volume

cylinder – a three-dimensional figure with two parallel bases that are congruent circles

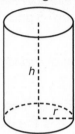

D

data – a collection of facts or information gathered by observing, questioning, or measuring, usually displayed on a chart, table, or graph

data point – a single fact or piece of information

debit card – a card issued by a bank that a customer uses to pay for purchases with money

debt – money, goods, or services owed to others

decimal number – a number that uses base-ten place value and a decimal point to show tenths, hundredths, thousandths, etc.

decompose – to break down or break apart into smaller parts

deductions – something that is or may be subtracted

degree (°) – a unit of measure for angles and temperature

denominator – the bottom number in a fraction; the total number of equal parts

dependent quantity – a quantity whose value is determined by the value of the related independent quantity

x	1	2	3	4
y	8	9	10	11

dependent quantities: {8, 9, 10, 11}

dependent variable – a variable whose value is determined by the value of the independent variable

$$y = 6x + 2$$

⬆

dependent variable

deposit – money placed into a checking or savings account at a bank

diagonal – a line that connects two vertices of a polygon that are not adjacent

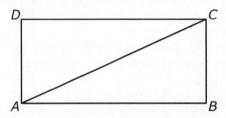

Line *AC* is a diagonal in rectangle *ABCD*.

diameter – the linear distance from a point on the circumference of a circle, through the center of the circle, to a point on the opposite side of the circle

difference – the answer to a subtraction problem

digit – one of the symbols 0, 1, 2, 3, 4, 5, 6, 7, 8, and 9 used to write numbers

dilation – a transformation which produces a figure similar to the original by proportionately reducing or enlarging the figure

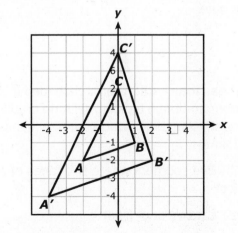

dimensions – the measures of sides in a geometric figure

direct variation – a relationship in which the ratio of two variable quantities is constant; when the value of one quantity changes, the second quantity changes proportionally; represented by the equation $y = kx$, where k is the constant of variation

discrete data – a set of finite data values with unconnected data points, such as a count or scores

distance – the measured space between two objects or points

distributive property – the property which states that multiplying a sum by a number is the same as multiplying each addend by the number and then adding the products
$$a(b + c) = ab + ac$$
$$3(4 + 2) = (3 \times 4) + (3 \times 2)$$

dividend – the number to be divided in a division problem

division – the operation of making equal groups to find the number in each group or to find the number of equal groups

division property of equality – a property that states that if a value is divided on both sides of an equality statement (equation), the sides remain equal

divisor – the number by which another number is divided

doctoral degree – the highest post-graduate degree awarded by a university

dot plot – a graph that uses dots above a number line to show the frequency of data

down payment – an amount of money paid at the time of a purchase with the remaining balance due at a later date

E

easy access loan – short-term cash loan that a borrower can obtain typically with no credit requirement; examples include car-title loans and payday loans

edge – the line segment where two faces of a solid figure meet

element – a member of a set

equality symbol (=) – a symbol that indicates two quantities are equivalent

equation – a number sentence that uses the equal sign to show two expressions are equivalent

equilateral triangle – a triangle with three congruent sides

equivalent – the same in value or amount

estimate – *noun*: an answer that is close to the exact answer; *verb*: to guess about

evaluate – to find the value of an expression

exclusive – not contained in a set; for example, the set of integers between -3 and 1, exclusive, is {-2, -1, 0}

expense – an amount of money used to buy goods or services

exponent – the number of times a base is used as a factor; for example, 4 is the exponent in 3^4

expression – a mathematical combination of numbers, operations, and/or variables

exterior angle – the angle formed by an angle of a triangle and the linear extension of an adjacent side

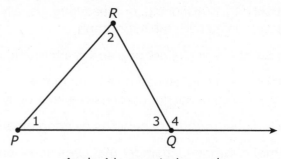

Angle 4 is an exterior angle.

F

face – a flat surface of a three-dimensional solid figure

factor – a number that is multiplied by another number to find a product

The factors of 6 are 1, 2, 3, and 6.

Federal Application for Student Aid (FAFSA) – free application used to determine eligibility for federal student aid

financial aid – money given or loaned to assist in paying for college expenses

financial institution – a business that deals with money, deposits, investments, and loans, rather than goods or services

finite – having a limited number of values

formula – a general mathematical statement or rule

fraction – a number that names a part of a whole or part of a group

frequency – the number of times an event happens

frequency table – a table listing each value that appears in a data set followed by the number of times it appears

function – a mathematical relationship in which there is exactly one output value for each input value

G

grant – a type of financial aid, typically based on need, not requiring repayment

grouping symbols – braces, brackets, or parentheses used to group numbers, symbols, and/or variables

H

height – the vertical distance from bottom to top

horizontal – the direction from left to right; parallel to the horizon

hundredth – one of 100 equal parts; the second place to the right of the decimal point

hypotenuse – in a right triangle, the side opposite the right angle

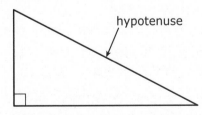

I

identity property of addition – the property which states that the sum of any number and zero is equal to that number

$$a + 0 = a$$
$$8 + 0 = 8$$

identity property of multiplication – the property which states that the product of 1 and any factor is equal to the factor

$$1 \cdot b = b$$
$$1 \cdot 9 = 9$$

image – the result of a transformation

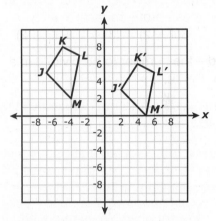

Quadrilateral $J'K'L'M'$ is the image of quadrilateral $JKLM$ after a translation.

improper fraction – a fraction in which the numerator is greater than or equal to the denominator

inclusive – contained in a set; for example, the set of whole numbers from 3 to 7, inclusive, is {3, 4, 5, 6, 7}

income – the amount of money received in a particular time (weekly, monthly, yearly) in exchange for work

independent quantity – a quantity whose value determines that of a dependent quantity

x	1	2	3	4
y	8	9	10	11

independent quantities: {1, 2, 3, 4}

independent variable – a variable whose value determines the value of the dependent variable

$$y = 6x + 2$$

↑
independent variable

inequality – a mathematical sentence that shows the relationship between quantities that are not equal using the symbols <, >, ≤, ≥, or ≠

inequality symbol (<, >, ≤, ≥, ≠) – a symbol that compares two quantities

> < means "less than"
> \> means "greater than"
> ≤ means "less than or equal to"
> ≥ means "greater than or equal to"
> ≠ means "not equal to"

inference – a conclusion drawn based on evidence

infinite – having an unlimited number of values

input – the value of the independent variable that is substituted into a function

input-output table – a table of values that follows a rule; used to show the pattern in *x*-values and their corresponding *y*-values

integers – the set of whole numbers and their opposites

interest – money paid by a borrower in exchange for using a lender's money for a certain period of time

interest rate – a percentage earned or paid on money invested or borrowed

interquartile range (IQR) – the difference between the upper quartile and the lower quartile

intersect – to meet or cross at a common point

interval – the distance or space between values; the set of points between two numbers

inverse operations – opposite operations; for example, addition is the inverse operation of subtraction

inverse property of addition – the property which states the sum of a number and its opposite is zero

$$a + (-a) = 0$$

$$3 + (-3) = 0$$

inverse property of multiplication – the property which states the product of a number and its reciprocal is one

$$a \cdot \frac{1}{a} = 1$$

$$6 \cdot \frac{1}{6} = 1$$

investment – money or items purchased with the expectation that the value will increase over time, yielding a profit

irrational numbers – numbers that cannot be written as the ratio of two integers; an irrational number cannot be represented by a repeating or terminating decimal number; examples include π and $\sqrt{2}$

isosceles triangle – a triangle with two congruent sides

J

justify – to explain why a solution was chosen

L

lateral faces – the faces of a three-dimensional figure that are not bases

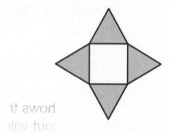

lateral surface area – the sum of the areas of all faces of a three-dimensional figure, not including the base(s)

leg (right triangle) – either side of a right triangle that forms the right angle

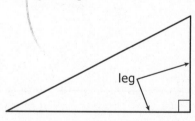

lender – a person or business that loans money

length – the distance from one end of an object to the other

line – a straight path that extends infinitely in opposite directions

linear angle pair – two adjacent angles that are also supplementary

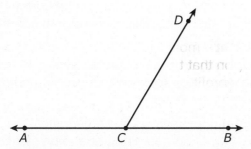

Angles *ACD* and *DCB* are a linear angle pair.

linear equation – an equation whose graph is a straight line

linear relationship – the relationship between independent and dependent quantities which shows a constant rate of change

loan – money that is borrowed by a person to purchase goods or services; the borrower agrees to repay the money over a set period of time with interest

loan term – length of time in months or years a borrower is given to repay a loan

lowest terms – the simplest form of a fraction in which the numerator and denominator have no common factor except 1

M

mapping – a representation that shows the relationship between input and output values

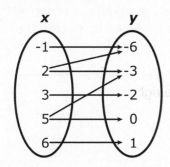

master's degree – a post-graduate degree typically earned after three years of study from a college or university

mean – the sum of the numbers in a set of data divided by the number of pieces of data; the average

mean absolute deviation – the average of the absolute values of the differences of each data point in a set of data and the mean of the data set; describes the variation of the data set in relation to the mean

measure – to find the size, weight/mass, or capacity of an item using a given unit

median – the middle number in a set of data when the data are arranged in order

minimum balance – the minimum amount a financial institution requires that a customer maintains in an account

minimum payment – the lowest amount that a borrower is allowed to pay each month toward a credit balance and remain in good standing

mixed number – a number composed of a whole number and a fraction; such as $2\frac{3}{4}$ or $5\frac{1}{8}$

mode – the number or category that appears most frequently

model – a drawing, diagram, or smaller version of something that represents the actual object

money market account – an account that earns interest, typically at a higher rate than a savings account, but may also require a higher initial deposit or daily balance

mortgage – a legal agreement to purchase a home or other real estate and repay the money borrowed over a period of time

multiple – the product of a given number and any whole number

Multiples of 5 include 5, 10, 15, 20, ...

multiplication – the operation using repeated addition of the same number; the combining of equal groups

multiplication property of equality – a property that states that if a value is multiplied to both sides of an equality statement (equation), the sides remain equal

multiplicative relationship – a relationship among a set of ordered pairs in which each *x*-value is multiplied by the same factor to find each corresponding *y*-value

The table shows a multiplicative relationship because each *x*-value is multiplied by 4 to find each *y*-value.

x	0	1	2	3
y	0	4	8	12

N

negative number – a number that is less than 0

net – a two-dimensional model that, when folded, forms a three-dimensional figure

non-adjacent interior angles – angles in a triangle that are not adjacent to the exterior angle

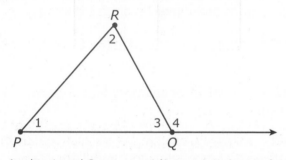

Angles 1 and 2 are non-adjacent interior angles.

non-linear relationship – a relationship in which there is not a constant rate of change between *x*- and *y*-values

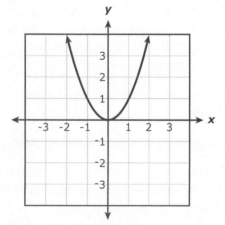

non-proportional relationship – a relationship in which the ratio of the dependent quantity to the independent quantity is not constant; for any non-proportional relationship, when $x = 0$, $y \neq 0$

number line – a line on which points correspond to numbers

number sentence – an equation or inequality that uses numbers and operation symbols

numerator – the top number in a fraction; the number of equal parts being considered

numerical data – values that can be counted or measured, such as dollars earned or minutes spent on homework

numerical equation – a number sentence that uses an equal sign to show that two numerical expressions are equal

numerical expression – a mathematical combination of numbers and operation symbols

O

obtuse angle – an angle measuring more than 90° but less than 180°

obtuse triangle – a triangle that has one angle greater than 90°

occupation – a job or profession

opposite numbers – two numbers that are the same distance from 0 on the number line but are on opposite sides of 0; 2 and -2 are opposite numbers

ordered pair – a pair of numbers, (*x*, *y*), used to locate a point on a coordinate plane

order of operations – the rules for the order of performing operations in expressions with more than one operation:
1) parentheses
2) exponents
3) multiplication/division from left to right
4) addition/subtraction from left to right

orientation – used to describe the location of an image after a transformation in relation to the pre-image; determined by the order of the vertices

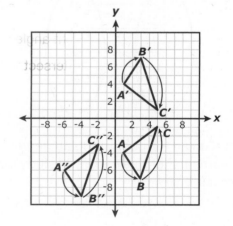

ILLEGAL TO COPY   motivation**math**™LEVEL 8   mentoring**minds**.com

origin – the point on a coordinate plane where the x-axis and the y-axis intersect; (0, 0)

outcome – one of the possible events in a sample space

outlier – a data value that is widely separated from the other data values in the data set

output – the value of the dependent variable after the independent variable is evaluated in a function

overdrawn – the status of an account where the money taken out is more than what is available

P

parallel – never meeting or intersecting; always the same distance apart

parallel lines – two lines in the same plane that never intersect

parallelogram – a quadrilateral with opposite sides that are parallel and congruent

parentheses – symbols used to group part of a mathematical expression or equation; ( )

partition – to divide or separate a whole into parts

pattern – a regularly-repeated arrangement of numbers, letters, shapes, etc.

payment plan – an agreement stating how a borrower will repay money to a lender over time

per – each or one

percent – the ratio of a number to 100

perfect square – a number that has a whole number square root; for example, 9 is a perfect square because $\sqrt{9}$ is 3

perimeter – the distance around a two-dimensional figure

perpendicular – intersecting at right angles

perpendicular lines – lines that intersect to form right angles

pi (π) – the ratio of the circumference of a circle to its diameter; approximate value is 3.14 or $\frac{22}{7}$

plot – to determine and mark points on a coordinate plane or number line

point – an exact location or position; a point may be represented by a dot

polygon – a closed figure made of line segments

population – the entire set from which a sample is drawn

positive number – a number that is greater than 0

powers of ten – any exponent written using a base of 10; for example, in 10^5, 5 is the power of 10

prediction – an educated guess as to what will happen

pre-image – the original figure prior to a transformation

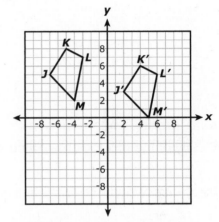

Quadrilateral *JKLM* is the pre-image of translated quadrilateral *J'K'L'M'*.

prime notation (') – used to indicate a point that is the result of a transformation; for example, *A'* indicates the point is the result of a transformation of *A*

prime number – a number that has exactly two positive factors, itself and 1

principal – initial amount of money invested or borrowed

prism – a three-dimensional figure with two parallel congruent bases; all lateral faces are parallelograms

product – the answer to a multiplication problem

profit – the amount of money earned after expenses are paid

proportion – a mathematical sentence stating that two ratios are equal; for example, $\frac{2}{6} = \frac{6}{18}$

proportional – having a constant ratio

proportional relationship – a relationship in which the ratio of the dependent quantity to the independent quantity is constant; for any proportional relationship, when x = 0, y = 0

pyramid – a three-dimensional figure in which the base is a polygon and the lateral faces are triangles

Pythagorean Theorem – the square of the hypotenuse of a right triangle is equal to the sum of the squares of the legs of the triangle

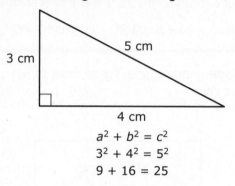

$$a^2 + b^2 = c^2$$
$$3^2 + 4^2 = 5^2$$
$$9 + 16 = 25$$

Q

quadrant – any of the four regions of a coordinate plane

quadrilateral – a polygon with four sides and four angles

quantity – an amount

quotient – the answer to a division problem

R

radical ($\sqrt{\ }$) – the operation symbol used to find the square root of a number

radicand – the number under the radical

radius – the distance from the center of a circle to any point on the circumference of the circle

random sample – sample in which every event has an equal chance of selection and each event is chosen by a random process

range – the difference between the highest and lowest values in a set of data

rate – a ratio in which two quantities with different units of measure are compared

rate of change – the ratio of the change in y-values to the change in x-values

ratio – a comparison of two quantities

rational numbers – numbers that can be written as $\frac{a}{b}$ in which a and b are integers, but b is not equal to 0; $\frac{2}{3}$, $\frac{7}{4}$, and $1\frac{2}{5}$ are examples of rational numbers

ray – a part of a line that has one endpoint and extends forever in the other direction

real numbers – the set of all numbers containing rational and irrational numbers

reasonable – logical or sensible

reciprocal – one of two numbers whose product is 1; the reciprocal of 2 is $\frac{1}{2}$

rectangle – a parallelogram with four right angles

rectangular prism – a three-dimensional figure with six rectangular faces

rectangular pyramid – a three-dimensional figure with one rectangular base and four lateral faces that are triangles

refinance – revise a payment plan to reflect a new interest rate or other terms

reflection – a transformation that produces a mirror image of a geometric figure; reflection over x-axis: $(x, y) \rightarrow (x, -y)$; reflection over y-axis: $(x, y) \rightarrow (-x, y)$

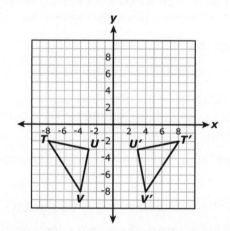

regular polygon – a polygon in which all sides are the same length and all angles have the same measure

relation – a set of ordered pairs

(0, 1), (1, 2), (3, 3), and (1, 0) are ordered pairs in a relation

relationship – a connection or pattern found between numbers

remainder – the number left over after dividing into equal groups

repeating decimal – a decimal in which one or more digits repeat indefinitely; $0.3333 \ldots = 0.\overline{3}$

representations – ways to display a math concept; may be in the form of an algebraic expression or equation, a graph, a table, or a verbal description

retirement savings – a savings plan funded by the employee and often matched by the employer; the savings deducted from income before taxes that accumulates until the employee reaches a set retirement age, at which time the funds are available to be withdrawn and used as needed

rhombus – a parallelogram in which all four sides are congruent and opposite angles are congruent

right angle – an angle with a measure of 90°

right triangle – a triangle with one right angle

rotation – a transformation of a figure by turning it about a fixed point called the center of rotation or axis; 90° rotation: $(x, y) \rightarrow (-y, x)$; 180° rotation: $(x, y) \rightarrow (-x, -y)$; 270° rotation: $(x, y) \rightarrow (y, -x)$; 360° rotation: $(x, y) \rightarrow (x, y)$

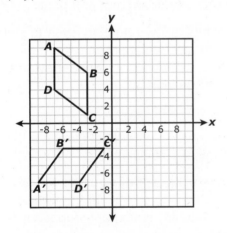

round – to approximate a number to a given place value

rule – a procedure that a pattern must follow

S

salary – a set amount of money paid to an employee by an employer for work completed

sales tax – a percentage of the cost of some goods and services, assessed by the government (local, state, or federal)

savings – amount of money not spent but accumulated or invested, typically with a financial institution

savings account – a bank account that allows a customer to deposit and withdraw money and earn interest from the bank

scale drawing – a drawing of a real object in which the actual measurements have been reduced or enlarged by a certain factor, known as the scale

scale factor – the common ratio for pairs of corresponding sides of similar figures

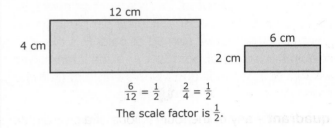

$$\frac{6}{12} = \frac{1}{2} \qquad \frac{2}{4} = \frac{1}{2}$$

The scale factor is $\frac{1}{2}$.

scalene triangle – a triangle with no congruent sides

scatterplot – a graph made by plotting points on a coordinate plane to show the relationship between variables in a bivariate set of data

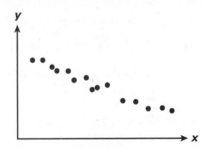

scholarship – money awarded based on academic or other achievement, not requiring repayment

scientific notation – a method of writing very large or very small numbers using powers of ten; for example, 3,400,000 is written as 3.4×10^6

service charge (fee) – a fee charged by a financial institution for a service provided to customers

set – a collection of distinct elements

shortfall – having less money than is needed or expected

similar figures – figures that are exactly the same shape with congruent corresponding angles and proportional corresponding sides

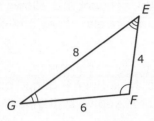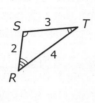

$$\triangle EFG \sim \triangle RST$$

simple interest – interest calculated only on the initial amount deposited, invested, or borrowed; the formula $I = Prt$ is used to calculate simple interest, where I is the interest earned or paid, P is the principal invested or borrowed, r is the interest rate written as a decimal, and t is the length of time the money is invested or borrowed, as a year

simplest form – the form of a fraction in which the greatest common factor of the numerator and denominator is 1

simplify – apply the properties of operations to an expression to make computation easier

simulation – a way to model a random event in which the outcomes of the simulation closely match the outcomes of the actual event

simultaneous – occuring at the same time

slant height – the altitude of a lateral face of a pyramid

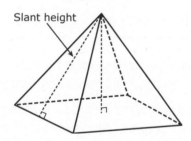

Slant height

slope – the measure of the steepness of a line; written as the ratio of the change in y-values to the change in x-values

For a line passing through (x_1, y_1) and (x_2, y_2),

$$m = \frac{\text{change in } y}{\text{change in } x} = \frac{y_2 - y_1}{x_2 - x_1}$$

solution – any value for a variable that makes an equation or an inequality true

solution set – the set of values that satisfies a given equation or inequality

sphere – a three-dimensional shape with all points an equal distance from the center

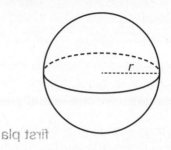

square – a special rectangle with 4 sides of equal measure

squared – raised to the power of 2; for example, 4 squared = 4^2

square root – a number that can be multiplied by itself to produce a given number; for example, $\sqrt{144} = 12$ because $12 \cdot 12 = 144$

square unit – a square with a side length of one unit, used to measure area

standard (decimal) notation – the customary method of writing decimal numbers, for example, 2.07, 0.003

stored value card – a payment method with money stored on a card, not at a bank

student loan – a low-rate loan given to students who need to pay for expenses related to post-secondary education, with repayment delayed until after graduation

subset – a set within a set

subtotal – the sum of a set of numbers that is then used in another calculation

subtraction property of equality – a property that states that if a value is subtracted from both sides of an equality statement (equation), the sides remain equal

sum – the answer to an addition problem

supplementary angles – two angles whose measures sum to 180°

surface area – the sum of the areas of each face and base of a three-dimensional figure

survey – gather information or data by asking multiple individuals the same question(s)

T

table – information organized in columns and rows

tax – money charged by the government (local, state, or federal) on income, goods, and services to fund government operations

tax rate – the percentage of income, goods, or services paid as a tax

tenth – one of 10 equal parts; the first place to the right of the decimal point

term (in an expression) – a number, variable, or product of numbers and variables

terminating decimal – a decimal that has a definite number of digits after the decimal point; for example, $\frac{1}{5} = 0.20$

thousandth – one of 1,000 equal parts; the third place to the right of the decimal point

three-dimensional figure – a solid figure that has length, width, and height

transformation – a change in size, shape, or position of a geometric figure

translation – a transformation that moves a geometric figure by sliding each of the points the same distance in the same direction: $(x, y) \rightarrow (-x + h, y + k)$

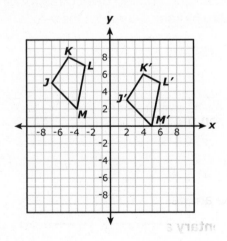

transversal – a line that intersects two or more additional lines

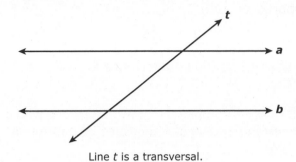

Line *t* is a transversal.

trapezoid – a quadrilateral with exactly one pair of parallel sides

trend – a pattern in a set of data

trend line – a line that shows the relationship of two sets of data on a scatterplot

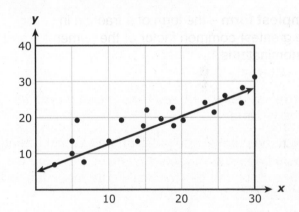

triangle – a polygon with 3 sides and 3 angles

Triangle Sum Theorem – the sum of the measures of the angles in a triangle is 180°

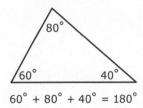

$60° + 80° + 40° = 180°$

triangular prism – a three-dimensional figure with two triangular bases and 3 lateral faces that are rectangles

triangular pyramid – a three-dimensional figure with 3 lateral faces that are triangles and one triangular base

truncated – to shorten by cutting off

tuition – a fee charged for instruction at an educational institution

two-dimensional figure – a plane figure that has length and width

U

unbiased – having no preference for one over another

unit rate – a comparison of two measures with one term having a value of 1; may also be called unit price or unit cost

V

valid – reasonable and justifiable

variability – measures how much data points differ from each other

variable – a letter or symbol used to represent a number

Venn diagram – a diagram showing relationships between sets

verify – to determine whether a value makes an equation true

vertex/vertices – the point where two rays meet, where two sides of a polygon meet, or where the edges of a three-dimensional figure meet; the top point of a cone or pyramid

vertical – straight up and down; perpendicular to the horizon

vertical angles – a pair of opposite congruent angles formed by intersecting lines

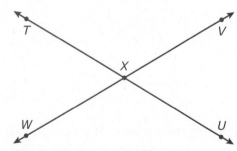

In the drawing, angles *TXW* and *VXU* are vertical angles.

vertical line test – a method used to determine whether the graph of a relation represents a function

volume – the number of cubic units needed to fill the space occupied by a solid

W

weight – the heaviness of an object as determined by its mass

whole numbers – the numbers used to count and zero (0, 1, 2, 3, 4, ...)

width – the measure or distance across something from one side to the other

withdrawal – money removed from a savings or checking account

work-study – a student aid program that provides a part-time job while in school to help pay expenses

X

***x*-axis** – the horizontal axis on a coordinate plane

***x*-coordinate** – the first number in an ordered pair, locating a point on the *x*-axis of a coordinate plane

Y

***y*-axis** – the vertical axis on a coordinate plane

***y*-coordinate** – the second number in an ordered pair, locating a point on the *y*-axis of a coordinate plane

***y*-intercept** – the ordered pair corresponding to the point where a graph intersects the *y*-axis

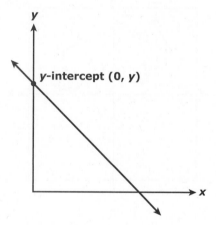

Z

zero pair – a number and its opposite; for example, 5 and -5

motivation**math**™LEVEL 8

Notes

Notes

motivation**math**™LEVEL 8

mentoring**minds**.com

Notes

Notes

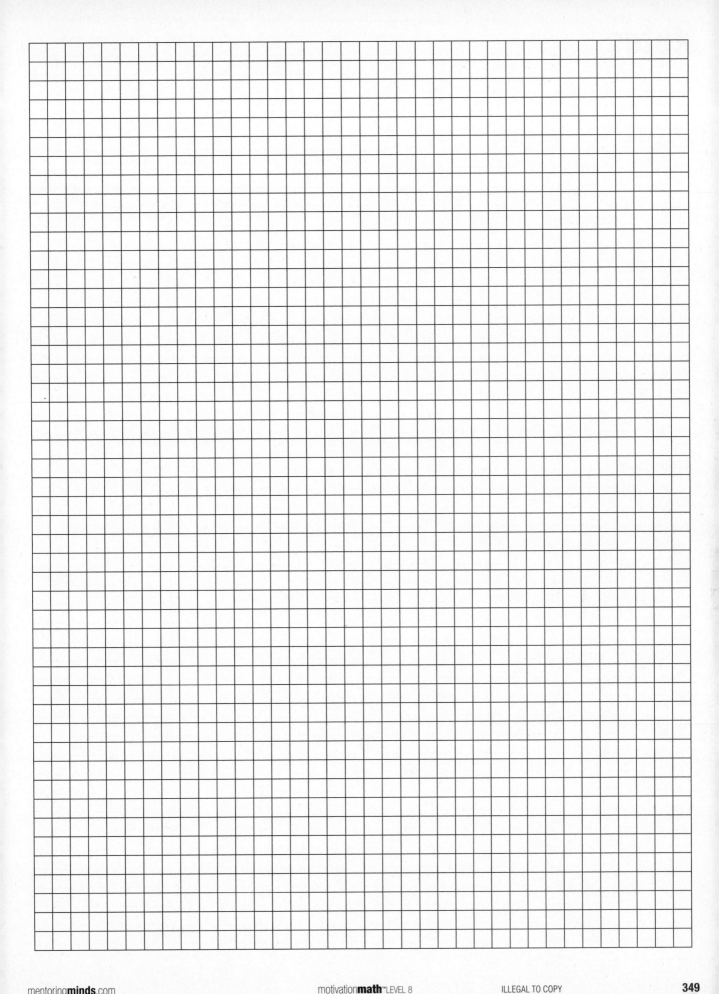

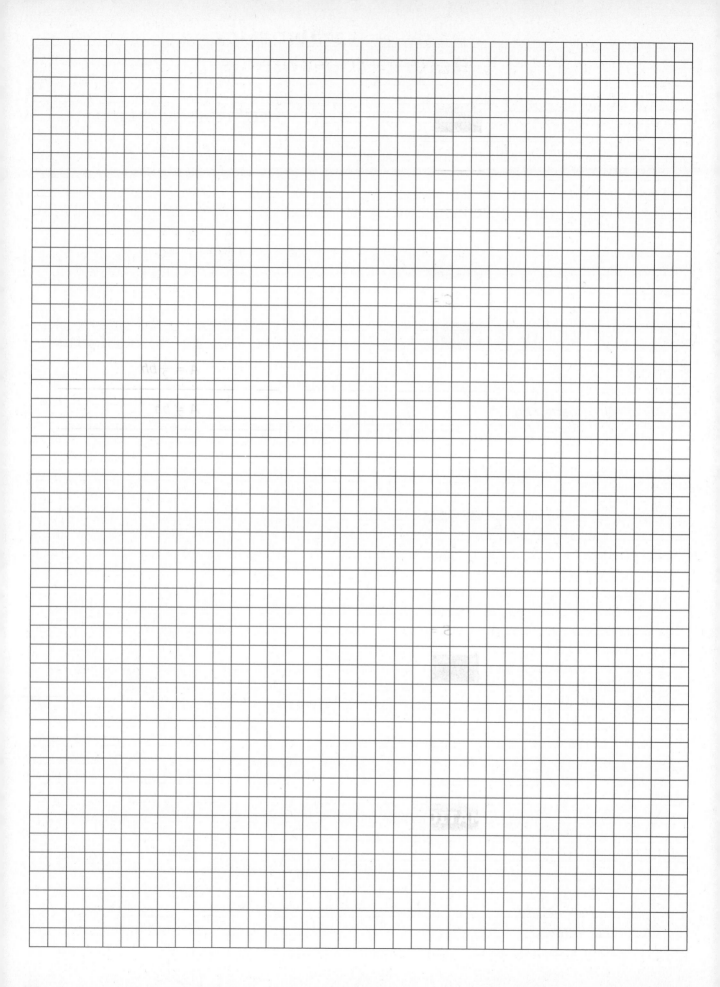

motivation**math**™LEVEL 8

mentoring**minds**.com

Grade 8 Mathematics
Reference Materials

LINEAR EQUATIONS

Slope-intercept form	$y = mx + b$
Direct variation	$y = kx$
Slope of a line	$m = \dfrac{y_2 - y_1}{x_2 - x_1}$

CIRCUMFERENCE

Circle	$C = 2\pi r$	or	$C = \pi d$

AREA

Triangle	$A = \frac{1}{2} bh$
Rectangle or parallelogram	$A = bh$
Trapezoid	$A = \frac{1}{2}(b_1 + b_2)h$
Circle	$A = \pi r^2$

SURFACE AREA

	Lateral	Total
Prism	$S = Ph$	$S = Ph + 2B$
Cylinder	$S = 2\pi rh$	$S = 2\pi rh + 2\pi r^2$

VOLUME

Prism or cylinder	$V = Bh$
Pyramid or cone	$V = \frac{1}{3} Bh$
Sphere	$V = \frac{4}{3}\pi r^3$

ADDITIONAL INFORMATION

Pythagorean Theorem	$a^2 + b^2 = c^2$
Simple interest	$I = Prt$
Compound interest	$A = P(1 + r)^t$

RR Donnelley/Owensville, MO USA/May 2015 - 18280_v15

motivation**math**™LEVEL 8

mentoring**minds**.com